新东方
XDF.CN

IELTS

雅思词组必备

俞敏洪 · 编著

浙江教育出版社·杭州

图书在版编目(CIP)数据

雅思词组必备 / 俞敏洪编著. —杭州：浙江教育出版社，2012.1

ISBN 978-7-5338-9536-5

Ⅰ. ①雅…　Ⅱ. ①俞…　Ⅲ. ①IELTS—词汇—自学参考资料　Ⅳ. ①H313

中国版本图书馆 CIP 数据核字(2012)第 003079 号

雅思词组必备

编　　著　俞敏洪
责任编辑　孔令宇　张　茜
责任校对　黄英妮
责任印务　陆　江
封面设计　大愚设计
出版发行　浙江教育出版社
（杭州市天目山路 40 号　　邮编：310013）
印　　刷　北京鑫海达印刷有限公司
开　　本　880×1230　1/32
印　　张　7
字　　数　216 000
版　　次　2012 年 2 月第 1 版
印　　次　2012 年 2 月第 1 次印刷
标准书号　ISBN 978-7-5338-9536-5
定　　价　22.00 元
联系电话　0571－85170300－80928
电子邮箱　bj62605588@163.com
网　　址　www.zjeph.com

前　言

对于大部分中国考生而言，雅思听力、口语一直以来都是弱项，这两部分难就难在发音不适应、语速跟不上、词汇量不够大，以及一些用法不熟悉。很多考生往往因为一两个单词、词组没听明白而丢分，实在令人扼腕叹息。在雅思听力、口语考试中，单词、词组的用法是最不容忽视的部分。先来看看下面这几个雅思考试中的常用词组，你是否掌握了它们的意思和用法：

catch sb. red handed	manual gear
nose dive	part exchange

这些词组中的单词本身都不难，但组合在一起后却让很多考生感到陌生。如果没掌握这些词组的意思，就会对理解文章造成障碍，影响做题，从而影响最终的考试成绩。它们的意思分别是："当场抓住"、"手动换挡，手动挡"、"俯冲；暴跌，急剧下降"、"部分抵价交易，以旧换新交易"。从上述例子可以看出，有时单单掌握了词组中的每个单词并不保证就能理解整个词组的意思与用法，而这正是许多考生徒有丰富的词汇量却无法在考试中取得高分的症结所在。雅思听力和口语材料模拟真实的交流语境，含有大量生动的习语和词组，对考生的词汇量更是提出了一个高要求。针对这一特点，本书结合雅思考试历次真题，全面收录考试中的常用词组，帮助考生彻底攻克难言难关。

本书特色

1. 紧扣真题，选词科学

本书在严格分析雅思考试特点的基础上，结合中国考生的弱项，从历次雅思听力原文与口语考试材料以及考试机经中精选大量词组，帮助考生学习真正实用的雅思常考词组，更加高效地备考。

2. 例句经典，原汁原味

本书精选大量雅思真题例句及与雅思常考内容相关、难度相当的例句，力求再现真实考试场景，帮助考生更好地熟悉考试难度，了解考查要点，为备考雅思打下坚实的基础。

3. 同义词组，扩充词汇量

熟悉雅思听力考试的考生会发现，将听力材料和题目对应起来是雅思听力的难点之一，这要求考生掌握大量的同义单词和词组，如用 depend on 代替 rely on；在口语考试中，考生应尽量丰富自己的语言表达，用不同方式表达相同的意思，给考官留下词汇量丰富的印象，从而获得高分。因此，掌握单词或词组的同义表达尤其重要。针对这一特点，本书特地编写了大量同/近义词组，帮助考生扩充词汇量，使表达更加多样化。

4. 要点提示，有力补充

本书总结听力、口语中的重点难点，如单词音变、连读、文化背景等相关知识，帮助考生掌握考试技巧，克服发音、用法上的障碍。比如 open ticket，该词组在真题中考过，但考生可能并不理解。本书补充了相关知识，介绍了这种不定期客票的信息（指票已经出了，但具体的出发日期、航班都没有确定，乘客在行程确定后需告知航空公司或铁路公司）。

此外，本书在该部分总结大量与主词组相关的表达，帮助考生学习相关词汇、词组，加强对相关主题的词组的掌握。

5. 幽默插图，巧妙助记

本书为词组配备约 100 幅生动有趣的插图，为考生营造一个轻松的学习环境，帮助考生变抽象记忆为形象记忆，在愉悦的氛围中高效学习词组。

本书旨在为考生解决雅思考试中词组这一难题，衷心希望它能帮助广大考生在雅思考试中取得优异的成绩！

新东方教育科技集团董事长兼总裁

目 录

Unit 1

a big potato 大人物

☞ ***A big potato*** is easy to distinguish, for he is always the last to arrive at a party. 大人物很好识别，因为参加聚会时他们总是最晚才到。

☞ a big shot

a box office smash （电影）票房很成功

☞ Though the film was far from ***a box office smash*** when it first hit theaters in 2005, it did receive generally positive reviews that time. 尽管这部电影在 2005 年刚上映时在票房上远远不算成功，但当时它的确得到了普遍的正面评价。

☞ The director is a talent and most of his films are ***box office smashes***. 这位导演是个天才，他的大多数电影都很卖座。

☞ a box office hit

在雅思口语考试中，常会涉及一些与 hobby（业余爱好）、leisure activity（休闲活动）等相关的话题，其中电影就是一个较常出现的内容，这里介绍一些和"票房"、"电影"相关的词组：

the highest grossing/top-grossing movie 票房冠军影片，票房最高的影片

weekend box office 周末票房 　 opening day box office 首日票房

daily box office 每日票房 　 box office battle 票房大战

a bunch of 一些

☞ A: I'm gonna ask you ***a bunch of*** questions and then you have to answer them real fast. Okay? So, clear your mind! Clear it right out!

B: Okay!

A：我要问你一些问题，你需要快速回答。可以吗？好，清醒下头脑！这就让你的脑子清醒下！

B：好的！

☞ a few of

a couple of 几个

☞ A: Did the lecturer suggest anything in particular?

B: Yeah. She recommended software called Vivat and I should book up for ***a couple of*** practice sessions using Vivat.

A：演讲者有什么具体的建议吗？

B：她推荐了一个名为 Vivat 的软件，而且推荐我预订参加几节使用该软件的训练课。

☞ A: Now, there are ***a couple of*** books I'd like you to look at. Have you got a pen? Right... *Approaches to Local History* by John Mervis.

B: Right...

A：现在我想给你推荐几本书。你有笔吗？好的，约翰·梅尔维斯的《当地历史研究方法》。

B：好的。

a cushion of air 气垫

☞ The main purpose of the first experiment is to show how hovercrafts work, and how things hover around on ***a cushion of air***. 第一个试验的主要目的是展示气垫船的工作原理和物体在气垫上是如何悬浮的。

a heavy demand for 对…有很大需求

☞ We do have a few rooms available for delegates at the conference centre. Those are very cheap but if you're interested you'll need to book soon, because there's always ***a heavy demand for*** them. 我们的确在会议中心为与会代表准备了一些房间。房间非常便宜，但是你们如果感兴趣的话就要马上预订，因为这种房间总是很紧俏。

☞ a big/great demand for

a host of 大量，许多，一大群

☞ Despite the harsh criticism and ***a host of*** skeptics, the preparation for the talk show is proceeding apace. 尽管面对苛刻的批评和众多的质疑者，这个脱口秀的准备工作仍在快速开展。

a matter of time 时间问题

☞ The police said that it was just ***a matter of time*** before the murderer was put into prison. 警方表示，将杀人凶手缉拿归案只是个时间问题。

a multitude of 许多，大量，众多

☞ Humans have adapted to ***a multitude of*** diets. The Western diet, however, is not one of them and we have higher rates of cancer and obesity than people on traditional diets. 人类已经适应了多种饮食。然而，西餐并不包括在内，西餐比传统饮食更容易使人患癌症和肥胖症。

🔍a multitude of 后面应当接可数名词的复数形式。

a piece of cake　小菜一碟；小事一桩

A: Don't forget to bring your ballet shoes for tomorrow's audition.

B: Ahhh! My teacher said it wasn't a dancing part.

A: Susan, all the roles got to dance a little. But believe me with your dance background it'll be ***a piece of cake***.

A：明天试演不要忘了带上芭蕾舞鞋。

B：啊！我的老师说这个角色不需要跳舞的啊。

A：苏珊，所有的角色都会有一些舞蹈。但相信我，以你的舞蹈基础，这只是小菜一碟。

a snap

一些和cake或其他食物有关的俚语：

a cake walk 轻而易举的事

have one's cake and eat it too 既要鱼，又要熊掌

like hot cakes 很受欢迎

the icing on the cake 锦上添花

have bigger fish to fry 有更重要的事要做

sugar-daddy 出手阔绰以博取年轻女子欢心的中年男人

limp as a noodle 无精打采

a range of　一系列；在…范围

A: And have you got any information on different train tickets types?

B: Yes. There's ***a range of*** ticket prices depending on when you travel and when you buy your tickets.

A：你能告诉我一些有关不同火车票种类的信息吗？

B：好的。票价不一，取决于你出行的时间和购票的时间。

We'd like to develop equipment with ***a range of*** size. 我们想开发各种型号的设备。

The famous talk show has attracted ***a*** wide ***range of*** audiences. 这个著名的脱口秀节目吸引了大量观众。

a 和 range 连读容易误听为 arrange，在考试时注意区分。

a series of　一系列

In the sixteenth century, the East End was still ***a series of*** separate, semi-rural settlements. 16 世纪时的伦敦东区仍是一系列独立的半乡村式住宅区。

a set of　一组，一套

CD players may be a good present for the dean, and also I thought maybe ***a set of*** dictionaries. I heard him say he needed a good one. 也许送院长一台 CD 机是个不错的选择，我认为一套词典或许也不错，听他说正需要一套好的词典。

a shortage of 缺少，缺乏

☞ There was ***a shortage of*** accommodation in East End, so marshland was drained and built on to house large number of people. 伦敦东区缺少住房，为解决大批民众的住房问题，人们抽干沼泽地来建房屋。

☞ be lack of

a slice of （尤指用刀切下来的）一片，一份

☞ A: The canteen was absolutely packed and I had to wait for ages. Then when I got to the front of the queue they had hardly any food left. So I had to get you ***a slice of*** pizza. I'm sorry.

B: Oh, that's OK. I could eat anything. I'm so hungry.

A：餐厅里人山人海，我等了很久。结果轮到我的时候，几乎没什么食物了，所以只得给你买份比萨。实在抱歉。

B：没关系，我什么都能吃，实在太饿了。

a sort of 一种；有点，有几分

☞ An old friend acted as ***a sort of*** transport organiser for everyone and the Hotel Ali in Markech was a good social base—I'd really recommend it, although I can't remember who runs it. 一个老朋友充当着一个类似交通组织人员的角色，为大家服务。马克奇的阿里宾馆是一个理想的社交基地——我要大力推荐一下，尽管我不记得经营者是谁了。

☞ I had ***a sort of*** feeling that he wouldn't come. 我隐约觉得他不会来。

☞ a kind of

a stone's throw away from 离…非常近

☞ Although we are just ***a stone's throw away from*** you, life for us is very different. 尽管我们只有数步之遥，但我们却生活得天壤之别。

a variety of 多种的，各种各样的

☞ Tourists want to find a place which offer ***a variety of*** shopping. 游客们想找到一个能购买各种商品的地方。

☞ various

a vicious circle 一个恶性循环

☞ I have many women patients who say they have completely given up exercise because the pain makes them so miserable. But of course that starts up ***a vicious circle***. 我的很多女性病人都声称她们难以忍受疼痛，以致完全放弃了锻炼，但是，当然这样就开始了一个恶性循环。

与"环境"相关的词组：

air pollution 大气污染　　ecological balance 生态平衡

food chain 食物链　　waste disposal 废物处理

a wealth of　大量的

☞ Once corals die, their skeletons would become the habitat for ***a wealth of*** marine organisms and settlements of new coral recruits. 珊瑚死后，它们的骨骼会变成大量海洋生物的栖息地和新珊瑚的生存地。

a wealth of 后面可以接 knowledge, information 等抽象名词。

academic atmosphere　学术氛围

☞ You can get an objective opinion of what you can expect if you come to live and study at Rexford not only the ***academic atmosphere*** but important details like what the leisure facilities are like and whether the English weather and food are really as awful as everybody says! 你将客观地了解到来雷克斯福德学习与生活会有什么收获。不仅仅是学术氛围，还有一些重要的细节，比如休闲设施以及英国的天气和食物是否真如所有人说得那么糟糕。

academic circle　学术界

☞ The corporate crime tends to be ignored in ***academic circle***—there's far more research on conventional crime and far more data available. 学术界总易于忽略公司犯罪——更多的是对传统犯罪的研究和可用的数据。

access to　有权使用；接近；通向…的入口

☞ A: Does the college library have ***access to*** computers?

B: Yes, your tutor will need to arrange with the technical support team for you to get a password, so ask him or her about it when you start the course.

A：学校图书馆可以用电脑吗？

B：可以，需要你的导师安排技术支持小组为你申请一个密码，所以开课时和他们说一下这事。

☞ ***Access to*** the auditorium is through the long corridor. 穿过长廊就能到达礼堂。

☞ A: Is there any difference between the two libraries?

B: Not in terms of their facilities. ***Access to*** online databases and the Internet is available at both sites and each site has a range of reference materials on education.

A：这两个图书馆有什么区别吗？

B：设施上没有区别，都可以进入在线数据库和网络，并且都有很多教育类参考资料。

☞ ***Access to*** the confidential documents is restricted to some managers in the company. 在这家公司，只有少数几位经理才能看到机密文件。

☞ have the right to; way in

account for (在数量方面)占;解释,说明

☞ I think I should start by emphasising that agriculture still ***accounts for*** a very important part of this country's economy. 我想我首先应该强调一下,农业仍是该国经济的重要组成部分。

☞ How do you ***account for*** your being late for school? 上学迟到这件事你怎么解释呢?

☞ make up, cover; make clear

adapt to 改造;改编,改写;(使)适应

☞ Some animals became extinct because they could not ***adapt to*** the changing environment. 一些动物因无法适应环境变化而灭绝。

☞ adjust to

add up to 总计达,合计

☞ The motorists must use detour routes through the national park which may ***add up to*** ten minutes of additional travel time. 车手们必须经过国家公园里的绕行路,这会增加十分钟的时间。

add...to 增加

☞ The modifications will ***add*** about $25, 000 ***to*** the price of a newly-built house. 这些装修将使新建房屋的价格增加约 25000 美元。

adept in 善于

☞ A: In your résumé you say you are ***adept in*** English.

B: Yes, I'm English major at university.

A:你在简历中称自己擅长英语。

B:是的,我大学时学的是英语专业。

☞ good at

adjacent to 邻近,接近

☞ Every house built on this site, not just those ***adjacent to*** the highway or nearest to the airport, will require high density insulation materials in the roof. 不只是那些靠近公路或离机场最近的房屋,该地区的每一间房屋的屋顶都需要用高密度绝缘材料建造。

☞ next to

adjust to 适应;调节

☞ You'll have to start ***adjusting to*** teaching and learning methods that may be unfamiliar to you, as well as the mounting pressure as the deadline for that first assignment creeps on you. 你必须开始适应对你而言可能陌生的教学方法,还有那不知不觉即将到来的第一次作业所带来的日益增加的压力。

☞ adapt to

adult education 成人教育

☞ Please turn down the radio. I'm preparing for the entrance examination for ***adult education***. 请将收音机声音调小一些，我正在准备成人教育入学考试。

🔍国外大学的教育种类繁多，常见的有高等教育（higher education）、职业教育（vocational education）、成人教育以及继续教育（further education）等。

advertising campaign 广告活动

☞ A: Having read through the case study, can you just summarise what the problems were that Box Telecom had to take on board?

B: Well, of course what first came to their attention was that, despite a new ***advertising campaign***, they were suffering from falling sales—and this is something that had many courses.

A：通过研读这个案例研究，你能简单总结一下博科斯电信必须注意哪些问题吗？

B：他们首先要注意的当然是虽然新开展了一个广告活动，但销售额却在下降——这里面有着很多原因。

🔍与“营销”相关的词组：

market research 市场调研	purchasing power 购买力
market potential 市场潜力	monthly report 月报
net income 纯收入	quality control 质量控制

advice on 关于…的建议

☞ There's ***advice on*** how to get the most from your lectures, as well as how to prepare for exams. 提供有关如何从讲座中获益最大的建议，以及备考的建议。

☞ A: Did you have a question?

B: Yes, does the Students Union also provide help with any problems, I mean ***advice on*** financial problems, for example? Or does the University provide that?

A: Yes, the Union runs their own advice service, offering help with financial matters such as grants.

A：你有什么问题吗？

B：是的，学生会也为任何问题提供帮助吗？我的意思是，比如就经济问题提供建议，或是学校提供这项服务？

A：是的，学生会有自己的建议服务，就补助金之类的经济问题提供帮助。

☞ suggestion on

aerial photograph 航拍照片

☞ Not every student is expected to tell the advantages and disadvantages of ***aerial photographs***. 并不是每个学生都需要说出航拍照片的利与弊。

afford to 负担得起，买得起

☞ I don't think I could ***afford to*** support myself with no salary for a whole year. 我觉得要是一整年没有薪水的话我无法维持生活。

agree on 就…取得一致，商定

☞ A: Do you want to talk me through what you've done on your dissertation?

B: Yeah, sure. Well, we have ***agreed on*** three main targets for me to aim for. The first one was to find out about suitable data analysis software.

A：你想和我说说你的论文的进展情况吗？

B：是的，当然。我们已议定我要完成三个主要的目标。第一个是找出合适的数据分析软件。

☞ consent to

agricultural workforce 农业劳动力

☞ The two factors I should mention are both very important, the first one is the high level of training amongst the ***agricultural workforce***, and secondly, the recognition by farmers of the value of investing in technology. 我必须提到两个非常重要的因素：一个是农业劳动力接受的高水平培训，另一个是农民们对科技投资的价值的认识。

ahead of time 预先

☞ All the performances have been rehearsed time and again ***ahead of time***. 所有的表演都已经预先彩排过很多次了。

☞ in advance

aim to 目的在于

☞ The Helpline was set up ten years ago by the Students Union and it ***aims to*** provide new students to the university with a service. 学生会十年前就开通了服务热线，目的是向大学新生提供服务。

air conditioning 空调

☞ A: Will audience find any difference in the auditorium?

B: Yes, we've increased the leg-room between the rows. And we've installed ***air conditioning***, so it won't get so hot and stuffy.

A：礼堂有什么变化吗？

B：是的，我们加大了排与排之间搁腿的空间，而且安装了空调，这样就不再那么闷热了。

all of a sudden　突然，忽然

☞ I thought the course was going to be really easy at the beginning and then ***all of a sudden*** in the second half of the course we got a whole load of work, reading to do and essays and things. 我认为刚开始的时候，这门课真是太容易了，然后到了课程的后半部分时，却突然要做大量的作业和阅读以及论文之类的事。

☞ all at once

all set　一切就绪

☞ All my luggage have been packed. I guess I'm ***all set*** to get on the bus. 我所有的行李都打包好了，我想我一切就绪，可以上车了。

☞ all ready

all walks of life　各行各业；各个阶层

☞ The members of the club come from ***all walks of life***. 俱乐部的会员来自各行各业。

all walks of life

all-talking film　完全的有声电影

☞ The film featured actors speaking only during parts of the film and was called *The Jazz Singer*, and it wasn't until 1928 that the first ***all-talking film*** was produced. 这部电影片名为《爵士歌手》，其特征是演员只在电影的某些部分说话，直到 1928 年第一部完全的有声电影才问世。

alter the course of one's life　改变了某人的生活

☞ We can at any time decide to ***alter the course of our lives***. 任何时候，我们都可以决定改变自己的生活。

alternative fuel　替代能源

☞ The salesman told me that the car ran on ***alternative fuel***. 销售人员告诉我，这款汽车用的是替代能源。

alternative work　其他可供选择的工作

☞ In the sixteenth century, the first dock was dug, eventually making the East End the focus of massive international trade. And in the late sixteenth century, when much of the rest of England was suffering economically, a lot of agricultural workers came to the East End to look for ***alternative work***. 16 世纪，伦敦东区建了第一个码头，最终使东区成为大规模国际贸易的中心。16 世纪晚期，英格兰其他很多地方遭遇经济创伤，很多农业工人都涌入东区寻找其他能做的工作。

annual fee　年费

☞ A: I noticed a fitness centre next to the college. Is that for students?

B: It's open to everyone, but students pay an ***annual fee*** that's much less than the general public pay.

A：我发现学校附近有一个健身中心，对学生开放吗？

B：对任何人都开放，但是学生付的年费要比公众少得多。

☞ annuity, yearly payment

🔍annual fee 曾出现在雅思考试申请银行卡的场景中。

annual interest rate 年利率

☞ In this country the average credit card has an ***annual interest*** rate of 15.3%. 该国的信用卡平均年利率是15.3%。

anything but 绝对不

☞ The food in this restaurant is ***anything but*** delicious. 这家餐厅的食物一点也不可口。

🔍与短语 nothing but (只是)相区别。

apart from 除…以外

☞ ***Apart from*** the rock salt, you only need a jar of water. 除了岩盐，你只需一罐水。

☞ Who else will quit the job ***apart from*** Tina? 除了蒂娜，还有谁要辞职？

☞ besides

appeal to 对…有吸引力；诉诸，求助于；呼吁，恳求

☞ It's important not to confine yourself to reading on your subject. You should also read things of general interest that ***appeal to*** you. 不要只读你所学科目的书，这点很重要。你也应该读一些让你感兴趣的大众读物。

🔍appeal 还可用做名词，如用在词组 take an appeal to 中。例：The lawyer decided to take an appeal to the high court. 这名律师决定向高级法院提起上诉。

appear to 似乎

☞ Shark-meshing does ***appear to*** be less effective than some other methods, especially when there are big seas with high rolling waves and strong currents and anything that lets the sand move—the sand that's holding the nets down. 网拦鲨鱼似乎没有其他方法有效，尤其是在那些有着巨浪、强水流等任何能让沙子移动的东西的巨大海域，因为沙子是用来固定网的。

☞ seem to

application form 申请表

☞ A: I've got the ***application form*** here. We have different types—I see you've got our leaflet there.

B: I've decided on the one called "Select."

A：我这里有申请表。我们有很多不同的类型——我看到你已经在那边拿到我们的宣传单了。

B：我已经决定办理“精选(服务)”了。

☞ You should first fill out the ***application form*** downloaded from the official website. 你应该先填好从官方网站上下载的申请表。

apply for　申请，请求得到

☞ A: The bookshop said the essays about classroom management were out of print and the library doesn't have a copy.

B: Oh right, and I'm afraid I've lent my copy to another student. What I suggest you do is try the library again this time—***apply for*** it through the service called special loan.

A：书店说关于教室管理的书籍已绝版，图书馆也没有。

B：哦，是这样，我的那本也借给另外一个学生了。我建议你再去图书馆找找——通过“特殊借阅”服务来申请借书吧。

☞ Please read the clauses carefully before ***applying for*** a personal loan. 在申请个人贷款前请仔细阅读条款。

approach to　(…的)方法，(…的)途径

☞ The seminar is aimed at students like you who are uncertain about what to expect at college, and looks at a fairly wide range of ***approaches to*** university learning, to motivate you to begin your study and build on your own learning strategies. 研讨会通过探讨大学学习的各种方法，旨在为像你这样不清楚自己在大学想做什么的学生提供服务：激励你们开始学习并形成自己的学习策略。

☞ a way of

argue over　争论，辩论

☞ Many believe that the story first began in America in 1877, when two friends were ***arguing over*** whether a horse ever had all four feet or hooves off the ground when it galloped. 很多人都相信这个故事最初于1877年发生于美国，当时两个朋友在争论马在驰骋时四个蹄子是否都离地。

☞ debate on

这里介绍一个和 argue 有关的词组：argue the toss 对决定提出异议。例如：There's no sense arguing the toss after the problems had been settled. 在问题解决后再提出异议毫无意义。

Unit 2

arise from　因…而造成，因…而引起；产生于，起源于

☞ The counselling service we offer deals with any problems ***arising from*** your studies, or your life outside the university. 我们就你在学习上或校外生活中遇到的任何问题提供咨询服务。

☞ There are many health problems in your life ***arising from*** smoking and drinking. 你生活中的很多健康问题都是由吸烟和饮酒引起的。

☞ result from

art exhibition　艺术展

☞ The program has sensational theatre, dance and also a large number of ***art exhibitions***, but the thing the festival is most famous for is its great street music. 该艺术节的节目包括情感剧、舞蹈，还有很多艺术展，但最为知名的当属它出色的街头音乐。

在英国，著名旅游景点之一就是国家画廊(National Gallery)，在那会举办各种艺术展。

art gallery 画廊，美术馆

☞ A large number of people were appreciating the paintings in the ***art gallery*** as it was raining outside. 外面正下着雨，很多人一直在美术馆欣赏绘画。

☞ picture gallery

与"美术"相关的词汇：

portrait 肖像，画像　　statue 雕像　　profile 外形，轮廓
aesthetic 审美的，美学的　　portray 描绘

as a result　结果，因此

☞ I didn't prepare for the examine; ***as a result***, I failed the exam. 我没有复习，所以考试没及格。

as a result of　由于

☞ ***As a result of*** the general success of the program in Sydney, shark-meshing was introduced to the state of Queensland around 1970. 由于该项目在悉尼大获成功，网拦鲨鱼在 1970 年前后被引进昆士兰州。

☞ because of

as a whole　总的来说，总体上

☞ There are marked differences between regions, but this does not prevent quite a strong sense of solidarity amongst the farming community ***as a whole***, right across the country. 地区间有着明显的差异，但这并不妨碍全国范围内的农业社区之间形成强烈的团结观念。

☞ on the whole

as far as　直到…为止；尽…，就…

☞ I will help you to mend your bike ***as far as*** I can. 我将尽我所能帮助你修车。

☞ so far as

as far as I know　据我所知

☞ ***As far as I know***, the two company have reached an agreement on that issue. 据我所知，这两家公司已经就该问题达成了一项协议。

☞ as far as I'm concerned

as far as sth. is concerned　就…而言

☞ ***As far as listening is concerned***, I find it hard to keep up sometimes in lectures, especially two-hour ones. I sometimes just seem to go off into a dream. 就听讲而言，我发现有时候在讲座上精力很难保持集中，尤其是一些长达两个小时的讲座。有时我就像进入梦境一样。

☞ on the part of; in terms of

as I see it　我想

☞ ***As I see it***, the President doesn't have any choice. 我认为这位总统没有选择余地。

☞ in my opinion

as long as　只要

☞ I don't think I'll need too much extra time, ***as long as*** I can get hold of some important references. 只要能找到一些重要的参考书，我想就不需要太多额外时间。

☞ so long as

as much as　差不多；多达

☞ A significant proportion of the lions' diet is made up of the livestock of these farmers—goats, chicken and so on—***as much as*** a third, in fact. 狮子的很大一部分食物来自这些农民养的牲畜——山羊、鸡等——实际上，多达 1/3。

as though　好像，仿佛

☞ Low-frequency noise goes through the trees ***as though*** they aren't there. 低频率的噪音从树林中穿过，仿佛树木并不存在。

☞ The little boy treats his elder brother ***as though*** he were a stranger. 那个小男孩视他哥哥如陌生人。

☞ as if

as usual 照常，照例

☞ ***As usual***, we hope to begin the season with a picnic next Saturday at the clubhouse. 和往常一样，我们希望以下周六在俱乐部会所举办野餐开始新赛季。

☞ Despite her problems, she carried on working ***as usual***. 尽管有困难，她照常继续工作。

as well as 也，又

☞ The base of this cot could be raised or lowered into two different positions making it safe ***as well as*** convenient. 这种婴儿床的底座可以被调高或降低到两个不同的位置，这使得床既安全又方便。

ask for trouble 自找麻烦，自讨苦吃

☞ Don't ***ask for trouble***. 别自找麻烦。

☞ borrow trouble

assembly line 流水线，装配线

☞ ***Assembly line*** is good for efficiency, but bad for creativity. 流水线有助于提高效率，却降低了创造力。

assist with 协助

☞ The sports psychologists help the athletes by improving motivation and concentration or ***assisting with*** stress management. 运动心理学家通过提高积极性和注意力或协助压力管理的方法来帮助运动员。

☞ help with

at a loss 不知如何是好，茫然；亏本

☞ Maybe we're often ***at a loss*** how to choose when facing various kinds of fashion clothes. 也许在面对各种款式的时尚服饰时，我们常常不知如何选择。

at a significant cost 以昂贵的花费

☞ Modifications to houses will be necessary but they come ***at a significant cost*** to the developer and home buyer. 装修房屋是有必要的，但是会给开发商和购房者都带来一笔不小的开销。

at all times 总是，始终，随时

☞ Locking doors ***at all times***...men didn't think it was quite as important as women, but both gave it a high safety rating. 在随时锁门这个问题上，男性不像女性那般重视，但二者都给予其高安全等级。

☞ all the time

at any time 在任何时候

☞ You're supposed to ask for a home visit before 10:30 in the morning, but obviously, if it's an emergency, you can phone ***at any time***, night or day. 你应该在上午 10:30 前要求医生出诊，但如果情况紧急，毫无疑问，你可以在白天或晚上的任何时候致电。

☞ at all hours

at least 至少

☞ ***At least***, we've done the oral presentation—I thought that was good, the way I got my feedback really quickly. 至少，我们已做了口头演讲，我认为那不错，能很快得到反馈。

☞ She may receive little education, but ***at least*** she is reliable. 她可能没接受过什么教育，但至少她很可靠。

☞ The interesting side of sports physiology, ***at least*** in my view, is the side that looks at the micro level, looking at cellular change. The researchers are doing cellular research, looking at changes in body cells when the body is under stress. 至少在我看来，运动生理学有趣的一面是其从微观上观察细胞变化。研究人员进行细胞研究，观察处于压力之下的人体细胞所发生的变化。

☞ no less than

at one time 一度，曾经；从前

☞ ***At one time*** the Asiatic lion was living as far west as Greece and they were found from there, in a band that spread east through various countries of the Middle East, all the way to India. 亚洲狮曾居住在遥远的西方，比如希腊，它们在那被发现，然后一路向东穿越中东的多个国家，最后到达印度。

☞ once

at one's service 愿为某人服务

☞ I'm glad to be ***at your service***, Sir. 先生，我很乐意为您效劳。

at risk 在危险中

☞ We know from modern farming that if the level of breeding stock falls below about three hundred females, the future of the species locally is ***at risk***. 根据现代农业的相关知识我们了解到，如果某一物种中雌性的数量低于 300，那么该物种在此地的未来堪忧。

☞ at stake, in danger

at some stage 在某些时候；在某阶段

☞ I want to ask where the staff room is in case I need to find a teacher ***at some stage***. 我想问一下教师休息室在哪里，以防我什么时候需要找老师。

at the end of 在…的尽头；…结束之时

☞ You've chosen to visit the rainforest in March, which is just ***at the end of*** the wet season, so you'll soon notice how well the waterfalls are running and also how damp the ground is. 你们选择三月来游览雨林，这正是雨季结束之际，那么不久你们就会发现瀑布有多么壮观以及地面有多么湿润。

☞ You will notice ***at the end of*** each corridor that there is another door but these are fire doors and are kept locked from the outside. 你会发现每条走廊的尽头都还有一扇门，但那是消防门，一直都是从外面锁上的。

at the expense of 以…为代价

☞ The rapid urbanisation in this country is occurring ***at the expense of*** both rural lifestyles and precious cultural heritage. 该国快速的城市化是以牺牲乡村生活方式和宝贵的文化遗产为代价的。

☞ at the cost of

at the moment 当下，目前

☞ ***At the moment***, your task is to get over the difficulties and start afresh again. 目前，你的任务是克服困难重新开始。

☞ at present

at the outset 开端，开始

☞ Your tutors will tell you ***at the outset*** how to set out the chapters they require but you will need to ask them how they would like you to organise the bibliography because it varies depending on your subject area. 你们的导师会在开始时告诉你们如何安排他们要求的章节，但是你们需要询问他们希望你们如何组织参考书目，因为这会因学科领域的不同而不同。

☞ at the beginning

at the top of 在…最高处，在…顶上

☞ ***At the top of*** the faculty we have a dean and below the dean we have three divisions. 系里最高的职位是系主任，主任管理三个部门。

at this stage 眼下，暂时

☞ I wouldn't bother with the article by Morris ***at this stage*** if I were you. 如果我是你，眼下我就不会因莫里斯的那篇文章而烦恼。

at work 在工作，在运转

☞ They are ***at work*** for a new plan. 他们在制订一个新计划。

attach...to 加上，使…依附于，附属于

☞ A: When you get your sticker, you must ***attach*** it ***to*** the front windscreen of your car. I m afraid it's not valid if you don't have it stuck on the window.

B: Right, I see.

A：你拿到停车证之后，必须把它贴在前面的挡风玻璃上。否则恐怕无效。

B：好的，我明白了。

☞ append...to

attempt to 试图

☞ When pain strikes, we ***attempt to*** keep the back as immobile as possible, which makes the muscles tense up. Research shows that they often go into spasm, which causes further twisting of the spine. 疼痛发作时，我们试图尽可能让背部保持不动，结果造成肌肉紧张。研究表明这经常会变成痉挛，导致脊柱更加扭曲。

attitude towards 对…的态度

☞ We've been looking at the ***attitudes*** of various social and cultural groups ***towards*** the management of their personal finances—how important they feel it is to save money, and what they save their money for. 我们一直都在关注不同的社会与文化团体对个人理财的态度——存钱的重要性及存钱的目的。

average salary 平均工资

☞ A: Do you know the ***average salary*** in the USA?

B: I don't know.

A：你知道美国的平均工资吗？

B：不知道。

baby cot 婴儿床

☞ Let's start by looking at ***baby cot***, that's for children of up to three years old. 我们从婴儿床开始吧，它适用于三岁以下的儿童。

baggage reclaim 行李提取处

☞ A: Excuse me, sir! Where is the ***baggage reclaim***?

B: Just in front of you.

A：先生，打扰一下，请问行李提取处在哪里？

B：就在你前面。

bail out 帮助…摆脱困境

☞ Government should ***bail out*** more poor people in the economy crisis. 政府应该帮助更多陷入经济危机的穷人摆脱困境。

☞ help out

bank statement 银行结单，银行对账单

☞ A: Shall I bring a ***bank statement***, would that do?

B: That'll be fine.

A：我带一份银行对账单就可以了吗？

B：那就行了。

☞ The man told me that my checkbook stubs didn't tally with my ***bank statement***. 那个男子告诉我，我的支票存根与我的银行对账单不一致。

bank transfer 银行转账

☞ You must understand that all payment can be in cash, cheque or ***bank transfer***. 你必须了解所有款项都可以通过现金、支票或银行转账的方式来支付。

🔍 transfer 还有"换乘"之意，如：transfer station 换乘站。

bar graph 条形图

☞ The ***bar graph*** shows reasons why people change where they live. 这个条形图反映了人们变换住所的原因。

🔍 table 和 graph 这两个词都有"图表"的意思，注意区别。table 主要指"表格图"，graph 主要指"曲线图"。

bare skin 裸露的皮肤

☞ The thing you should know is that certain plants can cause irritation if you touch them with ***bare skin***. 你应该知道皮肤直接接触某些植物会导致过敏。

be absent from 缺席

☞ There is no excuse for you to ***be absent from*** school at your graduation ceremony. 你没有借口缺席毕业典礼。

be accompanied by 由…陪伴

☞ Children should ***be accompanied by*** their parents to watch the show. 孩子们应该在家长的陪同下观看演出。

☞ consort with

be addicted to 沉溺于，对…上瘾

☞ Tracy ***was addicted to*** the computer games; as a result, she failed in the final examination. 特蕾西沉溺于电脑游戏，因此未能通过期末考试。

be against 反对

☞ We really do not instruct workers on how to ***be against*** companies. 我们真的不是教工人们如何去和公司对着干。

be alienated from 被疏离

☞ The manager ***is alienated from*** the rest of the company with various rumours surrounding him. 由于身边谣言不断，这名经理和公司的其他人疏远了。

be allergic to 对…过敏；对…极其反感

☞ I *am allergic to* some food. 我对某些食物过敏。

☞ The young lady seems to *be allergic to* hard work. 那位年轻的女士似乎对辛苦工作极其反感。

☞ be sensitive to

be around the corner （事情）很快就要发生

☞ The financial expert warns fiscal chaos in the industry *is* right *around the corner*. 这位金融专家警告说该行业即将出现财政混乱的局面。

be associated with 和…相关

☞ The increased risk of acute myeloid leukemia（AML）seems to *be associated with* the birth weight. 急性髓细胞白血病日益增加的发病率似乎和出生时的体重有关。

be attached to 附属于；喜爱

☞ The factory *is attached to* our school. 这个工厂附属于我们学校。

☞ The girl *is* very much *attached to* her boyfriend and she couldn't even live without him. 这个女孩非常喜欢她的男友，没有他甚至不能活。

be attributed to 归因于

☞ Up to one-third of the diseases that afflict people can *be attributed to* negative environmental factors, such as toxic chemicals, polluted air, dirty water, poor sanitation. 在困扰人类的各种疾病中，有 1/3 可以归因于负面的环境因素，如有毒化学物质、受污染的空气、脏水和糟糕的卫生条件。

☞ be ascribed to

be based on 基于

☞ The simple game *is based on* photos from students and teachers. 这个简单的游戏基于学生们和老师们提供的照片。

☞ on the basis of

be beneficial to 对…有好处，有益于

☞ The huge amount of green energy will *be beneficial to* the local area and will make a significant contribution towards the national energy targets. 大量的绿色能源对当地大有好处，并且会为实现国家能源目标作出巨大贡献。

be best with 最适用于

☞ In this case, I'd say pictures *are best with* individual children, because they give them an opportunity to let their imaginations run wild. 在这种情况下，我想图片最适用于孩子个体，因为它们给予孩子们一个自由想象的机会。

be blamed for 因为…而被责怪

☞ What does a course in sports studies involve? Well, you wouldn't ***be blamed for*** not knowing the answer to this question because sports studies as a discipline is still comparatively new. But it's a growing area and one which is now firmly established at our university. 运动研究课程包括哪些内容呢？你们不知道也无可厚非，因为运动研究还是一个相对较新的学科，但是该领域正处于发展中，也是我们大学目前正大力建设的一个学科。

🔍 be to blame 的意思是"应对…负责任，应受责备"，注意区别。

be bound for 前往

☞ A: Where ***are*** you ***bound for***, Jenny?

B: London.

A：珍妮，你去哪里？

B：伦敦。

🔍 be bound for 常用在旅行场景中。

be bound to 一定，必定

☞ A: That new Indian restaurant is supposed to be excellent.

B: But it ***is bound to*** be packed.

A：那家新开的印度餐馆应该很不错。

B：但那里一定客满了。

be broken beyond repair 坏到无法修理

☞ Before he knew it, his car had run into the rock in the lake and ***was broken beyond repair***. 他还没反应过来，他的车子就已经冲入湖中，撞在石头上，面目全非。

be broken beyond repair

be close to 接近，靠近

☞ I ***was close to*** tears when the tiger in the cage gave me quite a scare. 笼中的老虎差点把我吓哭了。

☞ There's I think at Rexford an excellent combination of physical and geographical advantages as well as having a rural setting and still ***being close to*** central London, and something that will certainly be of interest to you is that Rexford is just 35 minutes from London Airport. 我认为雷克斯福德集自然优势与地理优势于一身——既有乡村环境又离伦敦市中心很近，还有一点一定会让你感兴趣的，那就是它离伦敦机场只有35分钟的车程。

☞ approach to

Unit 3

be closely linked to 和…密切相关

☞ Access to clean water ***is closely linked to*** many factors such as pollution, human health and poverty. 是否能饮用到干净的水与诸如污染、人们的健康状况和贫困状况等因素密切相关。

be composed of 由…组成

☞ Now you'll note that all of the subjects which you undertake in the first year ***are composed of*** lectures and tutorials. 现在，你们将注意到，第一年要学习的学科，其课程都由讲座和辅导课组成。

☞ be consisted of, be comprised of

be concerned about 担心，忧虑；关注

☞ The whole society should ***be concerned about*** the health of children. 全社会都应该关注孩子的健康。

☞ be worried about

be concerned with 关于，牵涉；关心，挂念

☞ The book ***is*** primarily ***concerned with*** Soviet-American relations during the Cold War. 这本书主要讲的是“冷战”时期的苏美关系。

☞ The international community ***is*** more ***concerned with*** the country's military actions. 国际社会更为关注该国的军事行动。

be confronted with 面对(危机、挑战、困难等)

☞ Many consumers, especially the young ladies, ***are*** always ***confronted with*** the seemingly contradictory choice of wanting to help the planet and the desire to buy the latest so-called "must-have" products. 很多顾客，尤其是年轻女士们，总是面临一种看似矛盾的选择，一方面她们想保护地球，另一方面她们强烈地想购买最新的所谓“必需品”。

☞ encounter

be confused about 对…感到困惑

☞ If you ***are confused about*** subjects or how to combine them in your degree, then we can advise you and discuss the career you are aiming for. 如果你对科目或如何把科目与学位结合起来感到困惑，我们可以给你提供建议并对你打算从事的职业进行讨论。

be covered with 被…覆盖

☞ The shark's skin ***isn't covered with*** scales, like other fish: instead the skin ***is covered with*** barbs, giving it a rough texture like sandpaper. 与其他鱼类不同，鲨鱼的皮肤上没有鳞片，而是覆有一层倒刺，使得它们的皮肤像砂纸一样粗糙。

be crazy about 热衷于

☞ ***I'm crazy about*** opera while Thomas ***is crazy about*** cartoons. 我热爱歌剧，而托马斯热衷于漫画。

be dependent on/upon 依靠，依赖；取决于

☞ A: I'm really serious about improving my English so I'd prefer to be the only guest in the host family if that's possible.

B: No other guests...Yes, you get more practice that way. Anyway, obviously all this ***is*** partly ***dependent on*** how much you're willing to pay. What did you have in mind?

A: I was thinking in terms of about ￡60–￡80 a week, but I'd go up to a hundred if it was something special.

A：我真的很想提高英语水平，所以如果可能的话，我愿意寄宿家庭里只住我一个客人。

B：没有别的客人……是的，这样你就能多些练习了。无论如何，很显然，这部分取决于你愿意支付多少钱。你是怎么想的？

A：我计划是每周 60 到 80 英镑，但如果条件很好的话我愿意涨到 100 英镑。

be dotted with 遍布，点缀着

☞ The lake near my house which ***was dotted with*** various kinds of cartoon boats, attracts many children every day. 我家附近的那个湖里泊着各式各样的卡通小船，每天吸引来很多儿童。

be eligible for 对…有资格，具备条件

☞ All banks offer special student accounts. However, it's important to note that as an international student you'll not necessarily ***be eligible for*** all the facilities offered to resident students. 所有银行都提供特殊的学生账户，然而值得一提的是，并非所有为本国学生提供的设施都能为国际学生所用。

be embossed with 被压有…字样（或图案），凸印有…字样（或图案）

☞ All bed linen and towels ***are*** clearly ***embossed with*** the name "Smith House" so it's easily identifiable. 所有床单和毛巾都清楚印有"史密斯学院"的字样，所以极易分辨出来。

be entitled to（do） 使…有权利/资格获得，使…有权利/资格做

☞ What I suggest you do is try the library again—this time apply for it through the service called special loan. Have you done that before? ***You're entitled to*** six books a year. 我建议你再去图书馆试一下——这次通过所谓的"特殊借书"服务申请吧。你以前申请过吗？这样一年可以借六本书。

☞ All students at the college ***are entitled to*** become members of the Sports Center, for an annual fee of £9.50. 学院全体学生都有资格成为运动中心的会员，年费是 9.5 英镑。

☞ have access to

be equipped with 配备有，装备有

☞ Working becomes more convenient because offices have ***been equipped with*** modern facilities. 办公室里配备了现代设施，因此工作变得更加便利。

☞ be fitted out/up with

be expelled from 被从…赶走，被从…开除

☞ John ***was expelled from*** the school because he was absent from school five times in a month. 约翰被学校开除了，因为他在一个月内旷课五次。

☞ be dismissed from

be expelled from

be familiar with 熟悉

☞ You may ***be familiar with*** coffee processed by freeze-drying, which preserves the quality of the food product while making a large saving in weight. 你也许熟悉咖啡的冷冻干燥加工法，这种方法在减轻食物重量的同时能保证食物的品质。

be fascinated by 喜欢，为…着迷

☞ I ***am*** extremely ***fascinated by*** tattoos and see nothing but beauty and personality from them. 我极其喜欢纹身，我觉得它们非常漂亮，极具个性。

☞ be fond of

be flexible in 在…灵活的

☞ You need to ***be*** more ***flexible in*** your approach. 你的方法必须更加灵活。

be fond of 喜爱，喜好

☞ You know I ***am fond of*** collecting various stamps and I have already collected almost 2,000 stamps. 你知道的，我喜欢收集各种不同的邮票，已经收集了近 2000张了。

☞ show affection for

be fussy about 对…挑剔

☞ People ***are*** very ***fussy*** these days ***about*** the sound system and in general I think the new directors ought to do lots more of these kinds of interview, you know, talking with their potential customers. 如今，人们对音响系统非常挑剔，总的来说，我觉得新导演应该多做类似采访，你知道的，就是和潜在客户聊聊。

☞ be particular about, be critical about

"Don't be so fussy! "（不要太挑剔了！）是英美国家人士的口头语。

be going extinct 逐渐灭绝

☞ We know that unless we take action immediately, the species in rainforest will ***be going extinct***. 我们都知道，如果不立即采取行动的话，雨林里的物种将逐渐灭绝。

be going extinct 常用在生态环境的话题里，常见的导致物种灭绝的原因主要有：

greenhouse effect 温室效应
environmental pollution 环境污染
poach 偷猎
deforestation 乱砍滥伐

be good with 与…相处得好

☞ Dr Jones ***is*** very ***good with*** elderly people, but he tends to get a bit impatient with children. 琼斯医生与老人相处得很好，但是对孩子却常常有点不耐烦。

☞ get along well with

be honest with 对…说老实话，对…坦诚

☞ A: How did you find the whole experience?

B: I'll ***be honest with*** you. At the end of the first year I really wanted to leave West Africa and come home.

A: 你觉得整个经历怎么样？

B: 老实和你说，在第一年结束时，我真的很想离开西非回国。

be ideal for 对…是理想的，对…最合适

☞ Videos, ***are ideal for*** use with everyone present in the class, especially when children have individual activity sheets to help them focus their minds on what's in the video. 视频最适合在班级上使用，尤其是当孩子们各自都有活动单以帮助他们集中精力在视频内容上时。

be impatient with 对…没耐心

☞ She ***was*** always ***impatient with*** other people's advice. 她对他人的建议总是缺乏耐心。

be in charge of 负责

☞ Can you tell me who ***is in charge of*** the sales department? 能告诉我谁负责销售部吗？

☞ take charge of

be in good form/shape/health 状态/健康状况良好

☞ If you keep doing exercises every day, you can ***be in good form*** all the time. 如果你能坚持每天运动，就能保持良好的健康状态。

be incapacitated with 因…丧失能力，因…不能正常活动

☞ The most recent available figures show that about a quarter of a million people ***are incapacitated with*** back pain every day. 最新数据表明，每天约有 25 万人因背痛而不能正常活动。

be incompatible with 与…不协调；与…不兼容

☞ The experts think the rapid industrial growth ***is incompatible with*** environmental sustainability. 专家认为工业的飞速发展与环境的可持续性是不协调的。

incompatible 除了可以形容人际关系、人与自然的不协调外，也可用于指我们平时常说的电脑软件与硬件的“不兼容”，如：The anti-virus software is incompatible with the computer. 这种杀毒软件和这台电脑不兼容。

be innovative with 对…进行创新

☞ I think the company will recover. That advertising campaign they did was very strong and they ***are*** very ***innovative with*** their products—they set new trends. 我认为这家公司会复苏。它做的那个广告活动非常有效，商品也极具创新性——引领新潮流。

be keen on 喜爱，热爱，醉心于

☞ This country ***is keen on*** reaching bilateral agreements with its neighboring countries on various economic investments from oil to food. 该国热衷于和邻国达成经济投资的双边协议，投资内容从油到食品，种类繁多。

be likely to do 很可能

☞ The main priority for men when saving money is their retirement. When they're earning, ***they're*** far more ***likely to*** put money aside for their old age than women are. 男人攒钱优先考虑的是以备退休之用。在赚钱时，他们更可能存钱防老，此情况远远甚于女人。

be located on 坐落于

☞ The hotel ***is*** conveniently ***located on*** the center of the city. 这家酒店坐落在市中心，十分方便。

☞ be situated in/at

be mad about 对…疯狂，迷恋于

☞ Young people ***are*** always ***mad about*** playing computer games. 年轻人总是着迷于电脑游戏。

be mad at 对…发火，对…感到愤怒

☞ Here are the detailed steps that can help you determine whether a girl ***is mad at*** you. 这些详细的步骤可以帮助你确定一个女孩是否对你发火了。

☞ be angry about

be made into 被制成

☞ In Africa ostriches' feathers were used for tribal ceremonial dress and they were also exported to Europe and America where they ***were made into*** ladies' fans and used for decorating hats. 在非洲，鸵鸟毛被用在部落典礼用的服装上。它们还被出口到欧洲和美洲，在那儿被制成女士用的扇子，也用于装饰帽子。

be made of 用…建造

☞ When I was a little child, most of the buildings in town ***were made of*** red bricks. 在我的孩童时代，镇上大部分的建筑都是用红砖建造而成的。

与另一常考词组 be made from 的区别：be made of 所用的原料是看得出来的，而 be made from 则看不出来原材料。

be motivated to do 被激发做，被激励做

☞ We are discussing how children can ***be motivated to*** study foreign languages. 我们正在讨论如何激发儿童学习外语的兴趣。

☞ be spurred on to do

be nervous of 对…害怕

☞ There's no need to ***be nervous of*** the rainforest provided that you treat it with respect and common sense. 只要你怀着尊敬和常态的心理来看待雨林，就没有必要害怕它。

be on speaking terms （在争吵以后）关系好，友好；泛泛之交

☞ George's professional success was enormous, but his personal life wasn't as successful. He was no longer ***on speaking terms*** with his brother and had been devastated by the death at the age of seven of his elder daughter, Josephine. 乔治在事业上取得了巨大的成功，但是他的个人生活就没那么成功了。他和哥哥关系恶化，而且七岁的大女儿约瑟芬夭折，对他造成了毁灭性的打击。

be on the safe side 为保险起见

☞ A: First thing...numbers...have we got anything definite?

B: Well...I've been working it out and I think 40 to 43.

A: Shall we put 45 to ***be on the safe side***?

B: Yep, fine.

A：第一件事……人数……已经确定了吗？

B：哦……我一直在计算，我想是 40 到 43 人。

A：保险起见，定在 45 人，好吗？

B：很好。

be open to 对…开放；易受…攻击/影响；乐于接受

☞ During the course of this morning we hope to give you a clear idea of what we offer in our training programs and we will look at the types of course and the entry requirements, if any, for those courses. Some of these courses ***are open to*** school leavers, but for some you need previous qualifications, or relevant successful employment. 在今天上午的课上，我们希望你们能清楚了解我们的培训项目会提供哪些培训，我们也会看看课程类型及入学要求，如果有的话。一些课程是对毕业生开放的，但是有些课程需要你们有先前的资格证书或是相关的工作经验。

be opposed to 反对…

☞ A total of 70 percent of voters in this country said they ***were opposed to*** abortion with 48 percent saying they strongly opposed abortion. Just 15 percent of those polled said they favor legal abortions. 这个国家总共有70%的人反对流产，其中48%的人强烈反对流产。仅有15%的投票者支持合法流产。

☞ be against

be packed with 充满，挤满

☞ Flights from the UK to US destinations of San Francisco and Los Angeles ***were packed with*** the famous singer's fans. 从英国飞往美国旧金山和洛杉矶的航班上挤满了这位著名歌手的歌迷。

☞ be teemed with

be parallel to 与…平行/相类似

☞ The soldiers in this isolated island ***are parallel to*** those fighting in the battlefield. 驻扎在这个孤岛上的战士与在战场上冲锋陷阵的士兵一样(伟大)。

be popular among 在…中受欢迎

☞ The mini skirt ***was*** not very ***popular among*** the girls but nowadays the girls are crazy about them. 以前迷你裙不怎么受女孩们欢迎，但如今她们都为之疯狂。

☞ be popular with

be prepared to do 乐意做

☞ I think the company is much more cautious than we thought and expect they will start trying to find individuals who'd ***be prepared to*** back them with some of the capital they need. 我认为这家公司比我们原先想得谨慎得多，我也期望他们将开始努力找到乐意资助他们的个人，而资金正是他们所需的。

be prone to 易于

☞ Women ***are prone to*** be influenced by commercial ads of various forms. 女人容易受到各种形式的商业广告的影响。

☞ tend to

be proud of 为…自豪

☞ It's weird that Nancy ***is*** never ***proud of*** her motherland. 真奇怪，南希从不以她的祖国为豪。

be relevant to 与…相关

☞ There comments ***are*** not directly ***relevant to*** the enquiry. 这些意见与这项调查没有直接联系。

☞ A person's gender ***isn't relevant to*** whether he/she can do a good job. 一个人的性别与其能否做好工作无关。

☞ be related to

be removed from 与…远离，与…疏远；被免职；被从…排除

☞ There are fat soluble vitamins which can be stored for quite some time by the body and there are water soluble vitamins which ***are removed*** more rapidly ***from*** the body and so a regular daily intake of these ones is needed. 脂溶性维生素能在体内储存很长时间，而水溶性维生素从体内被清除则更迅速，因此需要每天摄取。

☞ keep...at arm's length

be replaced with 被…取代

☞ We would like the current reading room to ***be replaced with*** a small gym. 我们想把现在的阅览室改成小健身房。

☞ be substituted for

be responsible for 对…负责

☞ A: Do you think the hotel should ***be responsible for*** the loss?
B: Of course.
A：你觉得旅馆应该对损失负责吗？
B：当然。

☞ assume responsibility for

be satisfied with 对…感到满意

☞ A: ***Are*** you ***satisfied with*** the teaching method of my English teacher?
B: Not at all.
A：你对我英语老师的教学方法满意吗？
B：一点也不。

☞ be content with

be shocked to do　震惊地做

☞ We ***were quite shocked to*** discover that only 9% of people here in the UK make an effort to recycle their household waste. 我们非常震惊地发现，在英国只有 9%的人会回收家庭垃圾。

be shouted at　遭到怒斥

☞ As you can see, 93% of respondents had had some kind of problem. A surprisingly large percentage—24% had had their car damaged in some way, but the main type of incident was ***being shouted at***—69% had experienced that. 正如你们看到的，93%的受访者遭遇了某种问题。24%人的车在某种程度上遭到破坏，这一比例大得令人震惊，但最主要的是遭到怒斥——69%的人有过这样的经历。

be sick with　患…病

☞ A: Hi Mike, so what happened to you last week?

B: Oh, I ***was sick with*** the flu.

A：喂，迈克，你上周怎么了？

B：哦，我得了流感。

NOTES

Unit 4

be stuck on 贴上；被…迷住，特别喜欢

☞ The only problem anyone could find in this cot was that there were pictures which ***were*** simply ***stuck on*** and so could easily become detached. 显而易见，这种婴儿床唯一的缺点就是上面那些图片只是简单地贴上去的，因此很容易剥落。

☞ be fascinated by

be suited to 适合

☞ Single-speed cycles—that is bikes with no gears, ***are*** really only ***suited to*** short, casual rides. 单速自行车是指没有变速装置的自行车，只适合短途的休闲旅游。

表示“不适合的”可用 ill-suited，“极适合的”可用 well-suited 来表示。

be supposed to do 被期望(或要求)做；获准做；应该做；一般认为

☞ Back in 1928 the British writer George Bernard Shaw wrote in his *Intelligent Women's Guide to Socialism and Capitalism* that "A man ***is supposed to*** understand politics, economics and finance and is therefore unwilling to accept essential instruction." 1928 年，英国作家乔治·萧伯纳在他的《聪明女人的社会主义和资本主义指南》一书中写道：“男人自以为了解政治、经济和金融，因此不愿意接受基本的教育。”

be taken aback 使…大吃一惊

☞ A: What was the weather like?

B: It got us right from day one and we ***were*** pretty ***taken aback*** to find that it rained on quite a number of days, and so we were forced to start re-planning our route.

A：天气如何？

B：第一天还好，然后出乎我们意料的是，之后接连下了好几天的雨，以致我们不得不重新规划路线。

☞ be shocked by

take back 指“拿回，退回；接受”，注意和 be taken aback 相区分。

be taken to court 被告上法庭

☞ Parents of undisciplined pupils could ***be taken to court*** by teachers under act to be announced by the government. 一项由政府颁布的法案规定，老师可以把那些目无纪律的孩子们的父母告上法庭。

be teeming with 充满

☞ Deep into the forest are at least 100 lakes that may ***be teeming with*** microscopic organisms. 森林深处至少有 100 个湖泊，这些湖泊中也许充满微生物。

☞ be filled with

be told to do 被告知做

☞ A: Good morning, can I help you?

B: I ***was told to*** come over here to get a parking sticker. Is this the right place?

A: Yes, it is.

A：早上好，有什么能为您效劳的？

B：我被告知前来办理停车证，是这儿吗？

A：是的。

be torn between...and 在…和…间左右为难/难以抉择

☞ Everyone will ***be torn between*** being single ***and*** being married or in a relationship at their twenties. 每个人在 20 多岁时都会在单身和结婚或恋爱间左右为难。

be unfamiliar to 对…来说不熟悉/陌生

☞ This new invention ***is unfamiliar to*** most of the people. 这项新发明对大部分人来说还很陌生。

be unwilling to do 不愿意做

☞ He ***was unwilling to*** marry the young woman. 他不愿意娶那个年轻女人。

be vital to 为…所不可缺少，对…至关重要

☞ Water from these underground reservoirs bubbles to the surface as springs in some parts of the country, and these rare sources of permanent water ***were vital to*** early explorers of inland Australia, and to other pioneers last century, who used the springs for survival. 在这个国家的一些地区，地下水库的水以泉水的形式涌向地表，这些珍贵的永久水源对早期前往澳大利亚内陆的探险者及上个世纪的其他先驱者来说至关重要，因为这些泉水关系到他们的生死存亡。

☞ be essential to

be well off 富有；处境良好；顺利

☞ There are two practices near here, so we ***are*** quite ***well off*** for doctors in this part of Manchester. 这附近有两家诊所，在曼彻斯特的这个地区找医生很便利。

beauty saloon 美容院

☞ A: How long do you go to the ***beauty saloon***?

B: Once a week.

A：你多长时间去一次美容院？

B：一周一次。

🔍与"美容"相关的表达：

beautician 美容师	colour cosmetic 彩妆
perfume 香水	skincare 护肤
plastic surgery 整形外科	personal care 个人护理

bed linen 床上用品

☞ This store has a good reputation for selling ***bed linen*** with nice quality. 这家商店因销售质量上乘的床上用品而享有盛誉。

🔍常见的床上用品：

sheet 被单	pillow 枕头	quilt 被子
mattress 床垫	blanket 毯子	quilt cover 被套

belong to 属于

☞ The future does not ***belong to*** those who gather armies on battlefield; the future ***belongs to*** the people with the education and imagination to create. 未来不属于那些在战场上指挥军队的人，而属于受过教育并拥有创造能力的人。

🔍在说"某物属于某人"时，用 sth. belongs to sb. 来表示，不用被动语态。

bend over 使弯曲，弄弯

☞ You just need to ***bend*** the flaps ***over*** and stick them with glue or prittstick. 你只需把帽边弄弯，然后用胶水或胶棒把它们粘到一起。

benefit from 受益于，得益于

☞ We're always interested to hear of other places that would ***benefit from*** receiving a consignment of bikes, and welcome suggestions from people who've been to developing regions on their travels. 我们希望能得知有什么地区得益于我们运送的自行车，我们也欢迎曾去过发展中地区旅行的人给我们提出建议。

best buy 最合算的货品，最上算的买卖

☞ This cot will be safe in every way; we have made it our ***best buy***. 这种婴儿床在所有方面都很安全，我们认为是最好的选择。

☞ a good deal, an excellent buy

best man 男傧相，伴郎

☞ We want John to be our ***best man*** but he refuses us. 我们想让约翰做我们的伴郎，但他拒绝了。

beware of 当心，注意，提防

☞ Most of the animals and wildlife are gentle and harmless. There are some venomous snakes to ***beware of***, but really they're much more frightened of you than you are of them. 大多数动物和野生生物都很温顺，不会伤人。需要当心一些毒蛇，但实际上它们怕你要多过你怕它们。

bid for 投标；申办

☞ A: Have you heard that London has successfully ***bid for*** the next Olympic Games?

B: Of coursc, it deserves that.

A：伦敦已经成功申办下一届奥运会，你听说了吗？

B：当然，它实至名归。

☞ make bid for

blame for 为…负责

☞ The British diet could be partially to ***blame for*** increase in back pain. 背痛加剧应部分归因于英国的饮食。

☞ be responsible for

blood pressure 血压

☞ Let me feel your pulse and test your ***blood pressure***. 让我为你把把脉，测一下血压。

blow up 使充气；（使）爆炸；爆发；（丑闻等）曝光；夸大，放大

☞ A: What do you do with the balloons and the table?

B: Er, you ***blow up*** the balloons and balance the table on them.

A：你拿气球和桌子做什么用？

B：你给气球充气，使放在气球上的桌子保持平衡。

☞ explode; become public

boarding school 寄宿制学校

☞ Joe's mom wants to send him to the ***boarding school***. 乔的妈妈想送他去寄宿制学校上学。

🔍 在英国，学校分为公立学校(public school)和私立学校(private school)，许多学校都是寄宿制的。

book over the phone 通过电话预订

☞ ***Booking over the phone*** is not allowed, so you have to come here in person, with your card, when you want to book. 不允许通过电话预订，如果你想预订的话就要带上卡，亲自来办理。

book...in 为…预约

☞ A: What do I have to do if I want to join in this class?

B: Well, we ***book*** you ***in*** for an assessment with an instructor, who will show you how to use all the equipment.

A：如果我想学习这门课该怎么做呢？

B：我们为您预约了一位指导老师做评估，他会告诉你如何使用所有器械。

☞ make a reservation for

book up 预订，预购，预约

☞ A: The sessions sound really good and I'll certainly ***book up*** for the next two weeks.

B: Lovely. Thanks very much for ringing.

A：这些课听起来非常好，我一定会预订下两周的课。

B：太好了，非常感谢致电。

boost one's confidence 增强某人的信心

☞ Yoga is a best way to ***boost one's confidence*** and self-esteem. 瑜伽是提升自信和自尊的最好方法之一。

boost the efficiency of 提升…的效率

☞ The auto company aims to ***boost the*** fuel ***efficiency of*** its models 30 percent by 2020, and develop "electrical device solutions" and a new hybrid. 这家汽车公司的目标是在 2020 年前将其汽车的燃料使用率提升 30%，并开发"电力设备解决方法"和一种新型混合动力汽车。

bother to do 费力地做，特地做

☞ You needn't ***bother to*** come to my house and cook for us. 你不必特地来我家给我们做饭。

☞ take the trouble to do

bother with 为…担心，为…操心

☞ John didn't ***bother with*** his English homework. 约翰不为他的英语家庭作业担心。

☞ worry about

box office 售票处

☞ The tickets are available from the ***box office***, in person, by phone, fax or post, or online. 你可以通过售票处、本人亲自购买、电话、传真、邮递或在线的方式购票。

☞ ticket office, booking office

🔍box office receipts/takings 指"票房收益"。

brand name 商标

☞ A: Any marks or badges on the briefcase that make it stand out?

B: Only the ***brand name***.

A：公文包上有什么能突显它的标志或徽章吗？

B：只有商标。

雅思考试中，关于 brand 这个词还可能考到的词组有：brand switch 品牌转换，brand identification 品牌识别。

break down 分解；损坏，出故障

☞ Maybe you need to do something different every day, so if you ***break down*** your revision into small tasks, and allocate them to specific days, there's more incentive to tackle them. 也许你需要每天做不同的事，所以如果把复习任务分解成很多小任务，并把这些小任务分配到具体的每一天，就会有更大的动力去完成它们。

☞ take apart

break off （使）断开；中断；绝交

☞ Huge iceberg ***breaks off*** the continent each year, while in winter half the surrounding ocean freezes over, which means its size almost doubles. 巨大的冰山每年都会从大陆上脱离，在冬天这些冰山周围一半的海水会结冰，这意味着冰山的体积几乎要增加一倍。

☞ The overseas students may have interrupted personal relationships or even sometimes have ***broken*** them ***off*** to come overseas, and so the students often feel lonely, unhappy, unmotivated and unable to concentrate on studying. 为了出国，留学生可能会中断有时甚至断绝个人关系，这样一来他们经常会感到孤单、不开心、缺乏斗志而且无法专心学习。

☞ cut off

break records/the record 打破纪录

☞ The swimmer did everything he could to ***break the record*** in this match. 那名游泳运动员尽全力去打破这项比赛的纪录。

☞ beat the record

break with 与…绝交/关系破裂；破除

☞ Don't bother him. He's just ***broken with*** his girlfriend. 别去烦他。他刚和女朋友分手。

breeze through 顺利通过，轻松完成

☞ The little boy ***breezed through*** the tests. 这个小男孩顺利通过了测试。

bring about 导致，引起；带来…的结果

☞ The cultivation of crops and the husbandry of livestock ***brought about*** changes in people's lifestyle such as the type of shelters they made. 种植庄稼和饲养牲畜给人们的生活方式带来了变化，比如，人们所建造的住处的类型。

☞ lead to

bring along 把…一起带着

☞ A: If possible, could you ***bring along*** bottle tops which the children might be able to use in the models, you know, as decoration?

B: We'll certainly try to find some for you.

A: 如果可能的话，你能带一些瓶盖来吗？孩子们可能会用它们来装饰模型。

B: 我们会尽力找一些的。

☞ Well, it was very enjoyable and just to give you an idea of what the pupils produced. I've ***brought along*** three hats to show you. 这很有趣，为了让你们看看学生们做的东西，我带了三顶帽子来。

bring out 生产；出版；烘托出，衬托出

☞ A: Do you know the year or the model name of your car?

B: I think it's 1996, and it's called a Lion—like the animal.

A: Then it must be 1994, because the manufacture ***brought out*** the Fox after that.

A: 你知道你车子的生产年份或型号吗？

B: 我觉得是 1996 年，叫"莱恩"——就是狮子。

A: 那就一定是 1994 年了，因为制造商在它之后生产了"福克斯"。

☞ produce, manufacture; publish

bring up 培养，教育；使出庭受审；使突然停止移动或谈话

☞ In the first week, we run a series of talks which focus on different aspects of the library and its resources. You'll also find that to get the most out of the library you really do need to be computer literate and so all this term we run small classes which will ***bring up*** to speed on how to access the computer-loaded information. 在第一周，我们会进行一系列谈话，着重介绍图书馆的各个不同方面及资源。你们也会发现如果要充分使用图书馆资源，你就得会使用计算机，因此我们这学期将开设小班课程加深你们对如何通过计算机下载信息的了解。

☞ The manager was ***brought up*** and charged with drunk driving. 这名经理因为酒后驾车而出庭受审。

☞ The journalist's question ***brought*** the actor ***up*** short. 记者的提问使那个演员顿时哑口无言。

☞ cultivate

broadband connection 宽带连接

☞ A: What's wrong with my computer?

B: Maybe the ***broadband connection*** doesn't work.

A: 我的电脑怎么了？

B: 大概宽带连接坏了。

brush up lessons 复习功课

☞ As term examine is approaching, you'd better start ***brushing up your lessons***. 期末考试即将来临，你最好开始复习功课。

☞ go over lessons

budge price range 预算价格范围

☞ We tested three different cots all in the ***budget price range*** and, as usual, we will feature the good points, the problems. 我们对三种在预算价格范围内的婴儿床都进行了测试，和往常一样，我们会总结其各自的优缺点。

与"range"相关的词组：

working range 工作范围	middle range 中等距离
age range 年龄范围	a wide/narrow range of 大/小范围

build up 建立；形成

☞ A: What are the problems that you've been having?

B: Well, no one thing is really dangerous or anything, but you know, it's just been ***building up***.

A：你都有些什么问题？

B：嗯，没有什么是真正危险的事，但是你知道的，问题是逐步形成的。

build up one's confidence 建立某人的信心

☞ I think that I really need some help in preparing for the coming semester, especially to ***build up my confidence*** a bit and help me study effectively. 我想我真的需要一些帮助，为下学期做准备，尤其是要建立信心及高效地学习。

bullet point 项目符号

☞ ***Bullet point*** is an item which is printed with a square, diamond or circle in a document to show that it is important. 项目符号通常呈方形、菱形或圆形，用在文件里以显示重要性。

bump into 邂逅，偶然遇到；撞上

☞ I'm glad I've ***bumped into*** you. I've just found a great idea for the presentation we've got to do for Dr Banks next month. 真高兴碰见你。我刚刚为咱们下个月要在班克斯博士课上做的演讲想出一个好点子。

burn out 燃料用尽而熄灭，烧坏，停止工作；累垮

☞ ***Burning out*** often occurs among young people because they do not relax and enjoy their lives that they are busily creating. 年轻人经常被累垮是因为他们不休息，也不去享受他们匆忙创造的生活。

☞ be knocked up

bus route 公交线路

☞ Every morning there are many students and old people on this ***bus route***, so we need more buses. 每天早晨这条公交线路上都有很多学生和老人，因此我们需要更多的公交车。

🔍与“公交车”相关的表达：

get on/off 上 / 下车　　bus stop 公交站　　conductor 售票员

swipe card 刷卡　　stand clear 不要倚靠　　platform 站台

buy sb. out 买下某人的所有权(或产权、股份)

A: What do you think the company will do?

B: Hmm...Well, obviously they have the choice of accepting the very favourable terms that another company—KPMG—have given them to ***buy them out***. That would mean creating a new company with a new image.

A：你认为这家公司会采取什么方案？

B：这个，很显然他们可以选择接受另一家公司毕马威提出的极其有利的并购方案。这意味着创办一家有着全新形象的新公司。

by hand 用手工，用人力

☞ Toughened glass used for cooking doesn't fully melt at the temperature required for other glass, and so that also has to be picked out ***by hand***. 烹调用的钢化玻璃在其他玻璃必需的熔化温度下不能完全熔化，所以还要手工挑出。

☞ manually

by heart 熟记；凭记忆

☞ A: Do you need any ID or any thing like that?

B: Yes, we need your driver's license number, that is if you have one.

A: Yes, I know it off ***by heart***, it's an easy one, 2020BD. Do you need to see it?

B: I'm afraid I do.

A：你需要身份证或其他类似证件吗？

B：是的。我们需要你的驾照号码，如果有的话。

A：好的，我都熟记于心了，很好记，2020BD。你需要看一下吗？

B：我得看看。

☞ from memory

by installment 分期付款

☞ Don't worry! You can pay for the house ***by installment*** payment. 别担心！你可以通过分期付款的方式来付房款。

与"贷款"相关的常用表达：

an excessive amount 巨大的数目	mortgage 抵押
time loan 定期贷款	grant a loan 批准贷款
heavily in debt 负债累累	debt ceiling 债务上限

by means of 依靠，通过

☞ While most other animals, including fish, hunt their prey ***by means of*** their eyesight, sharks hunt essentially by smell. 包括鱼在内的大多数其他动物都靠视觉捕猎，而鲨鱼基本上靠嗅觉。

☞ by way of

by profession 专职

☞ A: And your occupation?

B: Well, I'm in Britain as a project manager, but that's not my main job. I'm an engineer ***by profession***.

A：您做什么工作？

B：我在英国做项目经理，但那不是我的主要工作。我是一名专职工程师。

by the middle of 到…中期

☞ ***By the middle of*** the 19th century, in 1850 that is, the figure had fallen sharply to 10%, and then to 3% ***by the middle of*** the 20th century. 到 19 世纪中期，也就是 1850 年，这个数字骤降至 10%，然后到 20 世纪中期则降至 3%。

by the way 顺便提起，顺便说说；在途中

☞ ***By the way***, if you want more information about any of the trips, have a look at the student newspaper. 顺便说一下，如果你想了解更多有关旅行的信息，请阅读学生报。

call...out （为处理紧急事件而）召唤某人；命令（或建议）工人罢工

☞ Our daughter, Anna, isn't well this morning and I may have to ***call*** somebody ***out***. 我们的女儿安娜今天早上不舒服，我得叫人来。

call slip 借书单，索书单

☞ Please fill out all the information required on this ***call slip***. 请填写这张索书单里要求填写的所有信息。

cancel one's reservation 取消预订

☞ Sorry, I'm afraid I have to ***cancel my reservation***. 对不起，恐怕我得取消我的预订。

☞ call off one's reservation

Unit 5

capable of doing　有能力做，能胜任

☞ As you know, sharks have a reputation for being very dangerous creatures ***capable of*** injuring or killing humans, and I'd like to talk about sharks in Australia. 众所周知，鲨鱼以极端危险著称，它们能伤害甚至杀死人类，我将谈论一下澳大利亚的鲨鱼。

☞ able to do

car exhaust fume　汽车尾气

☞ This kind of new fuel can help to reduce the emission of ***car exhaust fume***. 这种新型燃料有助于减少汽车尾气的排放。

☞ The target for the UK means that by 2008 we must reduce our carbon dioxide emissions by 12.5%, compared with 1990. 英国的目标是到 2008 年二氧化碳的排放量与 1990 年时相比必须减少 12.5%。

carry on　继续；进行下去

☞ We managed to ensure the bikes went out on time, but the other problems ***carried on*** for several months. 我们设法确保了自行车按时发货，但在接下来的几个月里其他问题接踵而至。

☞ go on

carry out　实行，进行；完成

☞ After three years of studying, I wanted adventure. I loved traveling, so I decided to join a voluntary organization and was sent to Ecuador to ***carry out*** land surveys. 在三年的学习之后，我想有惊险的刺激。我喜欢旅游，所以我决定加入一个志愿者组织并被派往厄瓜多尔进行土地调查。

不要和 carry-out（外卖食品）相混淆。

case study　个案研究

☞ A: Is there anything I should do before the course, like reading or anything?

B: We prefer to integrate reading with the course, so we don't give out a reading list in advance. But we like people to write a ***case study***, describing an organization they know.

A：在这门课开始前我应该做些什么呢，比如阅读或是别的什么？

B：我们会把阅读和这门课结合起来，所以我们不会提前给出阅读书单。但是我们希望学生能写一个个案研究，描述他们了解的一个组织。

case 和 study 在连读时只发一个［s］，类似词组还有：bus stop 和 take care 等。case study 是一个比较有"雅思特色"的词组，常出现在雅思考试的校园场景中，考生要充分了解其文化背景。

cash the check/cheque 兑现支票

☞ A: May I help you?

B: I'd like to ***cash the check***.

A：有什么需要帮忙的吗？

B：我想兑现支票。

cashpoint machine 自动柜员机

☞ You can withdraw cash from a ***cashpoint machine*** with a cash card. These are extremely useful as they enable you to withdraw cash from your account during the day or at night. 你可以用现金卡从自动柜员机中取钱。这些机器非常实用，不论白天还是晚上你都可以从账户中取钱。

☞ Automatic Teller Machine

cast one's eyes along 把视线投向

☞ During the economy crisis, people tend to ***cast their eyes along*** small amount of investments. 在经济危机中，人们倾向于小额投资。

☞ When we finally stop at the centre of an aisle, we pause and take stock, ***casting our eyes along*** the length of it. Now products displayed here sell well and do even better if they are placed at eye level so that the customer's eyes hit upon them instantly. 当我们最终在走廊的中心停住时，我们停下来挑选货物，将视线集中于走廊两边的货物。摆在这里的商品卖得很好，而且如果它们摆放的高度与视线同高就会卖得更好，因为它们一直都在顾客的视线内。

☞ take a glance at

catch a glimpse of 看到，瞥见

☞ The tour leaves at sundown and lets you ***catch a glimpse of*** some more of the rainforest's wildlife as it comes out at dusk to feed. 这次旅游在太阳落山时进行，让你看到更多生活在热带雨林里的野生动物，因为它们都在黄昏时分出来觅食。

catch sb. red handed 当场抓住

☞ I heard the thief was ***caught red handed*** in the supermarket. 我听说那个小偷在超市被当场抓获。

🔍英语里与"颜色"相关的常用表达：

green hand 新手
blue chip 蓝筹股
red letter days 节假日，纪念日，喜庆日
white elephant 累赘物
white sale 大减价
blue moon 不可能或稀有的时期或事情
black sheep 害群之马，败类
black letter days 倒霉的日子
white night 不眠之夜
white lie 善意的谎言

cater for 提供食品（或服务等）；满足，迎合

☞ A: Does the refectory ***cater for*** special diets? I have some food allergies.
B: Provided you warn the refectory in advance, it won't be a problem.
A：餐厅会提供一些特殊的饮食吗？我对有些食物过敏。
B：没问题，只要你提前告诉餐厅。

☞ Each day we offer three separate walks ***catering for*** all skills and fitness levels. 我们每天分别提供三次步行活动，以满足各种技能与健康水平的人的需求。

☞ provide for

🔍catering service（饮食服务）是雅思听力中的常见短语，catering 常和 accommodation 搭配出现：catering and accommodation 食宿服务。

certificate course 证书课程

☞ For Sports Administrators we provide a four-month ***certificate course*** but you should be aware that this is designed for those who are in employment. 我们为运动管理者提供一个为期四个月的证书课程，但是你必须清楚这专门针对在职人员。

change one's mind 改变主意

☞ A: I wanted to get my things moved into my room, and just take a look around here. So, did you decide to do English in the end?
B: No, I ***changed my mind*** and opted for history instead. And you're doing biology, if I remember correctly.
A：我想把东西搬进房间，然后到处转转。你最后选英语了吗？
B：没有，我改变主意了，选了历史。如果我没记错的话，你选的应该是生物吧。

charter flight 包机，专机

☞ There's the Ticket Shop, where you can get some very good deals on, well for examples, coaches to London or inexpensive ***charter flights***, as cheap as you'll get anywhere people say, or tickets for big pop groups playing here or at other venues all over the country. 那是"票券商店"，你可以在那买到一些相当划算的票，比如去伦敦的长途客车票或便宜的包机机票，票价和你在别处买到的一样便宜，还能购买知名流行乐队在这里或在全国其他地方演出的票。

🔍 与"飞机"相关的常用词组：

tourist class 经济舱
cabin class 二等舱
first class 头等舱
passenger cabin 客舱
boarding gate 登机口
boarding pass/check 登机牌
jet lag 飞机时差综合征
flight schedule 航班时刻表
forced landing 迫降

chase up 追讨，索要；催促；找寻

☞ We can ***chase up*** your tutor if you're not getting proper feedback on how you are getting on in your subject. 如果你在学科学习方面没有得到恰当的反馈，我们可以要求你的导师给你提供。

chat with 和…聊天

☞ You can ***chat with*** an artificial intelligence robot over the website. Please choose a robot to talk with. 你可以通过这个网站和一个人工智能机器人聊天。请选择你想要与其聊天的机器人。

check in 检查，登记，报到

☞ Passengers are supposed to ***check in*** at least an hour before airplane's departure. 乘客至少应该在飞机起飞前一个小时进行安检。

☞ sign in, book in

check on 查对；检查

☞ I think I'd better ***check on*** prices for CD player. 我想我最好查一下 CD 播放器的价格。

☞ A: Can you ***check on*** the deadline for my term paper?

B: Certainly, please wait for a moment.

A：您能确认一下我学期论文的最后期限吗？

B：当然，请稍等。

check out （从图书馆）借书；结账离开；检查

☞ A: What about the reading materials? Have you ***checked out*** the journal articles in the list?

B: Umm, no, not yet, there were about twenty of them, and I wasn't sure which ones would be most useful or important.

A：阅读材料呢？你借到书单上列出的期刊了吗？

B：没，还没呢，一共有 20 本左右，我不确定哪些是最有用的、最重要的。

☞ If you don't ***check out*** at the delivery desk, you will be fined. 未在借书台登记将被罚款。

🔍与“图书馆”相关的表达：

reference stacks 书库	delivery desk 借书台
call slip 索书单	admission card 借书卡
renew 续借	closed reserved 只读不借
not for circulation 不外借	out circulation 借出
in circulation 在书库里	return in time 及时归还
date of expiry 期限	inter-library service 图书馆馆际服务

check/cheque account　支票账户

☞ Can you remember last year's ***check account*** rate? 你记得去年的支票账户率吗？

cheer...up　让…开心

☞ The zookeeper ***cheered*** a depressed panda ***up*** by putting a TV set in its cage. 为哄一只情绪低落的熊猫开心，动物饲养员在笼子里放了一台电视机。

cheering section　拉拉队

☞ The ***cheering section*** is always the hottest association in high school. 拉拉队总是中学里最热门的社团。

church service　教堂礼拜

☞ Maybe we should go to the Cathedral today because it's Sunday tomorrow, and even though it's open every day it might be more difficult to get in tomorrow because of the ***church services***. 或许我们应该今天去大教堂，因为明天是星期天，尽管教堂每天开门，但因为做礼拜的缘故，明天也许会更难进入。

🔍与“教堂”相关的表达：

choir 唱诗班	hymn 赞美诗	preach 布道
priest 牧师	go to church 做礼拜	worship 做礼拜

civil servant　文职官员；公务员

☞ The supervisory system of ***civil servant*** is of importance to establish efficient, incorrupt government and select highly qualified civil servant's team. 公务员监督制度是建立高效、廉洁政府和选拔高素质公务员队伍的重要保证。

☞ public servant

classical literature　古典文学

☞ Do you know how many customs are described in the ***classical literature***? 你知道古典文学里描述了多少种习俗吗？

与"文学"相关的词组：

romantic literature 浪漫文学
realistic literature 现实文学
contemporary literature 现代文学
popular literature 大众文学
light literature 通俗文学
love story 爱情小说
detective story 侦探小说
mystery story 怪诞小说
deluxe binding 精装
flat stitching 平装

classical music　古典音乐

☞ The academy's theory is that, apart from being an excellent musician, success also means being an educator for ***classical music***. 该学院的理论是，成功不仅意味着成为一名优秀的音乐家，还意味着成为一名古典音乐的教育者。

与"音乐"相关的常用表达：

blues 布鲁斯
jazz 爵士乐
string 弦
wind instrument 管乐器
pop music 流行音乐

clean up　打扫，清理，梳洗；挣得(很多钱)

☞ A: Look, the room is in a mess. I don't know how to do.

B: What you should do is to ***clean up*** the toys and put them into the wardrobe.

A：看，房间乱七八糟的，我不知道该怎么办。

B：你要做的就是整理玩具并把它们放进衣柜里。

☞ tidy up

clear off　清除；摆脱；清偿

☞ After ten years' hard working, the poor man has finally ***cleared off*** the debt. 辛苦工作十年后，这个可怜的男子终于还清了债务。

☞ run away

closed reserve　只读不借

☞ A: Won't everyone take the books out of the library as soon as they get the reading list?

B: Well, yes, they might. But most of the important ones are held in ***Closed Reserve***...that's a part of the library where you can go to read books but you can't take them out of the building.

A：大家不都是在一拿到阅读书单后就把那些书从图书馆借走的吗？

B：或许是的，但是大多数重要的书都保存在只读不借区域里，放在该区域的书你只能阅读，却不能借出图书馆。

closed stacks　不外借书库

☞ Many foreign college libraries have both open and ***closed stacks***. 国外很多大学图书馆都分外借书库和不外借书库。

coffee break 上班间的休息时间，工间小憩

☞ A: We usually go round with an envelope to send invitations during ***coffee break***. Don't we?

B: Yeah, ***coffee break***'s always the best time.

A：我们经常在大家休息时间拿着一个信封四处走动去发请柬，不是吗？

B：是的，休息时间总是最合适的时间了。

come along 陪伴；赶快（用于催促或鼓励某人）；发生；进步，进展

☞ Thank you very much for ***coming along*** with us today. 非常感谢今天有你们的陪伴。

☞ ***Come along***! Let's go together. 来吧，咱们一起去！

come to an end 结束

☞ The project ***came to an end*** after five years and when I returned to the UK in 1998, I started planning the charity base. 该项目在五年后结束了。1998 年我回到英国，开始计划建立这个慈善基地。

☞ end up

come to nothing 彻底失败，失败

☞ A: What most concerns me is I'm still not doing very well in my assignments.

B: Well, I know that you plan your writing carefully, but this can ***come to nothing*** if the assignment doesn't answer the question.

A：最让我担心的是我的作业完成得还不是很好。

B：我知道你进行了细致的写作构思，但如果未能回答问题，就只能以失败告终。

☞ fall flat

come true 实现梦想

☞ A dream ***came true*** in 1995, when over 96 days of the spring and summer, and expedition of four men undertook what they believed to have been the first and only complete end-to-end crossing of Morocco's Attora mountains. 1995 年这个梦想实现了，在历经春夏两个季节 96 个日子后，四个人的探险队终于横越了摩洛哥的奥特拉山脉，他们相信这是人类首次终极翻越该山脉。

come up to 走进，上来；达到，符合

☞ I have a handout here with references on the subject, so if you are interested, please ***come up to*** the desk and take a copy. 我这里有些该学科参考书目的印刷品，感兴趣的话可以到讲台上来拿一份。

come up with　赶上；提供；想出

☞ Because not all paperclips are of the same length, students should ***come up with*** somc strange answers. 因为所有的回形针长度不一，所以学生们应该会得出一些奇怪的答案。

☞ A: If you could search out some silver paper to bring along to use in the sessions, you know, it's shiny—it looks like water, that'd be great.

B: Yes, of course. We'll see what we can ***come up with***. Well, thank you ever so much for all your help.

A：如果你能找到一些银色的纸带到课上来用，你知道的，就是闪闪发光的那种，看上去像水面，那就太棒了。

B：是的，当然。我们看看能想出点什么。非常感谢你提供了这么多的帮助。

☞ catch up with

commercial value　商业价值

☞ Those sports stars can achieve their ***commercial value*** by taking advertising for commercial company. 那些体育明星可以通过为商业公司拍广告来实现他们的商业价值。

commercial/merchant bank　商业银行

☞ A: Excuse me, how can I get to the nearest ***commercial bank***?

B: Sorry, I'm a stranger.

A：打扰一下，请问最近的商业银行在哪里？

B：对不起，我对这儿也不熟。

常见的银行种类：

agricultural bank 农业银行	communication bank 交通银行
industrial and commercial bank 工商银行	construction bank 建设银行
investment bank 投资银行	joint venture bank 合资银行

commit a crime　犯罪

☞ The employees may be involved in the crime, but they're acting in the first place for the company or they may not even realise they're ***committing a crime***. 员工可能会卷入犯罪，但是他们的行为首先是为了公司，或者他们甚至没能意识到自己是在犯罪。

与"犯罪"相关的词组：

crime rate 犯罪率	juvenile crime 青少年犯罪
continuous crime 继续犯罪	habitual criminal 惯犯
criminal motive 犯罪动机	criminal gang 犯罪团伙
criminal case 刑事案件	civil case 民事案件

common sense 常识

☞ You couldn't totally rely on your ***common sense*** to answer those questions. 你不能完全依赖常识来回答那些问题。

communicate with 与…沟通

☞ I think you should learn to ***communicate with*** your parents. 我认为你应该学会与你的父母沟通。

☞ exchange ideas with

compare with 和…相比

☞ The educationist found that some parents always ***compared*** their own children ***with*** other kids. 这名教育学家发现，一些家长总是拿自己的孩子和别的小孩作比较。

☞ in comparison with

compatible with 与…兼容的

☞ Google said that its web-based messaging platform is now more ***compatible with*** the Microsoft Outlook. 谷歌称他们基于网络的信息平台现在能更好地和微软邮件系统相兼容了。

compensate for 赔偿，弥补

☞ Unfortunately, the sound on this early film was not very good and I believe the producers put subtitles on the film—that is, they printed the dialogue along the bottom of the film to ***compensate for*** this poor sound quality. 不幸的是，这部早期电影的声效不是很好，我相信制片人给电影加上字幕——也就是，他们把对白打在电影的下方是为了弥补这糟糕的音效。

compete with 与…竞争

☞ Sport used to just ***compete with*** sport. Nowadays it ***competes with*** other leisure activities. The spectators go to sport to be entertained rather than out of loyalty to a team. 过去，运动只是和运动本身竞争。 现在它与其他休闲活动竞争。观众们去观看运动比赛是为了娱乐，而非出于对某支队伍的忠诚。

complain about 投诉，抱怨

☞ It is impolite to ***complain about*** the food in front of the cook. 在厨师面前抱怨食物不好吃是不礼貌的。

☞ make complaint about

compound apartment 复式公寓

☞ It is Christine's dream to buy a luxurious ***compound apartment*** at central New York. 克里斯汀的梦想是在纽约市中心买一幢豪华复式公寓。

computer literate 会用计算机的，懂计算机的

☞ It is quite necessary for young people to be ***computer literate***. 对年轻人来说，具备计算机知识是很有必要的。

concentrate on 全神贯注于；致力于

☞ Many students find it's hard to ***concentrate on*** their studying after long vacation. 很多学生发现，长假过后难以专心学习。

☞ be absorbed in

concessions for 对…的让步，面向…的优惠

☞ Now, by far the most useful type of account to open is a current account. When you do this, you will actually get what is called a student account which is a current account with special ***concessions for*** students. 迄今，最有用的账户类型就是活期账户。申请活期账户时，你实际得到的是个学生账户，这是个对学生有着特殊优惠的活期账户。

confine oneself to (doing) 把自己局限于

☞ You should not ***confine yourself to*** some general, ambiguous remarks on this occasion. 在这种场合下，你不应该只限于发表一些模棱两可的一般性言论。

confirm a reservation 确认预订

☞ I'd like to ***confirm the reservation*** for three rooms in this hotel . 我想确认一下在该酒店预订的三间客房。

consist of 由…组成

☞ Back in the first to the fourth century AD, when the Romans controlled England, London grew into a town of 45,000 people, and what's now the East End—the area by the river Thames, and along the road heading north-east from London to the coast—***consisted of*** farmland with crops and livestock which helped to feed that population. 回望公元一至四世纪，当时罗马控制了英格兰，伦敦发展成一个有着 4.5 万人口的城镇，现在的东区——泰晤士河沿岸，以及从伦敦顺东北方向直到海岸边的区域——到处都是农田，种植庄稼和饲养牲畜，养育着当时的人们。

☞ Two main cereal crops were introduced to Ireland during this time: wheat and barley, both in several varieties. The main evidence for their presence ***consists of*** impressions on pottery, where a cereal grain accidentally became embedded in the surface of a pot before it was fired. 当时两种主要的谷类作物被引进到爱尔兰：小麦和大麦，都有着好几个品种。它们存在的主要证据是陶器上的压痕，在陶器被烧制前一颗麦粒偶然嵌在了其表面。

☞ constitute, make up of

contact lenses 隐形眼镜

☞ My ***contact lenses*** fall out. Can you help me find them? 我的隐形眼镜掉出来了，你能帮我找找吗？

contrary to 与…相反

☞ ***Contrary to*** what you might imagine, the size of the cycle is not determined by the size of the wheels (except in children's cycles), but by the size of the frame. 可能与你想象的相反，自行车的尺寸不是取决于车轮(儿童自行车除外)，而是车架。

contribute to 是…的原因；捐献；有助于

☞ Few house had electricity at the beginning of twentieth century, so other sources of power were used, like coal for the fires which heated perhaps just one room. Of course, the smoke from these ***contributed*** a great deal ***to*** the air pollution for which London used to be famous. 20 世纪初，很少有房子通上电，所以人们就使用其他一些能源，比如烧煤来提高室温，或许只能暖和一个房间。当然，其产生的烟却是造成伦敦臭名昭著的空气污染的一个主要原因。

☞ Her positive attitude ***contributes to*** her success. 她的乐观态度促使她获得成功。

☞ be helpful to

convert into 转化成；改造成

☞ The original house was ***converted into*** a residential college for the university in 1940 and since then has continued to be added on to and modernized. 最初的房子于 1940 年被改建成这所大学的一个住宿学院，从那时起这栋房子就不断被扩建并变得现代化。

convince sb. of 使某人相信

☞ Mother tries to ***convince her daughter of*** the nonexistence of fairy tales. 母亲努力让女儿相信童话是虚构的。

cooperate with 与…合作

☞ I like playing basketball because it can make me stronger and train me to ***cooperate with*** others. 我喜欢打篮球，因为它能让我变得更加强壮并训练我与他人合作的能力。

☞ work with

cope with 应付

☞ Of course, you have to ***cope with*** all the pressure without your usual social network—you know, the social contacts, family and friends you could normally rely on for help. 当然，你得在没有正常的社会网的情况下应对所有压力——你知道的，社会网就是你通常寻求帮助的社会关系，包括家人和朋友。

☞ deal with

Unit 6

corporate loan　融资

☞ The problem is whether the *corporate loan* market is globally integrated. 问题在于融资市场是否在全球范围内进行了整合。

correspondence course　函授课程

☞ Peter has studied laws through a *correspondence course* in the past three years and now he becomes a lawyer. 在过去三年里彼得通过函授课程学习法律，如今他是一名律师。

cost sb. an arm and a leg　花费一大笔钱，付出昂贵代价

☞ I quickly told her that I knew that it would *cost me an arm and a leg* to buy a dress for her. 我很快就告诉她我知道给她买一件礼服会花掉我一大笔钱。

cough up　咳嗽；(将食物或钱)吐出来，勉强交出

☞ Then they bring up all the indigestible bits of skeleton and, of course, the wings in a pellet—a small ball of waste material which they *cough up*. 然后它们会把所有不能消化的骨骼，当然包括翅膀之类的东西，弄成一个小球吐出来。

☞ spit up, hand over

counselling service　咨询服务

☞ The organization offered *counselling service* for the students. 该组织为学生提供咨询服务。

count on　依赖，指望

☞ We must *count on* your support and cooperation, and we are certain that we—in the spirit of partnership—will be able to steer this case to a successful conclusion. 我们必须依赖你的支持和合作，而且我们都确信在合作精神的指导下，我们可以成功地完成这个项目。

☞ depend on

count towards　(按照获得某事物的条件)被包括在内，被算入(最终结果或数量)

☞ A: What kind of course work would I have to do?

B: Well, it's a mixture. You'd be expected to write an essay each month, which *counts towards* your final assessment.

A：我需要做哪种课程作业？

B：很多种。每个月要写一篇论文，这包括在你的期末评估里。

☞ figure in

course arrangement 课程安排

☞ Teachers are discussing the ***course arrangement*** for the next semester. 老师们正在讨论下学期的课程安排。

course code 课程编号

☞ A: Let's have a look at them. What do we have to do?

B: Let's fill in the top first, let's see, Course, ***Course code***.

A：让我们先看看吧，我们要做什么呢？

B：我们从最开始填起吧，看看，课程、课程编号。

course feedback form 课程反馈表

☞ A: Ben—I just remembered I never filled in that form for Nick—did you do it?

B: The ***course feedback form***?

A: Yes. If you want, we can do it together, and I've got mine here.

A：本，我刚刚想起我还没帮尼克填那个表呢，你填了吗？

B：是课程反馈表吗？

A：是的，如果你想的话，我们可以一起填，我的在这里呢。

cover an area of 具有…的面积

☞ The new park is under construction and it will ***cover an area of*** two square kilometers. 新公园正在建设中，其面积将达两平方公里。

cover the cost of 包含…费用

☞ I wonder if this amount will ***cover the cost of*** accommodation. 我想知道这个数目是否包含住宿费。

crack down 严加处置(或限制)，取缔，制裁

☞ Facing an increasingly serious official corruption, the government of every country has made a serial of policies to ***crack down***. 面对日益严重的官员腐败现象，各国政府都制定了一系列措施来严加制止。

cramming teaching 填鸭式教学

☞ ***Cramming teaching*** is harmful to the development of students' learning ability. 填鸭式教学不利于学生学习能力的培养。

credit card 信用卡

☞ A: Can I pay that by ***credit card***?

B: I'm afraid not. You'll have to send a cheque to us, or you can pay at the conference office.

A：我可以用信用卡支付吗？

B：恐怕不行。你需要寄给我们支票，或者去会议办公室付钱。

雅思考试中常考的付款方式有支票(check)、现金(cash)和银行转账(bank transfer)等。

credit point 学分

☞ Tomorrow I'll tell you the easy way to earn a ***credit point***. 明天我将告诉你一个挣学分的简单方法。

creep up on 不知不觉地来到…身边，悄悄靠近；(不知不觉)开始影响

☞ Tiredness can easily ***creep up on*** you while you are driving. 开车时会很容易不知不觉就累了。

crime rate 犯罪率

☞ Why is the ***crime rate*** in this area still on the rise? 为什么这一地区的犯罪率仍在上升?

与"犯罪率上升"相关的一些问题：

overpopulation 人口过剩	unemployment 失业
medical care 医疗保健	housing problem 住房问题
environmental pollution 环境污染	wealth distribution 财富分配
urban sprawl 城市扩张	social instability 社会动荡

cross-country race 越野赛

☞ Henry has beaten his opponent in the latest ***cross-country race***. 亨利在最近一次的越野赛中击败了对手。

culture shock 文化冲击

☞ When Chinese come to Western countries they may experience a great ***culture shock***. 中国人来到西方国家时可能会感受到巨大的文化冲击。

cup of tea 喜爱的人(或事物)

☞ The proposal made by the new comer is just my ***cup of tea***. 新来的那个人提的议案正合我意。

☞ The TV series is popular with a certain type of young girls, but to be frank it is not my ***cup of tea***. 这部电视连续剧很受一些年轻女孩的喜爱，但坦白地说我不喜欢。

currency exchange 现金兑换处；货币兑换

☞ A: Excuse me, can you tell me where the ***currency exchange*** is?

B: Over there.

A：打扰一下，你能告诉我现金兑换处在哪吗?

B：在那边。

current account　活期账户

☞ A: Is it a ***current account*** or a deposit account you wanted?

B: A ***current account***.

A：你想开一个活期账户还是储蓄账户？

B：活期账户。

☞ Saving your money in a ***current account*** gives you less interest than in a fixed rate bond for five years. 将钱存入活期账户五年所得利息要少于投入定期利率债券五年所得利息。

current affair　时事

☞ Internet brings us news about ***current affairs*** and thus helps us know what is happening at home and abroad. 网络带给我们时事新闻，帮助我们了解国内外动态。

curriculum schedule　课程表

☞ Make sure you get your ***curriculum schedule*** before the class begins. 确保在上课前拿到课程表。

curriculum vitae　简历

☞ Please send your ***curriculum vitae*** to our website. 请将简历发送至我们的网站。

🔍 这个词组常简写为 CV；"简历"也可以直接用 résumé 表示。

cut down　减少数量(或数额)

☞ About borrowing books, I'm living out of town, so I'm hoping I can borrow quite a few items, and ***cut down*** on the number of trips I have to make. 有关借书的事，我住在城外，所以希望(一次)能借很多书，这样就能减少来回的次数。

☞ decrease

cut out　阻挡；切掉；精减

☞ In those areas with sealed windows it will be necessary to fit fans with absorbers to ***cut out*** the noise. 在那些窗户密封的区域，有必要安装带噪音吸收器的电扇。

dash off　匆忙完成

☞ A: How long did you work on the whole draft?

B: Well, I spend about two or three weeks reading and doing general research and then I ***dashed*** the writing ***off*** very quickly...so about four weeks in all.

A：你完成整个草稿花了多久？

B：我花了大概两三周的时间阅读和做全面的研究，然后很快就写完了……一共用了大约四周时间。

date back to 始于，追溯到

☞ The custom ***dates back to*** medieval times. 这项风俗可追溯到中世纪。

date of expiry 借书期限

☞ He promises to see about the ***date of expiry*** and return the book in time. 他保证注意借书期限，并且按时还书。

daytime phone number 日间电话号码

☞ In the Yellow Pages you will find the ***daytime phone number*** of the company. 你能在(电话)黄页中找到这家公司的日间电话号码。

dead easy 极其简单

☞ Now, going on to suggestions for improvement, one thing that wasn't so good, I think we could have done a bit more work at the beginning, I mean at the beginning it seemed ***dead easy***. 现在让我们开始提些改进建议吧，有一点不太好，我认为在刚开始时我们应该多做些工作，我的意思是一开始实在是太简单了。

dead 作副词有"全然地，绝对地"的意思，如：dead sure 表示"非常肯定"，dead serious 表示"非常认真"。

deal with 关于；论及，涉及；处理问题，解决；应付，对付

☞ These books are all useful, but I don't expect anyone to read them all, because a number of them ***deal with*** the same issues. 这些书都很有用，但是我不希望有人把它们全部读完，因为有些书论及的是同样的问题。

☞ cope with

death toll 伤亡人数

☞ It's reported that ***death toll*** has increased in the earthquake. 据报道，地震中的死亡人数上升了。

debate on...with 就…与…辩论

☞ He has been ***debating on*** the Critical Period Hypothesis ***with*** the other linguists for a decade. 他已经与其他语言学家就关键期假说争辩了达十年之久。

department store 百货商店

☞ A: I don't think small shops can compete with large ***department stores***.

B: Every coin has two sides.

A：我觉得小商店竞争不过大百货商店。

B：事物皆有两面性。

departmental library 系图书馆

☞ If we tried to use interviews, I saw a book in the ***departmental library*** that'll be helpful: it's called *Interviews That Work*, by Wilson, published in Oxford in 1988. 如果我们试图采取采访的方法，我在系图书馆看到的一本书可能会有用：威尔逊的《采访指南》，1988 年牛津大学出版。

departure lounge 候机室

☞ The new ***departure lounge*** will open to the public next month. 新候机室将于下月对公众开放。

与"机场"相关的词组：

duty-free shop 免税店	excess charge 行李超重费用
vacant seat 空座	direct/non-stop flight 直达航班
connecting flight 中转航班	destination 目的地
flight number 航班号	flight record (记录飞机飞行信息的)黑匣子
departure time 起飞时间	airport terminal 航站楼
luggage locker 行李暂存箱	luggage claim 行李提取处

depend on/upon 取决于；依赖，依靠；指望

☞ I don't want to ***depend*** too much ***on*** my parents. 我不想过度依靠父母。

☞ It would ***depend on*** the circumstances. 这要视情况而定。

deposit account 定期存款账户

☞ I'd like to open a ***deposit account*** in that bank. 我想在那家银行开一个定期存款账户。

与"银行"相关的表达：

bank book 存折	earn interest 赚取利息
check account 支票账户	annual interest rate 年利率
blank check 空白支票	exchange rate 汇率

deposit money in a bank 存钱

☞ You should ***deposit money in the bank*** rather than put it at home. 你应该把钱存入银行而不是放在家里。

descend from 是…的后裔；起源于

☞ The early farmers kept various animals, including cattle and sheep. There's also evidence of pigs, but it is possible that these could have been ***descended from*** the native wild species. 早期农民饲养包括牛、羊在内的多种动物。也有证据显示猪的存在，但它们可能是当地的野生物种的后代。

☞ originate from

die a death 彻底失败；完全消失

☞ Our resident expert Liz will tell us which gadgets are worth buying and which will ***die a death***. 我们的常驻专家莉兹将告诉我们哪些物品值得购买，哪些完全不划算。

die out （家族、物种等）灭绝；（习俗等）消失

☞ The prince was very wealthy, and he managed to protect the lions—otherwise they'd probably have ***died out*** completely. 这位王子非常富有，他想方设法保护了狮子，否则它们可能已经完全灭绝了。

☞ become extinct

dip into 把手伸进(…里取东西)；翻阅，浏览；动用(存款)

☞ Levis ***dipped into*** the old newspaper for inspiration. 莱维斯翻阅旧报纸，寻找灵感。

☞ look through

diploma course 文凭课程

☞ Mary is studying a higher ***diploma course*** of computer in a private school. 玛丽正在一所私立学校攻读计算机高级文凭课程。

direct line number 直拨号码

☞ If you want to organize a trial session and look around the center, you'll need to speak to David Kynchley. I'll give you his ***direct line number***. 如果你想试听一节课并来这个中心转转的话，需要和戴维·肯奇力说一下。我会把他的直拨号码给你。

雅思曾考过以下和 number 相关的词组：

emergency contact/telephone number 紧急联系电话

passport number 护照号　　master card number 万事达卡号码

credit card number 信用卡号码　　ID number 身份证号

direct/non-stop flight 直达航班

☞ Susan is going to take a ***direct flight*** to Paris. 苏珊打算乘直达航班去巴黎。

discussion group 讨论小组

☞ A：Would you like to join our ***discussion group***?

B：I'd like to, but I have promised John to join theirs.

A：你想加入我们讨论小组吗？

B：我很想，但是我已经答应约翰加入他们组了。

🔍在国外，上课的形式多种多样，如讲座(lecture)、陈述(presentation)、导师指导(tutorial)、实地考察(field trip)等。

dispute against/with 与…辩论

☞ I have no time to ***dispute with*** you over such a naive topic. 我可没时间在这个幼稚的话题上跟你争论。

☞ debate with

distance education 远程教育

☞ There are pros and cons about ***distance education***. 远程教育优缺点并存。

divide into 把…分成

☞ The fourth experiment is called "Spinning Color Wheel." It looks like you get some cardboard and draw a circle on it, ***divide*** it ***into*** six equal segments and color each one in using different colors, then you thread a piece of string through the middle. 第四个实验叫做"旋转色轮"。在一张硬纸板上画一个圆，把它六等分并涂上不同的颜色，然后在纸板中心穿一条线。

To help things run smoothly, we have ***divided*** you ***into*** four teams—the blue team, the green team, the red team, and the yellow team. 为了让事情顺利进行，我们把你们分成了四队——蓝队、绿队、红队和黄队。

☞ split into

divide up 分割，分散

☞ First, I'll explain how the teams are ***divided up*** and then we'll be giving you color-coded T-shirts so we can identify you more easily. 首先我会解释如何进行分组，然后我会发给你们不同颜色的T恤，以便更容易识别。

divorce rate 离婚率

☞ The high ***divorce rates*** in North America are creating a poverty cycle for women. 北美地区的高离婚率导致女性的贫困循环。

do a face-to-face interview 进行面谈，做面对面的采访

☞ A: Do we have to use any particular method to get our data? Can we mail out a questionnaire, or ***do face-to-face interviews***, or maybe even observations?

B: Well actually, it looks like we don't have a choice. We have to do telephone interviews.

A：我们需要用什么特殊的方法来收集数据吗？邮寄调查问卷，或做面对面的采访，甚至是通过观察呢？

B：实际上，看起来我们别无选择，必须做电话采访。

do a presentation on 做…方面的介绍

☞ Today Vivien is going to ***do a presentation on*** the hat-making project she did with her class during her last teaching practice. 今天维维安将就她上次教学实习时和她的学生们进行的制帽项目作个介绍。

do background reading 进行背景知识阅读，背景阅读

☞ The course requires students to ***do*** a huge amount of ***background reading***. 这门课要求学生进行大量的背景阅读。

do further study 深入学习，深造

☞ That is all we have for this morning, but you will be able to ***do further study*** on this important area in the library. 这就是我们今天上午要讲的全部内容，但是你们需要去图书馆就这一重要领域做更深入的学习。

☞ pursue further education

do housework 做家务

do housework

☞ A: Who ***does housework*** in your family?

B: My mother.

A：你们家谁做家务？

B：我妈妈。

do one's homework 指"做家庭作业"。

do jogging 慢跑

☞ A: When did you start to ***do jogging***?

B: About one year ago.

A：你什么时候开始慢跑的？

B：大约一年前。

常见的相关表达：

go hiking 徒步旅行
make an excursion 远足
stay/keep in shape 保持健康
gain/put on weight 增加体重
sports center 运动中心
sports facilities 运动设施
health club 健身俱乐部
team sports 团队运动

Unit 7

do...a favor 帮助

☞ A: Could you ***do me a favor***, if it's not too much trouble?

B: Yeah, anything.

A：如果不是太麻烦的话，你可以帮我个忙吗？

B：好的，什么都可以。

☞ help/assist...

do some trips 旅行

☞ A: My family and I are staying in Trebirch for a week or two and we wanted to know about the train services. We're hoping to ***do some*** local ***trips***.

B: Ok. Well, I can give you lots of details about all the trains going from Trebirch.

A：我们一家人要在垂博克待一两周时间，因此想了解一下其铁路服务。我们希望能在当地旅行旅行。

B：好的。我会详细告诉你所有从垂博克始发的火车的情况。

do...on one's own 自己做

☞ I mean the biggest difference between college and school is that new college students really have to ***do*** a lot of work ***on their own***, and it's sometimes useful to get advice on how to take control of your time and work effectively. 我认为大学和中学的最大区别在于大学新生需要自己去做很多事情，所以有时获得一些有关如何控制时间并有效工作的建议是很有用的。

domestic market 国内市场

☞ A: Do we export lots of bananas overseas, to Europe and Asia for instance?

B: Well, oddly enough, no. They're mostly grown for the ***domestic market***, which is surprising when you think about it because we grow an enormous number of bananas each year.

A：我们大量出口香蕉到国外吗，如欧洲和亚洲？

B：非常奇怪的是，很少。它们大多数都供给国内市场，这会让你很吃惊，因为我们每年都大量种植香蕉。

☞ national market

double lock 上双锁

☞ The little girl ***double locked*** her door and had been in her room for two hours. 那个小女孩把房门反锁起来，在房间里待了两个小时。

double unit　双课时量

☞ A: I lecture on that program. What do you need to know?

B: Quite a few things, actually. Firstly, how many lectures a week do I have to attend?

A: Ah, well, the Economics I course is a ***double unit*** so there are two lectures a week and one tutorial.

A：我教那门学科，你想知道些什么？

B：实际上有很多问题。首先，我一周需要参加多少次讲座？

A：我所教的经济学 I 是双课时量，所以一周有两次讲座和一节辅导课。

在国外，学生每年都要读满一定数量的 unit，每所学校要求的 unit 数量各不相同。有些科目比较大，可以作为 whole unit，有些很小的科目只能算 half unit。

double-bed room　带双人床的房间

☞ A: What can I help you?

B: I want to book a ***double-bed room***.

A：有什么能为您效劳的吗？

B：我想订一间有双人床的房间。

single room 指"单间"。

draft an outline　起草大纲

☞ A: Have you ***drafted an outline*** for your program?

B: Not yet.

A：你起草计划大纲了吗？

B：还没有。

draft plan　草案

☞ Please present your ***draft plan*** the day after tomorrow. 请你后天把草案交给我。

☞ A: Do we have to have our own ***draft plan*** by 31 January?

B: No, your ***draft plan*** is due on 7 February, which is a week later, so that should give you plenty of time.

A：我们需要在 1 月 31 日前列出草案吗？

B：不用，递交草案的截止时间是 2 月 7 日，也就是在那一周之后，所以你应该有充裕的时间。

draw out　抽出；提取（现金）；拖延；（天黑得）渐晚，（白昼）渐长

☞ If you want to ***draw out*** cash for yourself you can make the cheque payable in your own name or to cash. 你可以通过让支票以你的名义支付或兑现达到提取现金的目的。

draw the line 划界限

☞ A: Do we invite faculty heads?

B: No, better ***draw the line*** between the dean and the ordinary teacher.

A: 我们要邀请系领导吗?

B: 不要了,(我们)最好在系主任和普通老师间划清界限。

draw up 草拟,拟订,制订;(车辆)到达某处停下

☞ The SU (student union) Committee collated the results and ***drew up*** a report. 学生会核对了结果并草拟了一份报告。

☞ Maybe we could ***draw up*** a table and look at examples of each medium in turn. 也许我们可以列出一张表,分别看一下各种媒体的例子。

☞ A: The target was to ***draw up*** a survey checklist which I...

B: Yes, you e-mailed me it last week.

A: Have you had a chance to look...?

B: Of course, um I think it's good. Very much on the right lines.

A: 目标是起草一个调查清单,这个我……

B: 对,你上周已经在邮件里发给我了。

A: 您抽时间看了吗?

B: 当然,我认为很好,很切合主题。

☞ sketch out, make out a draft of

dress rehearsal 彩排

☞ I am stunned by your performance at the ***dress rehearsal***. 你在彩排中的表现让我叹为观止。

dressing room 更衣室,化妆室

☞ A: Is there anything different in the auditorium for the performers?

B: Yes, we've made a number of improvements backstage. The small, dark ***dressing rooms*** we used to have have been converted into two large airy rooms, so they're much more comfortable now.

A: 演员们所用的礼堂有什么变化吗?

B: 有的,我们在后台做了一系列改进。过去阴暗、狭窄的更衣室已经被改成了两间宽敞通风的房间,现在舒适多了。

☞ fitting room, changing room

与"化妆"相关的表达:

dressing table/dresser 梳妆台	bedside cabinet 床头柜
candlestick 烛台	wardrobe 衣橱
cosmetic products 化妆品	skin care 护肤

drop down　掉下，下落；倒下；迅速低下身子

☞ On the minus side, our testers did not like the fact that the side of the cot did not ***drop down***, making it difficult to pick up newborn babies. 测试者觉得这张婴儿床不好的一点是，不能降下侧板，要抱起新生儿很困难。

drop in　顺便走访，拜访

☞ I think the counselling sessions would be useful for everybody but well, everybody has their own way of going about things. I prefer people just to ***drop in*** when they can. 我认为咨询课程对每个人都会有用，但是每个人都有不同的做事方式。可能的话，我希望大家都来看看。

drop out of　退出

☞ If you fail a subject or ***drop out of*** a course because it's too difficult then your self-esteem can suffer. 如果你一门功课不及格，或因为课程太难而退出，那么你的自尊心就会受损。

drop-out rate　辍学率

☞ The ***drop-out rate*** of schools in this region is appalling. 该地区学校的辍学率高得惊人。

各种常见的"率"：

unemployment rate 失业率	interest rate 利率
birth rate 出生率	death rate 死亡率
exchange rate 汇率	divorce rate 离婚率

dry up　干涸；耗尽，枯竭；（突然）讲不出话来；擦干（刚洗的碗碟）

☞ You generally think of Africa as being a very hot and dry place, but it is not in comparison with Australia. In many parts of Australia standing water, that is dams, puddle and so forth, ***dry up*** rapidly and some rainfall barely penetrates the soil. 你们普遍认为非洲是一个既炎热又干旱的地方，但实际上它与澳大利亚不能相提并论。在澳大利亚的很多地方，诸如水库、水坑等死水都干涸得非常快，降水很少渗入土壤。

☞ run dry

due to　由于，归因于

☞ The student's failing in the examination was ***due to*** the headache. 该学生由于头疼而没有通过考试。

☞ because of, owing to

duty-free shop　免税店

☞ There are some ***duty-free shops*** in my city and I like to go there for shopping. 我所在的城市有一些免税店，我喜欢去那里购物。

🔍一些常见的“店”：

grocer 杂货店	toy store 玩具店
flower shop 花店	leather shop 皮革店
antique shop 古董店	stationery shop 文具店
book store 书店	snack bar 快餐店
pharmacy 药店	food store 食品店

eager to do　渴望做

☞ Playing football makes Jason energetic and ***eager to*** engage in the work of the day. 踢足球令贾森充满活力，并渴望投入工作。

☞ keen to do

eat out　外出就餐

☞ A: What exactly do we have to do?

B: Well, it says here we have to look at one area of the entertainment industry. There's a list of the different types.

A: What are they?

B: Music, cinema, theatre, sport, and ***eating out***.

A：我们具体要做些什么呢？

B：要求上说我们需要关注娱乐产业的某一方面。有一个类别清单。

A：都是些什么呢？

B：音乐、电影、戏剧、运动和外出就餐。

ecological balance　生态平衡

☞ The protection of ***ecological balance*** counts on everyone of us. 保护生态平衡要靠你我他。

🔍与“生态”相关的词组：

protected species 受保护的物种	endangered species 濒危物种
conservation area 保护区	national reserve 国家保护区
food chain 食物链	biological diversity 生物多样性
environment-friendly products 环保产品	

education system　教育体系

☞ I think the ***education system*** in our country focuses enough on science and technology. 我认为我们国家的教育体系充分注重科技。

🔍与“学习”相关的表达：

curriculum 课程
syllabus 课程大纲
ways of examining students 考试方法
required/compulsory course 必修课
basic course 基础课
teaching method 教学方法
the credit system 学分制
quality of school 学校质量
elective/optional course 选修课

either...or （在两个可能性中进行选择）要么…要么，不是…就是，或者…或者

☞ If you don't want to do the whale watch cruise, your guide will take anyone who is interested ***either*** on a bushwalk through the national park near the hotel, and there's no extra charge for that, ***or*** on a fishing trip. 如果不想参加观鲸游览，感兴趣的话，导游会带你们去宾馆附近的国家公园体验一把丛林行走，是免费的，或者去钓鱼。

electronic gadget 电子器件；电子产品

☞ Children today like to play indoors because all their favorite ***electronic gadgets***, computer games and toys are all there. 如今，孩子们喜欢待在室内玩耍的原因是室内有他们最喜欢的所有电子产品、电脑游戏和玩具。

eligible to do 有资格做

☞ A: What about facilities for young children? I'd like to bring my daughter here while I'm studying.

B: How old is she?

A: Three.

B: Then she's ***eligible to*** join the nursery, which is supervised by a qualified nursery nurse. The waiting list for a place is quite long though, so you ought to apply now.

A：面向小孩子开放的设施怎么样？我想在我学习时把女儿送到这里来。

B：她多大了？

A：三岁。

B：那么她可以进托儿所，这家托儿所由高素质的保育员管理。很多人都想申请呢，你应该现在就申请。

☞ entitled to do

embark on/upon 从事；着手，开始

☞ Setting up an ostrich farm isn't something to ***embark on*** lightly. 开办鸵鸟农场不是一件轻易就能开始的事。

☞ Richard, a famous walker, ***embarks on*** his new journey to the Africa. 理查德，一个著名的徒步旅行者，踏上了他探索非洲的新旅程。

☞ go about

emphasize on　强调，注重

☞ As an English teacher, you should ***emphasize on*** practical skills rather than too much theoretical knowledge. 身为一名英语老师，你应该注重实践技能的培养，而不能过于强调理论知识。

☞ place an emphasis on

enable...to do　使…能够做

☞ The new programme ***enables*** older people ***to*** study at college. 这个新计划使老年人有机会在大学学习。

☞ Insulin ***enables*** the body ***to*** use and store sugar. 胰岛素使人体能够利用和贮存糖分。

end up　以…终结，以…收场；最后处于

☞ If you go on like this you will ***end up*** in prison. 你如果继续这样，早晚得进监狱。

☞ It is ironic that he dreams of becoming an astronaut but ***ends up*** being a waiter. 具有讽刺意味的是，他梦想成为一名宇航员，结果却当了服务生。

☞ A: I've been looking at some of last year's dissertations. Is that a good idea, sir? I heard...

B: Well, I don't think you should read them in details too early or you might ***end up*** taking more of their ideas than you realize.

A：我一直在看去年的一些论文，老师，这种做法好吗？我听说……

B：我觉得你不应该过早开始详细阅读那些论文，这样最终你可能会过多受他们想法的影响。

☞ wind up

end with　以…结束

☞ The day doesn't ***end with*** the return to base...after our dinner at communal tables designed to make all our guests feel part of a family atmosphere...entertainment is laid on nearly every night. 每天的活动不是返回基地就结束了，我们为客人精心设计的共享桌能让所有客人感受家庭氛围，晚饭后几乎每晚都会安排娱乐活动。

☞ finish with

endangered species　濒危物种

☞ The global crisis for ***endangered species*** is more serious than the financial crisis, with numbers of endangered animals and plants rising at high rates. 随着濒危动植物数量的不断增加，全球濒危物种危机要比金融危机来得更为严重。

enjoy a superb reputation 享有好口碑，享有盛誉

☞ The annual movie festival continues to ***enjoy a superb reputation*** with many visitors planning their weekend to the resort. 这个一年一度的电影节依旧享有盛誉，很多游客都选择到这个度假胜地过周末。

☞ enjoy a good reputation

enquire about 询问

☞ A: Hello. Er, I'm Dawn Mathews.

B: Yes, hello. I've been referred to you because I'm ***enquiring about*** the refresher course that you run.

A：您好。我是唐·马修斯。

B：您好。有人介绍我向您咨询您开设的进修课程的情况。

☞ inquire about

enrol on 加入，参加；注册；入学

☞ This college is one of the educational institutions which offer night classes in money management, and increasing numbers of women are ***enrolling on*** such courses. 这所大学是提供晚间理财课程的教育机构之一，越来越多的女性注册学习这类课程。

☞ register, join (in), become a member, enter

enrollment fee 注册费

☞ A: Is there an ***enrollment fee***?

B: Well, er, just a minute, let's see...the cost is thirty pounds, which includes all course materials and morning tea. You have to arrange your own lunch.

A：要交注册费吗？

B：请稍等，让我看看……费用是 30 镑，包括所有的课程资料费和早茶费。午餐自备。

enrollment form 登记表

☞ A: I'd better go home and fill in the ***enrollment form***. Thanks for all your help.

B: You're welcome. Goodbye.

A：我最好回家填这张登记表。谢谢你的帮助。

B：不客气，再见。

☞ registration form

enrollment form 常出现在雅思听力注册或申请场景中，相关表达有：

admissions office 招生办　　faculty 系

letter of recommendation 推荐信　　application form 申请表

score report 成绩单

entertainment facilities 娱乐设施

☞ The stores and ***entertainment facilities*** were all gone after the riot. The city had lost its functioning as a city. 在那次动乱后，这座城市中的商店和娱乐设施都不见了，它已经丧失了作为城市应有的功能。

entertainment industry 娱乐业

☞ In 1968, a shy, talented pop singer made his mark on the global ***entertainment industry***. 1968 年，一名害羞却很有天分的流行歌手在全球娱乐业上写下了属于他自己的一笔。

even though 即使

☞ There was no hesitation and Sebastian George bought the house immediately, for £9,300, ***even though*** the house had no bathroom, no running water upstairs, and no electricity. 塞巴斯蒂安·乔治毫不犹豫地以 9300 英镑的价钱买下了这幢房子，尽管屋里没有浴室，楼上没有自来水，也没有电。

☞ even if

every walk of life 各行各业

☞ In my spare time I prefer to hang out with my friends, and going to a bar for a couple of beers is one of my favorites. Through this I can expand the circle of my social relations, as I meet people from ***every walk of life*** in the bar. 闲暇时，我喜欢和朋友泡在一起，去酒吧喝几杯啤酒是我最喜欢的 件事。通过这种方式，我能在酒吧里遇见各行各业的人，拓宽社交面。

☞ all kinds of occupations

一些常见的“行业”：

sales industry 销售行业	power industry 电力行业
insurance industry 保险行业	Internet industry 互联网行业
food industry 食品行业	TV industry 电视产业

evolve into 发展成，进化成

☞ The professor told us how the early football ***evolved into*** its modern form. 教授告诉我们早期足球是如何发展成现代足球的。

☞ develop into

except for 除了

☞ A: Would you be willing to attend any of our special promotions for the new channel?

B: Yes, I'd be very happy to, as long as they're held here in my area.

A: OK, I'll make a note of that. And finally, may we put you on our mailing list?

B: Well, I'd prefer not...***except for*** the information about the promotion you mentioned.

A：您愿意参加新频道的任何特别推广活动吗？

B：是的，我很愿意，只要在我住的这个地区举办就可以。

A：好的，我会记下来的。最后一点，我们能把您添加到我们的邮件发送列表中吗？

B：最好还是不要了……除非是接收与你刚才提到的推广活动有关的消息。

excess charge 超重费用

☞ Just bring the necessaries with you, then you can avoid an ***excess charge*** at the airport. 只带上必需品，这样你就能避免在机场行李超重了。

exchange rate 汇率

☞ The ***exchange rate*** was looking healthy, but when I went to the teller, they told me the computer system was temporarily down. 汇率看起来很稳定，但是当我到银行职员那时，他们却告诉我计算机系统暂时出故障了。

☞ When did China begin to use a floating ***exchange rate***? 中国是什么时候开始使用浮动汇率的？

受全球金融危机(financial crisis)的影响，各国汇率大幅下调。与"货币"相关的表达有：

coin 硬币	penny 便士	nickel（美、加的）五分硬币
unit 货币单位	value/worth 面值	franc 法郎
dollar 美元	euro 欧元	pound 英镑
yen 日元		

exchange student 交换生

☞ It is the university's policy to give priority in the allocation of residence places to three categories, and those are: visiting students, ***exchange students*** and new postgraduate students. 大学政策规定，三种学生可以优先选择住处：访问生、交换生和研究生新生。

expand one's knowledge 开阔眼界

☞ The female candidate needs to ***expand her knowledge*** of national and global issues. That was a significant weakness in the 2004 campaign, for which she was obviously insufficiently prepared. 这位女性候选人需要拓宽在国内及国际问题上的知识面。在 2004 年的竞选中，她在这方面极其薄弱，显而易见她并没有为此次竞选做充分的准备。

expect...to do 希望/期望/预计…做

☞ The professor ***experts*** his students ***to*** finish reading all the references he listed within one month. 教授期望他的学生能在一月内读完他列出的所有参考书。

☞ anticipate...to do

extended family　数代同堂的家庭，大家庭

☞ The ***extended family*** has lived in the big wooden house for almost a decade. 这个大家庭已经在一幢大木房子里住了近十年。

extensive reading　泛读

☞ ***Extensive reading*** is of great help for grasping the main idea of the article. 泛读非常有助于掌握文章主旨。

extra cost　额外成本

☞ You'll also find that the library has loaded several CD-ROMs onto the computers from specialist reference sources such as the MLA. It means we can expand what we offer you at very little ***extra cost*** and saves us having to invest in more and more books. 你也会发现图书馆给电脑安装了一些只读光盘，它们来自一些专家参考资源，如现代语言学会。这意味着我们能够以极低的额外成本扩大我们所能提供的信息，而且不必投入大笔资金购买更多的书。

eye contact　目光交流，眼神交流

☞ It is very important to have ***eye contact*** with the one you have conversation with. 在交谈时与对方有目光交流是很重要的。

face up to　诚实勇敢地面对（困难或不快之事）

☞ On top of that immediate problem, what had also happened over the last years was that, although the Box Telecom had invested in an expansion plan, they had to ***face up to*** increased competition. 除了那个紧急的问题外，在过去的几年曾经出现过这样的问题：尽管博科斯电信在扩张计划上有投资，但他们必须面对日益严峻的竞争。

☞ be confronted with/by

faculty head　系领导

☞ I don't think it's necessary to invite ***faculty heads*** to party. 我认为没有必要邀请系领导参加宴会。

与"教师职位"相关的常用表达：

headmaster 校长	head teacher 班主任	dean 院长
assistant 助教	lecturer 讲师	professor 教授

fall in love with　爱上

☞ A: John has ***fallen in love with*** Ann. Have you heard that?

B: That's amazing.

A: 约翰爱上了安。你听说了吗？

B: 真不可思议。

fall to　下降到；开始做；（责任等）落在…身上

☞ My partner has resigned one week ago, so all the work ***fell to*** me. 我的搭档一周前辞职了，所以工作全落在了我身上。

fall upon/on　落在…身上，由…负担；开始进攻，扑向，袭去；依靠

☞ The full cost of the wedding ***fell upon*** us. 整个婚礼费用由我们负担了。

☞ The starving children ***fell on*** the food and ate it greedily. 饥饿的孩子们扑向食物，狼吞虎咽地吃起来。

familiarize oneself with　使自己熟悉

☞ At this library we hold materials relating to primary education, as well as special needs, but of course you'll need to ***familiarize yourself with*** both the two libraries to make the most of our resources. 在这个图书馆里我们有关于初级教育的资料，也有别的资料能满足你的特殊需求，但是当然，为了最大限度地利用我们的资源，你需要了解这两个图书馆。

family album　家庭相册

☞ This ***family album*** is full of photos of the family members. 这本家庭相册里都是家庭成员的照片。

"家庭成员"：

grandfather 祖父	grandmother 祖母	father 父亲
mother 母亲	uncle 叔叔，伯父，舅舅，姨丈	aunt 姑姑，伯母，婶母，舅妈，姨
cousin 堂兄弟	brother 兄弟	
sister 姐妹	nephew 侄子，外甥	niece 侄女，外甥女

NOTES

Unit 8

family bonds 亲情，家庭纽带

☞ The director hopes the program's emphasis on rebuilding ***family bonds*** can keep the next generation on the straight and narrow. 导演希望这个节目对重建家庭纽带的强调能让下一代过诚实正派的生活。

🔍 family bonds 常用于介绍家庭的场景里，一些和"家庭"相关的表达：

marriage 婚姻	spouse 配偶	couple 夫妻
single 单身者	stepson 继子	stepdaughter 继女
family member 家庭成员	family tree 家谱	family photo 全家福
family history 家族史		

family planning policy 计划生育政策

☞ ***Family planning policy*** has been carried out for ten years in that area. 在该地，计划生育政策已经实施了十年。

family reunion 家庭团聚，家庭聚会

☞ I remember that when I was growing up, the third Tuesday of July was the day of our annual ***family reunion*** at the small village. 我记得长大后，每年七月的第三个星期二我们都会在那个小村庄举行家庭聚会。

☞ family gathering

feel bored with 对…感到无聊

☞ The report said 50% of graduates had considered teaching as a career, with 42% of foreign language degree holders ***feeling bored with*** their current jobs. 这份报告称50%的毕业生将教书作为他们的职业，42%拥有外国语专业学位的学生认为他们目前的工作很无聊。

feel free to do 随便做，随意做

☞ ***Feel free to*** ask any questions during the talk and I'll do my best to answer them. 在谈话中请自由提问，我会尽力回答。

field research 实地调查，野外研究

☞ A: Have you been given any written assignments yet?

B: Yes, I've got to write about animal language.

A: Hmm! That sounds a challenge. I suppose you'll be off to the zoo to do ***field research***.

A：你有什么书面作业要写吗？

B：有，我要写有关动物语言的作业。

A：听上去很有挑战性。我猜你要去动物园实地调查吧。

🔍 design research "设计调查"、scientific research "科学调查"也是雅思听力中的高频词组。

field trip 实地考察

☞ The paper you're submitting for the Geography Society ***field trip*** competition has got through. 你交上来的参加地理协会实地考察比赛的方案已获通过。

☞ field survey

fill out 填写；填满，塞满；膨胀，扩大；长胖

☞ A: Could you tell me what I have to do to join the library?

B: Well, you'll need to come in to the library and ***fill out*** some forms.

A：你能告诉我怎样才能成为这个图书馆的会员吗？

B：你需要来图书馆填写一些表格。

☞ fill in

fill...in (on) 向…提供(情况)

☞ Jane is going to ***fill*** us ***in on*** what's in store for us at this year's Summer Festival. 简将向我们介绍今年夏季节上会有些什么活动。

financial assistance 经济援助

☞ Don't solely count on the ***financial assistance*** from the government; you have to make your way out. 不要单纯指望政府的经济援助，要自己想办法摆脱困境。

☞ Farmers are to receive ***financial assistance*** to help see them through the worst drought in over 50 years. 农民们会收到经济援助，以度过 50 多年来最严重的干旱期。

☞ financial aid

financial budget 财务预算

☞ I am entrusted with the job of writing ***financial budget*** for my company. 我被指派制定公司的财务预算。

🔍 与"金融贸易"相关的常用表达：

financial crisis 金融危机	trade barrier 贸易壁垒
trade surplus 贸易顺差	trade deficit 贸易逆差
trade balance 贸易平衡	budget deficit 预算赤字

financial circumstance 经济状况

☞ I think each course type has its advantages and disadvantages, so it really depends on you—your own study habits, and your ***financial circumstances***. 我认为每种课程都有优缺点，所以这完全取决于你自己——你自己的学习习惯和经济状况。

☞ financial situation

financial crisis 金融危机

☞ Here many countries have the most serious economic and ***financial crisis*** in decades—possibly since the Great Depression. 现在很多国家都正经历着几十年来最严重的经济和金融危机——也许是"大萧条"后最严重的。

find it's difficult to do 发现做…有困难

☞ When we look at the effects of corporate crime we may ***find it's difficult to*** assess the costs. 当审视公司犯罪的影响时，我们可能会发现难以估算其代价。

finish off 结束，完成；完全吃光

☞ We'll ***finish off*** the morning with lunch, which should give everyone a chance to meet and get to know each other, and we'll be serving you a buffet lunch in the Main Hall, which is on the first floor. 我们将以午饭结束上午的内容，大家可以趁午饭这个机会互相认识，午饭采用自助餐的形式，设在主餐厅。主餐厅位于一楼。

☞ Who has ***finished off*** the cakes my mother bought yesterday? 谁吃光了我母亲昨天买的蛋糕？

☞ end up

fire away （一般用于祈使句）开始说话（或做事）

☞ A: I suppose you're going to tell me the whole history of banana growing now, aren't you?

B: Well, it'd be a good practice run for my tutorial next week. I'll do the same for you some time.

A: OK. ***Fire away***.

A：我想你会告诉我香蕉种植的整个历史，对吗？

B：这也许在我下周的辅导课上讲比较好。以后我会给你讲的。

A：好了，快说吧！

fire away 在听力中发生连读时容易误听成 far away，考生注意辨别。

fire exit 消防出口

☞ Peter Chan will also go through the security arrangements with you and show you the ***fire exits***. 彼得·陈还会与你们讨论安全保障方面的安排并告诉你们消防出口的位置。

☞ fire door

fire exit 常出现在英美国家的标识语中，如：Fire exit only. 仅作火警出口用。

常见的相关表达：

fire service 消防队 fire door（建筑物内的）防火安全门

fire drill 消防演习 fire extinguisher 灭火器

first aid 急救

A ***First Aid*** Volunteer Team was established right after the earthquake happened and it saved many people's lives. 地震发生后立即成立了一支急救志愿服务队，挽救了很多性命。

first of all 首先

First of all, as you probably know, the children workshops run every Saturday. 首先，如你所知，儿童作坊每周六开放。

in the first place

fix up 修理，修补，整理；安排

Can you ***fix up*** the typewriter for my daughter? It means a lot to her. 你能帮我女儿修好这台打字机吗？它对她很重要。

Although the couple was ***fixed up*** by their parents, they led a happy married life. 虽然这对夫妻是奉父母之命结婚的，但是他们婚后生活得很幸福。

repair, mend; arrange

flag down 挥手使（车辆）停下

Yesterday I ***flagged down*** a cab to take me to the office—and had to direct the driver all the way. 昨晚我坐出租车去办公室，一路上还得指引司机怎么开。

floppy disk 软盘

You'd better use a ***floppy disk*** to save your blueprint. 你最好用软盘保存你的蓝图。

hard disk 指"硬盘"。

focus on 集中（注意力、精力等）于

I'll start with a brief history of East End, and then ***focus on*** life in the first half of the twentieth century. 一开始我将简要介绍一下伦敦东区的历史，然后集中讲 20 世纪上半叶伦敦东区的生活。

concentrate on

在雅思听力中，focus on 后面接的一般都是考点，其他类似信号词有 suggest、indicate 等。

for instance 例如

☞ Now, there are several hypotheses about the origins of the first Neolithic settlers in Ireland, but most of these contain problems. ***For instance***, there are considerable archaeological difficulties about the theory that they came from England. The evidence doesn't really add up. 现在，关于爱尔兰的第一批新石器时代居住者的起源有几个假设，但是大多数的假设都存在问题。例如，有一个理论认为这些早期居民来自英格兰，但该理论存在许多考古方面的困难，证据完全不合情理。

for lease/rent 出租

☞ There's an apartment ***for lease***. Let's go and have a look. 有公寓出租。我们去看看吧。

for one thing （用于列举原因）一来，一则

☞ There are great practical problems about the theory that the settlers came directly from continental Europe. ***For one thing***, it's not clear just how sufficient numbers of men and women could have been transported to Ireland to establish a viable population. 居住者直接从欧洲大陆过来这一理论存在很多实际的问题。一来，不知道要运送多少男人和女人到爱尔兰才足以建立起一个可存活种群。

☞ on the one hand

for the sake of 为了…；符合…的利益

☞ I feel you've often used complex structures and long sentences ***for the sake of*** it. 我感觉，你过于频繁地使用复杂结构和长句子，为用而用。

☞ in the interests of

freak out 处于极度兴奋中，行动反常

☞ People often fume over the mistreatment of animals by merchants but and ***freak out***, at an uptick in food prices. 人们经常对商人虐待动物的行为感到愤怒，又会对食品价格的小幅升高反应强烈。

freeze over （使）被冰覆盖，封冻

☞ The lake ***froze over*** in winter, so the children could go skating there. 冬天时湖面结冰了，孩子们可以去滑冰了。

frequency of buses 公交车发车频率

☞ There are few people on this bus route so the ***frequency of buses*** on this route will be reduced. 这条公交线路的乘客很少，因此将降低此线路公交车的发车频率。

from/at the outset 从最开始时，一开始

☞ You should tell him the truth ***from the outset***. 你一开始就该告诉他真相。

☞ from the very beginning

full address 详细地址；地址全名

☞ A: Are the children workshops held in the main museum?

B: Not exactly. They're nearby.

A: Could you give me the ***full address***? I don't know the area very well.

B: Yes, it's Winter House.

A：儿童作坊在主博物馆内举办吗？

B：不是，在附近。

A：你能给我详细地址吗？我对那块不太熟。

B：好的，在冬屋。

full refund 全额偿还，全额退款

☞ You can submit your unused tickets to the place of purchase and have a ***full refund*** of your money. 你可以去售票处退掉未用的票，获得全额退款。

full-time student 全日制学生

☞ A: Are you working at the moment?

B: No, I'm a ***full-time student*** at Sydney University.

A：你现在工作吗？

B：不，我是悉尼大学一名全日制学生。

相关词组：

commuting student 走读生

resident student 住校生

auditor/guest-pupil 旁听生

honors student 优等生

foreign student 外籍学生

targeted-area student 定向生

fundamental differences between...and 两者间的根本差异

☞ Though these days people might question a lot of the assumptions contained in the statements, recent research does suggest that there are some quite ***fundamental differences between*** men ***and*** women in their attitudes to economic matters. 尽管现在人们也许会质疑声明中的很多假设，但最近的研究表明男人和女人在对待经济问题的态度上确实存在着许多根本差异。

further education 继续教育

☞ Are you planning to pursue ***further education*** on the field of linguistics? 你打算在语言学领域继续深造吗？

gain a reputation for 因…而出名

☞ Angelina Jolie broke onto the scene in the mid-1990s, quickly ***gaining a reputation for*** her on-screen work. 安吉丽娜·朱莉在 20 世纪 90 年代中期走红荧屏，因在影视方面表现出色而快速成名。

gear change 换挡，变速；变速装置

☞ A: Is there anything else to do with the engine? What kind of ***gear change*** do you want? I presume you'd want a manual.

B: I'd want automatic—I've never driven a car with manual gears.

A：对发动机还有什么别的要求吗？你想要什么样的变速器？我猜是手动挡的。

B：我想要自动挡的——我从未开过手动挡的车。

雅思听力考试中曾出现过这样一个词组：downhill gear 下坡变速器。

gene pool 基因库

☞ Indian lions are particularly vulnerable because they have a limited ***gene pool***. The reason for this is interesting—it's because all of them are descended from a few dozen lions that were saved by a prince. 受限于有限的基因库，印度狮的生命尤其脆弱。造成这种情况的原因很有趣——因为它们是一位王子救下来的一些狮子的后代。

gene pool 常出现在雅思考试的自然科学场景中，相关词组：

genetic background 遗传背景
gene expression 基因表达
gene mapping 基因图谱
gene therapy 基因治疗
gene code 遗传密码
gene transfer 基因转移
gene marker 遗传标记
candidate gene 候选基因

general practitioner 全科医生

☞ The first thing you have to do is find a family doctor—sometimes we call them ***general practitioners*** as well when someone was sick. 有人生病时，你要做的第一件事是找家庭医生，他们有时也被称为全科医生。

☞ It is quite hard to make an appointment with the ***general practitioner***. 要预约全科医生非常困难。

雅思听力"看病"场景常用表达：

mental hospital 精神病医院
clinic 诊所
dispensary 药房
physician/internist 内科医生
oculist/eye doctor 眼科医生
surgeon 外科医生
dentist 牙医
tablet 药片
syrup 糖浆
capsule 胶囊
symptom 症状
therapy 疗法
prescription 处方
case history 病史
check up 检查
side effect 副作用

generally speaking 一般而言

☞ ***Generally speaking***, everyone here has a chance to perform in the stage. 一般而言，这里的每个人都有机会上台演出。

get a good view of　看到…的美景

☞ From where we're standing you've ***got a good view of*** the river over there. 从我们站的这个地方看出去，能看到那条河的美景。

get a move on　赶紧，加快

☞ First of all you've got to work on your basic bibliography, and that's due in to your course tutor by 31 January...which is just two weeks away, so you'd better ***get a move on*** that. 首先你必须开始做基本参考书目，这要在 1 月 31 日前交给导师……只剩两个星期了，最好加快速度。

☞ speed up

get a refund　退款

☞ A: I just tried to book a ticket yesterday for Perth and would you believe there are three different prices for the flight?

B: And what was the rationale for that?

A: Well, the travel agent said it depended on when you booked and the length of the stay, like it's cheap if you stay away for a Saturday night, presumably because this isn't business travel and even cheaper if you buy a ticket where you can't ***get a refund*** if you have to cancel; in that case the ticket costs about half the price.

A：我昨天想订一张去珀斯的机票。你相信吗？居然有三种不同的票价。

B：票价制度是什么？

A：旅行社说票价取决于预订的时间和停留时间的长短，如果你周六晚上走票价就会便宜，大概因为这不是商务旅行，而且如果取消行程不能获得退款的票会更便宜，那样的话，票价才是正常票价的一半。

get admitted to　被…录取

☞ I am very happy to get the letter from you saying that I had ***got admitted to*** this famous college. 从你那收到信件，告知我被这所著名的大学录取，真是太高兴了。

get along with　与…相处

☞ If the new employees start work and don't ***get along*** well ***with*** everybody else, the interviewer may be backing a loser in staff selection. 如果新员工开始工作后和其他人相处得都不好，那么面试官可能挑选了不合适的人。

get an extension of time　延期

☞ A: You mean you'd like to ***get an extension of time*** to finish your assignment?

B: If that's possible, but I don't know...

A: Well, yes, it is possible, but extensions are normally given only for medical or compassionate reasons, otherwise it's really a question of organising your study, and we don't like giving extensions to students who simply didn't plan their work properly.

A：你的意思是想延长交作业的期限？

B：如果可能的话，但是我不知道……

A：嗯，有这个可能性，但是我们通常只在学生生病或其他情有可原的情况下才延长期限，不然就是学生真的在组织学习过程中遇到了麻烦，但我们也不愿意给那些仅仅是不能合理安排学习时间的学生延长期限。

get behind with 落下；支持

☞ It's our first performance next week, so we're rehearsing frantically, and I've ***got behind with*** my work, but it's worth it. 下周是我们第一次演出，所以我们正在疯狂地排练。我的功课有点落下了，但是值得。

☞ fall behind, back up

get hold of 控制；掌握；找到某人，与某人联系；找来某物以供使用

☞ A: Do you have a daytime phone number?

B: Well, I work at the hospital but it's a bit difficult to ***get hold of*** me. I can give you a number just for messages, and then I'll get back to you when I can.

A：你有白天能找到你的电话号码吗？

B：我在医院工作，但是打电话很难找到我。我可以给你一个只用来发短消息的电话号码，然后情况允许的话我就会给你回电话。

☞ Little was done by the government to confront the drought until the press ***got hold of*** the story. 媒体掌握了真相之后，政府才采取措施应对干旱。

☞ A: What sort of trouble are you having? Is the assignment question a problem?

B: Well, that's part of the problem. I'm also having been having trouble ***getting hold of*** the books. I've been to the library several times, and all the books are out.

A：你有什么麻烦吗？理解不了作业的问题？

B：这只是部分问题，而且我一直找不到可用的书。我去过图书馆好几次了，可是所有的书都被借走了。

☞ get in touch with

get hurt 受伤

☞ Don't you think it's a bit risky to get a group of eight-year-olds pushing each other around a classroom? Someone could ***get hurt***. 你不觉得让一群七八岁的孩子在教室里互相推来推去很危险吗？有人可能会受伤。

☞ be injured

get into 进入，陷入；控制，影响(某人)；学会

☞ A: Can you give me any idea about the content of the first year of Economics so that I can ***get into*** some reading?

B: Well, you'll be getting the reading list next week when lectures start. All the books are in the library.

A：你可以告诉我第一年经济学都有些什么内容吗，这样我就可以开始做一些阅读了。

B：下星期课程开始时你会拿到阅读书目，那些书图书馆都有。

get into some reading 相当于 do some reading。

get into the habit of 养成…习惯

☞ With reading, there'll be sessions aimed at ***getting into the habit of*** analyzing material as you read it. 在阅读方面设置了这样一些课程，旨在让学生在阅读时养成分析材料的习惯。

☞ form the habit of

get into trouble 陷入困境，惹出麻烦

☞ Get away from me! I don't want to ***get into trouble***. 离我远点！我可不想惹麻烦。

☞ be trapped in

get married 结婚

☞ I can't believe that Tracy will ***get married*** next year! 特蕾西明年要结婚了，真让人难以置信！

与…订婚：engage oneself to

get on one's nerve 令人不安/心烦

☞ Stop screaming! You are ***getting on my nerve***! 别尖叫了！扰得我心烦！

get on with 继续；取得进展，进行，前进；与…相处

☞ Well, thank you, Mark, for the overview that was well researched. Now let's ***get on with*** your main topic for today. 好了，谢谢你，马克，这个概述经过了充分的研究。现在我们开始你今天的主题吧。

☞ A: Hello, Sandy. How have you been ***getting on with*** your dissertation?

B: Fine, and I've been working hard on the various points we agreed on our last tutorial.

A：你好，桑迪。你的论文进展如何？

B：很好，我一直致力于上次指导课上我们达成共识的各点。

☞ go on with, get along with

get promoted 得到提升，晋升

☞ You won't ***get promoted*** unless you work hard. 只有努力工作才能得到晋升。

get...down 使…沮丧/疲倦/不安

☞ If things are ***getting*** you ***down***, don't go and hide. Come and talk to us about it. 如果觉得沮丧，不要封闭自己。来和我们聊聊。

get separated from 和…分开；走散

☞ The information desk, marked with the small letter i on your plan is located right here in the foyer, so if you ***get separated from*** your friends, I suggest you make your way back to the information desk because we'll be returning to this spot at the end of the tour. 问询处在你们的导游图上用小写字母 i 标出，就位于休息室，所以如果走散了，我建议你们回到问询处，因为参观结束后我们会回到这里。

get straight down to 开门见山地说

☞ A: OK, everybody, good morning! It's Mark's turn to talk to us today, so Mark, I'll ask you to ***get straight down to*** business.

B: Right!

A：好了，大家早上好！今天轮到马克给我们作讲座了，马克，你直接开始吧。

B：好的！

☞ get to the point

get stuck 被困住，被卡住；陷入困境

☞ We run to the ticket counter immediately after we heard the broadcast, but we ***get stuck*** behind a group of old people who are walking very slowly. 我们听到广播后，直奔售票口，却被一群步伐极其缓慢的老人堵在了路上。

get the best deal 最划算

☞ Well, last week we talked about buying camping equipment and today I'd like to talk to you about buying a bicycle. A simple enough exercise, you might imagine, but there are lots of things to look out for to make sure you ***get the best deal*** for your money. 上星期，我们谈了购买野营设备。今天，我要和你们谈谈购买自行车的问题。你们可能会想，这个再简单不过了，但是要想买到最物有所值的自行车，需要注意很多问题。

☞ get a good deal

Unit 9

get the hang of 掌握，得知，基本了解

☞ Fans of the original game will definitely enjoy this updated version, especially once they ***get the hang of*** the secret to get through it. 旧版游戏的爱好者们一定会喜欢这个新版本的，尤其是在他们掌握了通关的诀窍后。

☞ get hold of

get through 用完，用光；做完；通过；打通电话

☞ A: What's your book list like?

B: Well, it's not as long as yours, but it's still pretty big. There are 43. I don't know how I'm going to ***get through*** them all.

A：你的书单怎么样呢？

B：虽然没有你的长，但还是很多，一共 43 本。我不知道如何才能读完这些书。

☞ finish up

get to grips with 开始应付，认真应对，勉力对付

☞ Before they had a chance to ***get to grips with*** the effects of increased competition, they were stalled by a strike and it was just when they were thinking about making a colossal investment in new machinery for their plants. 没等他们来得及应对日益严峻的竞争所带来的影响，他们(的行动)就被一场罢工阻止了，当时他们正考虑为工厂进行一项大投资，购买新设备。

☞ deal with

get used to 习惯于

☞ I think the people speak at natural speed, so it forces me to ***get used to*** it. And they use a lot of slang. 我认为这些人是以正常语速在说话，这迫使我去适应，而且他们用了很多俚语。

get used to 和 be used to 两者间其实存在着细微的差别：get used to 是从不习惯到习惯，其中有一个适应的过程；be used to 是从来就习惯，没有适应这个过程。

give a prescription　开药方

☞ I can't ***give you a prescription*** if you refuse to tell me your problem. 如果你不告诉我你的问题所在，我就无法给你开药方。

give comments on　对…提出意见

☞ A: Now let's have a look—"Please ***give your comments on*** the following aspects of the course," what's the first one? Oh, course organization. What do you think?

B: I think the organization was clear.

A：现在让我们来看一下，"请就课程如下方面提出意见"，第一点是什么呢？课程组织。你觉得怎么样？

B：我觉得课程组织很清晰。

give off　发散，放出

☞ This kind of key can ***give off*** a high pitched noise and flashes light when you whistle so you can find it. 当你吹口哨时，这种钥匙可以发出尖锐的声音并且闪光，这样就能找到它了。

give out　发出，分发；发表，公布；用完；出故障

☞ The spokesperson of the financial center has refused to ***give out*** any information on the scandal. 金融中心的发言人拒绝就这桩丑闻公布任何信息。

☞ The research materials ***gave out*** this morning. 调查材料今天早晨用完了。

☞ hand out, allot; declare, announce, make known; run out, come to an end

give over to　把…留作特定用途

☞ As for crops, the east is the UK's great cereal-producing region. However, increasingly significant areas are now also ***given over to*** high quality vegetables for supply direct to the supermarkets. 至于农作物，东部是英国主要的谷类生产区。然而，现在越来越多的区域被留作种植高品质的蔬菜以便直接向超市供货。

give priority to　优先考虑(或处理)，把…当成首要任务

☞ The country must ***give priority to*** customer service if the country wants to be a favored shopping paradise. 该国若想成为令人向往的购物天堂，就必须把客服质量置于首位。

give...a sack　解雇

☞ I don't know if my boss will ***give*** me ***a sack*** or another opportunity. 不知道老板是想解雇我，还是再给我一次机会。

☞ kick...out of work, dismiss

give...a miss 不予理睬，不理会；决定不做

☞ I think I'll ***give*** basketball ***a miss*** this afternoon. 我今天下午不想打篮球了。

give away 捐赠，赠送；分发，颁发；泄露

☞ We collect second-hand bikes in the UK and send them to some of the poorest regions in the world. When we distribute bikes overseas we don't ***give*** them ***away*** for free. 我们在英国收集二手自行车，然后把它们送往世界上最穷困的一些地区。这些自行车并不是免费捐送的。

give up 放弃

☞ I have many women patients who say they have completely ***given up*** exercise because the pain makes them so miserable. 我的很多女性病人称疼痛让她们痛苦得完全放弃了锻炼。

glance down at 低头看一眼

☞ As we entering the ward room, we ***glanced down at*** the bed and already a different patient was lying there. 我们走进病房时都低头向床上看了一眼，躺在那儿的已是另一个病人。

global warming 全球变暖

☞ The problem of ***global warming*** is on the agenda of almost all the international climate conferences. 全球变暖问题已被提上几乎所有国际气候会议的议程。

go ahead 前进，继续；先走，先行；开始

☞ I have come to the conclusion that this development of this kind of house should ***go ahead***, but with various acoustic modifications according to the position of the block in relation to the highway and intersection. 我得出的结论是应该继续开发这种房子，但是要根据楼房与公路及十字路口的距离来调整声效。

go away 离开，走掉

☞ My job is to make sure that you all have a great stay here with us and ***go away*** feeling relaxed and refreshed. 我的工作就是确保你们在这里度过一段美好时光并且身心轻松、精神焕发地离开。

go back （在时间或空间上）回到先前某点，追溯（到…）

☞ A: When will you ***go back*** to your work in London?

B: I've gotten a large amount of work to do here.

A：你打算什么时候回到伦敦工作？

B：这还有一大堆事情等着我做呢。

☞ If we ***go back*** ten thousand years we would find that there were lions roaming vast sections of the globe. But now, unfortunately, only very small sections of the lions' former habitat remain. 我们如果回到一万年前，就会发现狮子自由奔跑于全球大部分地区。但不幸的是，狮子早先的栖息地现在所剩无几了。

☞ date back

go back 常出现在雅思听力的问路场景中，相关表达有：

cross over 穿过…
go east/west/south/north 向东/西/南/北
go on/along...till you meet 沿…一直走，直到…
directly opposite 和…正相对
be in the corner of 在…转角处

go bad 变坏，变酸

☞ A: How do the farmers stop the bananas ***going bad*** before they reach the shops?

B: Well, the banana bunches are picked well before the fruit is ripe. Once you cut the bunch, the bananas stop growing but they do continue to ripen.

A：在香蕉到达商店前，农民是怎样防止它们变坏的？

B：香蕉还没成熟就被成串摘下。它们被成串摘下后，就会停止生长，但是会继续变熟。

go for a dinner 去吃饭

☞ Let's ***go for a dinner***! What is your favourite restaurant? 我们去吃饭吧！你最喜欢哪一家餐厅？

go for an/the interview 参加面试

☞ I bet you will ***go for the interview***; it is just meant for you. 我打赌你会去参加那个面试，它简直就是为你设置的。

与"求职"相关的表达：

job hunter 求职者
résumé 简历
job application 职位申请表
employment rate 就业率
talent market 人才市场
work experience 工作经历
second job 第二职业
job hopping 跳槽

go hand in hand (with) 和…齐头并进

☞ We've got the strand which I referred to as sports management and this ***goes hand in hand with*** the area of sports marketing. 我所指的体育管理已经开始，它和体育营销齐头并进。

☞ Poverty and poor health often ***go hand in hand***. 贫困和健康不佳常有连带关系。

☞ keep pace with

go off 爆炸；走开；中断，停止运行；发生，进行；(食物)变坏

☞ The lights ***went off***. 电灯熄灭了。

☞ The milk has ***gone off***. 牛奶变酸了。

go on a date　约会

☞ The young man asked the girl several questions about her age and what school she went to before telling her he wanted to ***go on a date*** with her. 这个年轻人在告诉女孩他想和她约会之前，问了她几个有关年龄和就读学校的问题。

🔍 与"约会"相关的表达：

make a date 确定约会　　schedule a date 确定约会时间

blind date 别人代为安排的男女初次会面

double date 两对男女一起约会或出游

在西方很流行的 blind date，指不相识的男女经第三方安排而进行的约会，类似于我们所说的"相亲"。

go on strike　举行罢工

☞ A: Do you know the taxi drivers have been ***going on strike***?

B: Really? That's amazing.

A：你知道出租车司机一直在举行罢工吗？

B：真的吗？真是不可思议。

☞ come out on strike

go out of fashion　过时

☞ Later, feather fans and big, decorated hats ***went out of fashion*** but ostriches were still bred this time for their hide. 后来，羽毛扇和装饰华丽的大帽子过时了，但人们仍饲养鸵鸟，目的是获得鸵鸟皮。

go over　察看；查阅；复习；（演出等）受欢迎，获得成功；转播（to）

☞ A: Lucy, we really need to get working on this marketing assignment. We've only got five weeks left to the end of term to design it, carry it out, and then write up the result.

B: Sure. Well, let's get started right now. Let's ***go over*** the instructions.

A：露西，我们真的要开始写营销作业了，在学期结束前我们只剩五周的时间来设计、实施并写出结果。

B：好的，我们马上开始吧。先看看说明。

☞ You'll hear from Peter Chen, our conference manager, and he will be ***going over*** a plan of the conference center with you, which will help you to orient yourself. 你们会听到我们的会议经理彼得·陈的讲话，他会和你们一起回顾一下会议中心的平面图，这将有助于你们熟悉环境。

☞ look through

go rock climbing　攀岩

☞ A: What do you do in your spare time?

B: I'd like to ***go rock climbing***.

A：你闲暇时做什么？

B：我喜欢去攀岩。

go round 四处走动；蔓延，传播；足够分配

☞ I am afraid there aren't enough chairs to ***go round***. 恐怕没有足够的椅子分给每个人坐。

☞ go around

go surfing 冲浪

☞ If the waves are big enough, I'll ***go surfing***. 如果浪够大，我就去冲浪。

go through 遭受，经历；讨论；仔细检查；排练（演出）；（法律等）被通过

☞ The Helpline is able to ***go through*** things with you and see what the outcome is. 热线电话可以和你一起讨论并查看结果如何。

☞ A: Maybe I'd better ***go through*** the article again, just to be sure. Can you remember what it was called?

B: Sample Surveys in Social Science Research, I think. By Mehta.

A：也许我最好再仔细查阅一下那篇文章，再确定一下。你还记得文章标题吗？

B：我记得是梅赫塔写的《社会科学研究中的抽样调查》。

go under 倒闭，破产，失败；沉没

☞ The company's problems cross all types of industries and it's lucky it's so big—a smaller or even medium sized company would have ***gone under*** by now. 这个公司的所有产业都存在问题，幸运的是这家公司够大，换作一个规模更小或甚至中等规模的公司到现在肯定已经破产了。

☞ That huge ship finally ***went under*** that evening. 那个晚上那艘大船最终沉入海底。

另外一个表示"破产"的词是 bankruptcy，其常用表达有：bankruptcy cost 破产成本，bankruptcy proceedings 破产程序。

go up 上升，增长；建起；启幕，开演

☞ A: Is this kind of membership very expensive?

B: Well, you pay a £250 joining fee and then it's £450—oh no, I'm sorry, it's just ***gone up*** by £50—it's now £500 for the annual subscription fee.

A：要想成为这种会员费用会很昂贵吗？

B：你需要付 250 英镑的入会费，然后要交 450 英镑，哦不，抱歉，年费刚刚涨了 50 英镑，现在的年费是 500 英镑。

☞ be on the up, increase

go with 进展；伴随；与…相配，协调；同意，接受

☞ Disease often ***goes with*** poverty. 疾病与贫穷常常相伴而生。

☞ Your hairstyle doesn't ***go with*** your dress. 你的发型与衣服不搭调。

☞ get along with

graduate from 从…毕业

☞ I got the idea of exporting bicycles to developing countries while I was in Ecuador. I went there in 1993 just after ***graduating from*** university. 在厄瓜多尔时，我产生了向发展中国家出口自行车的想法，1993 年我大学毕业后就去了那里。

graduation ceremony 毕业典礼

☞ What a pity that I can't attend your ***graduation ceremony***. 真遗憾，我不能参加你的毕业典礼。

🔍与"毕业"相关的表达：

diploma 毕业证书	degree 学位	dissertation 论文
bachelor 学士	master 硕士	doctor 博士
graduation gown 毕业礼服，学士服	graduation project 毕业设计	

greenhouse gas emission 温室气体排放

☞ Recycling can help to achieve UK's goal in two main ways: the production of recycled glass and paper uses much less energy than producing them from virgin material, and also recycling reduces ***greenhouse gas emission*** from landfill sites and incineration plants. 回收主要可以通过两种方式帮助英国实现目标：生产可回收的玻璃和纸所耗费的能量要比用原材料来生产它们少得多，并且回收可以减少垃圾填埋场和焚化厂排放的温室气体。

greenhouse effect 温室效应

☞ In recent years winter has become warmer and warmer because of the ***greenhouse effect***. 近年来，由于温室效应，冬季变得越来越暖和。

🔍温室效应是由温室气体(greenhouse gas)的排放引起的，最常见的温室气体就是二氧化碳(carbon dioxide)，温室效应会导致全球变暖(global warming)。

gross national product 国民生产总值

☞ We are used to hearing the UK's society and economy described as being "industrial" or even "post-industrial," but we mustn't let this blind us to the fact that agricultural and its supporting industries still account for around 20% of our ***gross national product***. 我们已经习惯于听到英国的社会和经济被描述成"工业的"甚至是"后工业的"，但是我们不能因此就无视农业及其支撑产业仍占国民生产总值约20%这一事实。

GDP 是 gross domestic product（国内生产总值）的缩写。

ground floor 底层，地面层；一楼

☞ At 10:30, there will be a coffee break in the staff canteen, which is located down on the ***ground floor***. 在 10:30，位于一楼的员工餐厅会有一个休息时间（聚会）。

group discussion 小组讨论

☞ I didn't think it was all that wonderful when we had great long ***group discussion*** sessions that went on for hours and hours. I don't mean we shouldn't have ***group discussion***, just that they shouldn't go on too long. 我觉得大量地进行持续数小时的小组讨论课并没那么好。我不是指我们不应该进行小组讨论，只是讨论不应该持续那么长时间。

group discussion 常出现在学习场景中，其他相关表达：

coursework 课程论文
exam preparation 准备考试
reference 参考书
overdue book 过期图书
course arrangement 课程安排
field trip（学生）实地考察

group interview 集体面试

☞ In the second part of the interview you go for a ***group interview***. 在面试的第二部分，你要进行一场集体面试。

grow up 长大

☞ A: Do you have any women living alone, retired women on your book?

B: Yes, I have quite a few whose children have ***grown up*** and left home.

A：你的名册中有独居的退休女性吗？

B：有，我这有好几位女士，她们的孩子长大后都离开了家。

guided tour 有导游带领的旅游

☞ We go for places where we know there are ***guided tours***, because this gives a good focus for the visit. 我们去一些我们知道有导游带领游玩的地方，因为这样旅游起来目标明确。

相关词组：

tourist guide 导游
travel agency 旅行社
package tour 包办旅行
trip route 出行路线
tourist attraction 旅游景点
tourist destination 旅游目的地
summer resort 避暑胜地
natural landscape 自然景观
theme park 主题公园
virgin forest 原始森林
garden architecture 园林建筑
ancient architectural complex 古建筑群

hall of residence 学生宿舍

☞ Most of the students in this college live in ***hall of residence***. 这所学院的大多数学生都住在学生宿舍里。

在美语中常用 dormitory 或其缩写 dorm 表示“学生宿舍”。该词组的复数形式是 halls of residence，考试时要注意。

hand in 上交，提交

☞ A: If you do things with a plan, then you'll find that you still have time for yourself and your hobbies as well.

B: Yeah. I've heard from Thomas that you made him a sort of plan like this, and he's going away for the weekend with all his work ***handed in***, whereas I haven't started.

A：如果你做事有计划，就会发现仍有时间留给自己和自己的爱好。

B：是啊。我听托马斯说你为他制订了一个类似计划，他已经交了所有的作业，打算周末出去玩，而我的作业却还没有开始。

☞ turn in, submit

hand out 分发，散发

☞ Anne works in the accounts department and she looks after all temporary staff, and so she is the person to see if you have any problems regarding pay. She will also be ***handing out*** your tax form. 安妮在会计部工作，负责管理所有的临时工作人员，所以如果你们有什么关于报酬的问题就可以找她。她还会给你们发税表。

☞ All the times of each day's activities are printed on the blue sheet you should have got in the information guides that were ***handed out*** on the coach. 每天的活动安排都印在了信息指南中蓝色的单子上，信息指南在长途车上就发给你们了。

☞ distribute

hand 的其他常见搭配：

at first hand 第一手地，直接地	hand to hand 短兵相接地
at hand 在手边，在近处	by hand 用手工
in hand 手头有的	hands up 举起手来

hand over 移交，交出

☞ A: So, I'll ***hand over*** now to Julie Brooks.

B: Thank you. Welcome to the Sports Centre. It's good to see that there are so many people wanting to find out about our sports facilities.

A：那么，我现在把话筒交给朱莉·布鲁克斯。

B：谢谢。欢迎来到体育中心。很高兴看到有这么多的人想了解我们的体育设施。

☞ The floor seniors will introduce themselves later today and answer any questions you have. But for now I'm going to ***hand*** you ***over*** to Marney who is going to give you the orientation packs and keys. 今天晚些时候，楼长会进行自我介绍并回答你们的任何问题。但是现在我要把你们交给马尼了，他会给你们资料包和钥匙。

handicapped toilet 残疾人专用厕所

☞ I'd just like to point out one or two things of general interest which were in the museum. ***Handicapped toilets*** are located on this floor and the door shows a wheelchair. 在这个博物馆里，我只想指出一两件大家可能关心的事。残疾人专用厕所就在这层楼，门上有轮椅标志。

hang on 不挂断(电话)，等待片刻；抓紧；决定于，有赖于；坚持

☞ A: What are the opening times for the two tourist places?

B: According to this guide book, the Cathedral is only open from nine-thirty in the morning until midday. No, ***hang on***. That's the Cathedral Museum. The Cathedral itself is open morning and afternoon. The Castle is just open from one to five.

A：这两个旅游景点的开放时间是什么时候？

B：这本导游手册上说，大教堂只从上午 9: 30 开放到中午。不，等一下，这是大教堂博物馆的开放时间。大教堂上午和下午都开放。城堡只从下午 1 点开到 5 点。

☞ hold on

hang on to 保留某物；紧紧抓住

☞ A: How long can I ***hang on to*** the books for?

B: The borrowing period is one month, but of course books can be renewed. You can renew an item a maximum of three times.

A：这些书我能保留多久呢？

B：借期是一个月，但是当然可以续借。一本书最多可续借三次。

☞ reserve; hold back

> hang on to your hat 是一个俚语，意思是"这里有惊人的消息，你要准备好，不要太惊奇让帽子从头上掉下来"。如：Hi, honey. Now hang on to your hat—the manager told me that he wanted me to take charge of the new project next month. 嗨，亲爱的。准备好哦，经理说下个月让我接管新项目。

hang out with 和…一起玩(或闲逛)

☞ I normally ***hang out with*** my little sister at the park. 通常我和妹妹在公园里玩。

☞ play with

hang over 笼罩；威胁，逼近

☞ A: Right...let's try and get the matter sorted out today so we don't have it ***hanging over*** us. OK?

B: Good idea.

A：好了，我们今天试着把这事解决了吧，这样它就不会一直缠着我们了。好吧？

B：好主意。

hatch out 孵出

☞ Almost all the fertilized eggs will ***hatch out*** into chicks which will in turn reach maturity. 几乎所有的受精卵都会孵出幼鸟，继而发育成熟。

have a baby 生孩子

☞ A: John, I've just had some good news. Susan has ***had her baby***.

B: Do you know when she had it?

A: Yesterday. The tenth of August.

A：约翰，我刚得知个好消息。苏珊生了孩子了。

B：你知道她什么时候生的吗？

A：昨天，8 月 10 号。

☞ give birth to a baby

have a blast 玩得很开心

☞ I want to say that I like watching the videos of your trip in Australia. You all ***have a blast***, huh?! 我想说的是我很喜欢看你们在澳大利亚旅行时的视频，你们都玩得很开心吧！

☞ have a great time, have fun

🔍blast 最常用的意思是"大风；冲击波"等，在这个词组里指"欢乐而刺激的经历，寻欢作乐的时刻，狂欢会"等，为美国俚语。have a blast 既可用在写作中，也可用于日常口语。

have a check 做检查

☞ We doubt if it would be feasible to ***have a check*** at reception of all people coming in. 我们怀疑在接待处对所有进来的人进行检查是否可行。

have a fever 发烧

☞ Don't worry! Your baby just ***has a*** slight ***fever***. 别担心，你的孩子只是低烧。

☞ have a temperature

have a good relationship with 与…关系良好

☞ It is of great importance for human beings to ***have a good relationship with*** nature. 人与自然的和谐相处极其重要。

☞ get along very well with

have a look around 随便看看，到处看看

A: You can borrow videos now, if you like, but your card won't be ready until next week. You can come and pick it up when you bring your first videos back. That's OK if you want to take some now.

B: Yes, I'd like to. I'll ***have a look around***.

A：如果你愿意，你现在就可以借录像带，但是你的卡得到下星期才能办好。如果你现在借的话，可以在还录像带时把卡取走。

B: 好的，我很愿意。我想四处看看。

NOTES

Unit 10

have a look 看一看

☞ May I ***have a look*** at the new products? 我能看看新产品吗?

have a reputation for 因…而著称

☞ That small bank has long ***had a reputation for*** poor service. 那家小银行的服务质量一向口碑不佳。

☞ be famous for

have a significant effect/impact on 对…有深刻影响

☞ There are two major areas that I will focus on in my talk: how vegetation can ***have a significant effect on*** urban climate, and how we can better plan our city using trees to provide a more comfortable environment for us to live in. 我的讲话将重点讨论两个问题:植被如何对城市气候产生重要影响,以及我们如何通过树木来更好地规划城市从而为我们提供一个更舒适的生活环境。

have a sore throat 嗓子痛

☞ A: What's wrong with you?

B: I ***have a sore throat***.

A:你怎么了?

B:我嗓子痛。

have a stuffed nose 鼻子不通气

☞ A: Nancy, are you alright?

B: Oh, I ***have a stuffed nose***.

A:南希,你还好吧?

B:我鼻子不通气了。

have access to 有权(或方法、手段)接近(或取得、使用)

☞ These are what we call the audio forms of media. CDs and radios are probably the best examples, because a lot of children ***have access to*** these...especially radios. 这些就是我们所说的视听媒体,其中 CD 和广播很可能是最好的例子,因为许多孩子都能用上这些,尤其是广播。

☞ approach to

have an overdraft 透支

☞ You may want to take more money out of the bank than you have in it. This is called ***having an overdraft***. Be very careful with this: you should not do this without permission from your bank. 也许你想从银行提取的钱比你存进去的多。这就称为透支。这样做的时候一定要非常谨慎：未经银行允许不要这么做。

have disagreement on 在…方面有分歧

☞ It is a pity that you ***have disagreement on*** payment. 很遗憾，你们在佣金方面意见不一。

☞ have difference in

have (a) taste in 讲究

☞ His girlfriend ***has*** very expensive ***tastes in*** clothes. 他的女朋友讲究穿高档的服装。

have faith in 相信，信任

☞ People have to ***have faith in*** each other's ability to carry out the task their boss has set them. 在执行老板分配的任务时人们必须相信大家有能力完成它。

☞ have belief in

have links with 与…联系

☞ A: Well, I'm going to transfer £2,000 from my account, just till I get paid. In fact, I wanted to ask you about that. What's the best way to do it?

B: It depends on which bank you're with.

A: It's the Fransen Bank in Utrecht.

B: OK, fine. I'll check that in a minute. If we ***have links with*** them we can do a direct transfer.

A：我打算在发工资前从账户里转 2000 英镑。实际上，我想问问有关转账的问题。怎样做最好呢？

B：这取决于你的账户是在哪一家银行。

A：是乌得勒支的弗兰森银行。

B：好的。我马上给你查查，如果我们和这家银行有业务联系的话，就可以直接转账。

☞ be in touch with

have no choice but (to) do 除了做…别无选择

☞ The bosses ***have no choice but to*** admit that they are bankrupt and default on the debt, and then they will be forced to make some necessary changes. 这些老板别无选择，只能承认破产且无力偿还欠款，然后会被迫做出一些必要的改变。

have problems with 在…上有问题

☞ You may find that you can't meet a deadline for an essay or perhaps you're ***having problems with*** attendance. 你可能会发现，自己无法在期限内完成论文，或有些事情可能导致你无法出席。

have...done （让别人）做…；遭遇

☞ A: Lost Property. Can I help you?

B: Oh, yes. I've ***had*** my briefcase ***stolen***.

A：这里是失物招领处，有什么可以帮你的吗？

B：我的公文包被偷了。

🔍 这种句型一般有两种解释：一是表示主语有意志的行为，have 具有使役意义，如：You'd better have that bad tooth pulled out. 你最好去把那颗坏牙拔掉。二是表示"遭遇，经历"，此时句子所表示的动作是违背主语的意愿的，例句就是这种用法。

have trouble in doing 做…有困难

☞ Jenny ***has trouble in*** finding a satisfying job. 珍妮很难找到一份满意的工作。

☞ have difficulty in doing

have trouble with 在…上有困难

☞ A: How can I help you?

B: I'm ***having*** a bit of ***trouble with*** the second assignment, and it's due in twelve days.

A：我能帮你什么吗？

B：我在第二次作业上遇到了一点困难，而且 12 天后就要交了。

having said that 即便如此

☞ ***Having said that***, I still find it hard to get along with her. 虽说如此，我仍然觉得和她很难相处。

health system 卫生保健系统

☞ I don't know how the ***heath system*** works in UK. All I know is that it's very different from ours back in Canada. 我不知道英国卫生保健系统是如何运作的，我只知道和加拿大的截然不同。

healthy diet 健康饮食

☞ ***Healthy diet*** is good for people to keep fit. 健康饮食有助于保持健康。

hear about 听说，得悉

☞ At that time, news of the new projection system in America traveled fast and a number of rival European systems started to appear once people had ***heard about***. 那时，美国出现新投影系统的消息不胫而走，消息传出后，欧洲许多与之抗衡的系统开始出现。

help with 帮助…做

☞ A: Well. Ann ***helped*** me ***with*** some of the electronics work.

B: Then you must put her name in as well.

A：安帮助我温习了一些电子学功课。

B：所以你必须也把她的名字填上。

☞ aid with

help out 帮助…摆脱困境

☞ My friends ***helped*** me ***out*** when I lost my job. 我失业期间朋友们帮了我一把。

☞ He's always willing to ***help out***. 他总是急人之难。

high heels 高跟鞋

☞ The man over there is a Portuguese designer who has created many ***high heels*** for men. 那边的那个人是一位葡萄牙设计师，他设计了很多男性穿的高跟鞋。

high heels 常用在描述人物的话题里，这里补充一些常见的描述人物衣着、外表的表达：

overweight 过胖的	tubby 矮胖的	muscular 强壮的
slim 苗条的	slender 修长的	skinny 极瘦的
well dressed 衣着光鲜的	neatly dressed 衣着干净整洁的	

high jump 跳高

☞ A: Which one do you like, ***high jump*** or long jump?

B: ***High jump***.

A：跳高和跳远，你喜欢哪一个？

B：跳高。

historical viewpoint 历史观点

☞ So far, in these lectures, we've been looking at crimes like robbery and murder—both from a ***historical viewpoint*** and also in contemporary society. 迄今，在这些讲座里，我们都以历史观点，从当代社会的角度来看待抢劫和谋杀等犯罪行为。

hit on/upon 偶然碰到，偶然发现

☞ They ***hit upon*** a good method to solve that tough problem. 他们灵光一现，想到一个好方法来解决那个棘手的问题。

☞ encounter

hold a reception 举行欢迎会，举行招待会

☞ The school staff ***held a reception*** to their new principal. 学校员工为新校长举办了一个欢迎会。

相关表达：

distinguished guest 贵宾	eye salute 注目礼
farewell ceremony 欢送仪式	generous hospitality 盛情款待
goodwill visit 友好访问	guest of honor 主宾
propose a toast 祝酒	play host to / receive 接待

hold up 推迟，(使)耽搁；举出…作为榜样(as)；支撑

- A: My flight to New York has been ***held up*** due to bad weather.
  B: Bad luck.
  A：由于天气恶劣，我去纽约的航班延误了。
  B：真倒霉。
- Although at the clinic we recognize that a short rest in bed can be helpful, up to two days. Any longer makes our back muscles become weaker and unable to ***hold up*** our spine. 尽管我们在诊所里得知短暂的卧床休息会有用，但是最多两天。过多的休息会使得我们背部的肌肉更虚弱并且无法支撑脊柱。
- ☞ delay

home visit 出诊；家访

- If you want a doctor to visit you at home, you have to ask for a ***home visit***. 要想让医生到你家来给你看病，就得要求医生出诊。

host family 接待留学生的家庭，寄宿家庭

- Many ***host families*** are willing to board Chinese students. 许多寄宿家庭都愿意为中国学生提供食宿。
- A: Good morning. How can I help you?
  B: Good morning. Umm, I understand you help fix up students with ***host families***.
  A：早上好，有什么可以帮助你的吗？
  B：早上好。我听说你可以为学生安排寄宿家庭。

host family 是愿意为国际学生提供食宿、帮助他们更好适应国外生活的家庭。

house/household appliance 家用电器

- Traders from the countryside bring harvests of dragon fruit, departing with ***house appliances*** and medical supplies to sell back home. 农村小贩们来时带着火龙果，离开时带着家用电器和药品回去出售。
- The Britain ***household appliances*** manufacturer has confirmed plans to cut its workforce in London by up to a fifth over the next nine months to relieve financial pressure. 这家英国家用电器厂商已证实未来九个月内计划在伦敦裁员 1/5 以缓解经济压力。

常见的家用器具：

fluorescent 荧光灯
electric iron 电熨斗
vacuum cleaner 吸尘器
electric oven 电烤箱
broiler 烘烤用具
egg beater 打蛋器

household budget 家庭预算

☞ The study have found that men tend to save for a car, which by the way takes a surprisingly large amount of the ***household budget*** in North America. 这项研究表明男人倾向于为买车攒钱，顺便提一下在北美这部分开支在家庭预算中所占的比例高得令人吃惊。

household waste 家庭垃圾

☞ My group has been doing a project on how ***household waste*** is recycled in Britain. 我们组正致力于在英国是如何回收家庭垃圾的这一项目。

☞ household garbage

hover around 徘徊在，盘旋在

☞ The main purpose of the first experiment is to show how hovercrafts work, and how things ***hover around*** on just a cushion of air. 第一个试验的主要目的是演示气垫船的工作原理以及物体如何在一个气垫上悬浮。

hunt for 寻找

☞ People usually come to big cities to ***hunt for*** fame and wealth. 人们通常去大城市谋求名誉和财富。

☞ look for

hustle and bustle 忙碌喧嚣

☞ To escape the ***hustle and bustle*** of the city, many rich men head to the tranquil villages where they can feel the wide spaces yet enjoy the city lights from afar. 为逃离城市的喧嚣，许多富人都搬到了宁静的乡村，在那他们拥有宽敞的空间，同时也能远远欣赏城市的灯光。

在雅思口语考试中，曾考过 difference between living in city and a village 这个话题。考生可以用 hustle and bustle 来表达“(城市的)喧嚣”。

illegal profit 非法利润

☞ For the company, some deception might result in massive ***illegal profit***. 对公司而言，有些欺骗行为可能会带来巨额非法利润。

与“利润”相关的词组：

profit and loss 盈亏；损益	gross profit 毛利，总利润
net profit 净利润	profit drawing 利润提成
profit margin 利润率	trading profit 贸易利润
pre-tax profit 税前利润	non-profit firm 非营利公司

immigrate to　移入

☞ Do you know why people in the developing countries want to ***immigrate to*** the developed countries? 你知道发展中国家的人为什么想移民发达国家吗?

☞ emigrate to

immune system　免疫系统

☞ Your ***immune system*** functions as a defender protecting you against infections. 免疫系统行使着防卫者的职责，保护你免受感染。

impose on/upon　把…强加于，征(税)；趁机利用，占便宜；打扰

☞ I have no intention to ***impose on*** you. 我没想占你便宜。

in a dilemma　处在两难中

☞ The nurse is ***in a dilemma*** as to whether to tell the patient the truth about his condition immediately or not. 这位护士进退两难，不知道是否要立即告诉病人他的真实病情。

in a mess　处在混乱状态

☞ The book is about the relevance and use of environmental statistics—it does not deny that the global environment is ***in a mess*** and may still be getting worse. 这本书是关于环境统计数据的价值和使用——它没有否认全球环境正处于混乱状态而且可能仍在恶化这一点。

in a position to　处于能…的境况，能够…

☞ A: Can I just ask you about finance? The cash price is going to be somewhere in the region of seven and a half thousand. How would you like to pay? Are you ***in a position to*** pay cash, or would you need credit?

B: I'd like credit provided the terms are reasonable.

A：我可以问一下你的经济状况吗？现金价大概是 7500 元。你想如何支付？用现金还是用信用卡支付?

B：如果价钱合适的话我想用信用卡支付。

☞ be able to

in a slump 在衰退

☞ The economy of this area is ***in a slump*** and citizens are complaining about it. 这个地区的经济有所衰退，市民对此颇有怨言。

☞ in recession

in a way 在一定程度上

☞ A: Someone told me the article by Cooper is important.

B: Well, yes, ***in a way***, but just look at the last part, where he discusses the research results.

A：有人告诉我库珀写的那篇文章很重要。

B：在一定程度上是的，但只要看最后一部分，也就是他讨论研究结果的部分。

in a word 总之，一言以蔽之

☞ ***In a word***, I'm deeply impressed by your performance. 总之，你的表现给我留下了深刻印象。

☞ to sum up

in accordance with 依照；与…一致

☞ What is important is that illegal actions of either individual or a group within the company are normally ***in accordance with*** the goals of the company. 重要的是，公司内部个人或团体的非法行为通常是为达到公司的目标。

☞ according to

in addition 另外

☞ ***In addition***, taking a reasonable amount of exercise every day can help one to sleep well at night. 另外，每天适度运动有助于在夜间拥有良好的睡眠。

☞ besides

in addition to 除了…

☞ I've already mentioned that you must be able to support yourself. ***In addition to*** this most banks ask you to bring your passport and your letter or certificate of enrollment. 我已经提过你必须能维持自己的生活。此外，大多数银行还会要求你提供护照及入学信或入学证明。

in advance 预先，提前

☞ Booking ***in advance*** is strong recommended as all Daybreak tours are subject to demand. 强烈推荐提前预订，因为所有的日间游都根据需求来安排。

☞ There's a range of ticket prices depending on where you travel and when you buy your tickets. There's a standard open ticket which doesn't have any restrictions. This can be bought ***in advance*** or on the day. 票价取决于你的目的地以及购票时间。还有一种标准不定期客票，没有任何限制，可以提前购买，也可以当天购买。

☞ previously

in broad terms 宽泛地讲，总体来说

☞ A: What about the word limit of the dissertation?

B: We try to be pretty flexible in this, but ***in broad terms*** it's 18,000–22,000.

A：论文有字数限制吗？

B：我们努力在这方面灵活些，但宽泛地讲是 18000 到 22000 个词。

☞ ***In broad terms*** you can spend anything from $50 to $2,000 on a bike, so you'll need to know what you are looking for. 宽泛地说，自行车的价钱可以从 50 美元到 2000 美元不等，所以你需要知道自己想要什么样的自行车。

☞ broadly speaking

> come to terms with“协商，与…妥协；勉强接受”和 in terms of“至于，关于；从…角度来看”是雅思听力中比较常见的两个短语。

in case 以防万一

☞ The deposit is as insurance, ***in case*** you break something. 押金是一种保障，以防你损坏东西。

☞ for fear that

in case of 防备；假如…；如果发生…

☞ These fire doors should only be opened from the inside ***in case of*** emergency. 这些消防门只有在紧急情况下才会从里面被打开。

☞ in the event of

in circulation 未借出，在书库里；在流通

☞ A: Where can I find the book I need?

B: ***In circulation***.

A：我在哪儿能找到我需要的那本书？

B：书库里。

in comparison 相比之下

☞ There are about six doctors in our practice and three in the other, so ours is quite big ***in comparison***. 我们的诊所大约有六名医生，另一家则只有三名，所以相比之下我们诊所规模较大。

☞ by comparison

in comparison with 与…相比

☞ Corporate crime has been relatively ignored by the mass media—for example, it tends to be under-reported ***in comparison with*** conventional crime in news broadcasts, and in crime serials and films and so on—they very rarely deal with corporate crime. 相对说来，大众媒体一般会忽略公司犯罪。比如，和传统犯罪相比，新闻广播、犯罪系列片和电影等对公司犯罪的报道就不够，大众媒体很少涉及公司犯罪的题材。

☞ ***In comparison with*** your sarcastic words, your behavior is more agreeable. 和你尖酸刻薄的言辞相比，你的行为更讨人喜欢。

☞ compared with

in danger 在危险中

☞ In this film there is a superman who can fly and will help those ***in danger***. 这部电影中有个能飞且会帮助那些身处险境的人的超人。

☞ at risk

in detail 详细地

☞ All the trip are planned ***in detail*** by our highly trained guides, who all work in a variety of different locations, so we can guarantee standards. 所有行程都由我们受过高级培训的导游详细安排，他们都在各个不同地方工作过，因此我们能够保证服务质量。

☞ at length

in employment 在职的

☞ These courses are designed for those who are ***in employment***, so you cannot register. 这些课专门针对在职人员，所以你不能注册。

☞ on-the-job

NOTES

Unit 11

in full blossom 开花

☞ May will be perhaps our most spectacular month with the arrival of the Canada geese and when our fruit trees will be ***in full blossom***, but there are interesting events on all year round. 五月可能是我们这里最热闹的月份，届时会有很多加拿大黑雁过来，而且果树也会繁花满枝，不过我们这里全年都有有趣的活动。

与“开花”相关的词汇：

crossbreed 杂交　　pollination 授粉　　shoot 发出，发芽
sprout 发芽，抽条　　photosynthesis 光合作用　　bud 发芽；花蕾
petal 花瓣

in favour of 支持，赞成

☞ There was a large number of respondents ***in favour of*** a travel agent and insurance centre. 很多受访者都支持成立旅行社和保险中心。

in general 总的来说，一般而言，大体上

☞ Well, ***in general***, Asiatic lions are not as big as African lions. The colour is more or less the same, but the appearance of the mane is different—that's the hair around the lion's face and neck. 总的来说，亚洲狮没有非洲狮那么大。颜色几乎一样，但是鬃毛也就是狮子脸部和脖子周围的毛不同。

general 是雅思听力中的高频词汇，除 in general 这个常见词组外，还有下列常见搭配：

general practice 全科医疗服务　　general science 普通科学
general information 一般信息　　general course（英国大学中的）普通课程

in (great) demand 需求量很大

☞ A: It is said that the leather boots are ***in great demand***.
B: So it is.
A：据说这些皮靴需求量很大。
B：的确如此。

☞ Good secretaries are always ***in demand***. 优秀的秘书总是很抢手。

in harmony 协调一致，相配；融洽，和睦

☞ I will be very happy if all the people here live ***in harmony***. 如果这里所有人都能和睦共处，我会很高兴的。

☞ in accord

in line with 与…一致

☞ A: I think I'd be better off starting from the basics and looking at all the strategies, don't you?

B: Yes, from what you've told me, I think that's more ***in line with*** your situation.

A: 我觉得最好从基础开始，看一下所有的方法，你觉得呢？

B: 是的，根据你告诉我的，我觉得那样更符合你的情况。

☞ in accordance with

in moderation 适度地，有节制地

☞ On the middle of our diet pyramid we find the things that we can eat ***in moderation***. Not too much though! And that's where we find milk, lean meat, fish, nuts, eggs. 在饮食金字塔的中间层，我们发现一些可以适度摄取的东西。但是也不能过量！那就是牛奶、瘦肉、鱼、坚果和鸡蛋。

☞ moderately

in most cases 在大多数情况下

☞ ***In most cases*** the tragedy could be prevented if cars had been overhauled. 在大多数情况下，如果车辆经过彻底检修，悲剧是可以避免的。

in need of 需要

☞ I expect by this time you may also be ***in need of*** a rest and some refreshment. 我想你们现在也需要休息放松一会儿吧。

in other words 换句话说

☞ ***In other words***, the greenhouse effect is a natural course which is to some degree helpful to us. 换句话说，温室效应是个在某种程度上对人类有益的自然过程。

☞ ***In other words***, when the wind is blowing at 300 metres per second, most houses will be blown down. 换句话说，当风速达到每秒300米时，大多数房屋都会被吹倒。

☞ namely

in part 部分地，在某种程度上

☞ This solidarity comes ***in part*** from the need to present a united front in dealing with other powerful interest-groups, such as government or the media. 这种团结部分来源于一种要表现出统一阵线以应对其他强大的利益集团，如政府或媒体的需要。

☞ to some degree

注意和 in parts（有些部分）相区分。

in particular 特别，尤其；专门的，具体的

☞ A: Could I ask you about the college facilities, please?

B: Anything ***in particular***?

A：我能问您关于学校设施方面的事情吗？

B：有什么特别要问的吗？

☞ Is there anything ***in particular*** you'd like to say? 你有什么具体要说的吗？

☞ particularly

in person 亲自

☞ If you want to make an appointment you can phone or call at the office ***in person***. 如果你想预约的话，可以亲自打电话到办公室。

☞ personally, in the flesh

in place 在适当的地方；适合的，恰当的；准备好投入使用的

☞ A: What happens if I return the books late?

B: Like all libraries there's a fine system ***in place***. The minimum fine is ￡1.50 but it can be much higher for some items—up to ￡5 per week.

A：如果我书还晚了会怎么样？

B：和所有图书馆一样，我们有一个罚款制度，罚款的最低额度是 1.5 英镑，但是一些书的罚款可能会高很多，最高的为每周 5 英镑。

in reaction to 作为对…的回应

☞ This kind of flower changes direction ***in reaction to*** light source. 这种花能随着光源的变化改变方向。

☞ The manager said the changes were not ***in reaction to*** the company's recent losses. 经理说，这些变动不是针对公司最近的损失而作出的反应。

☞ in response to

in/with relation to 关于，涉及

☞ I have a lot to say ***in relation to*** that book. 关于那本书我要说的有很多。

☞ with regard to

in short supply 供应短缺

☞ You'd better be quick; the new toy is now ***in short supply***. 你最好迅速点，新玩具现在已经数量不多了。

in spite of 不管，尽管

☞ Last academic year, ***in spite of*** staff cuts, we counselled two hundred and forty international students for a total of twenty-six hundred hours counselling. 上一学年，我们尽管裁员了，但还是为240名国际学生提供了总计长达2600小时的咨询服务。

☞ despite

in stock 现存；现有，备有

☞ A: And then the last thing on the list is the kitchen curtains. They're torn.

B: Oh, right. We do have quite a few spare ones ***in stock*** and can get those to you in the next week, if that's alright with you?

A: Yes, that'd be fine.

A：清单上的最后一件是厨房用帘子，它们都破了。

B：我们的确还有不少余货，下周给你，可以吗？

A：好的。

☞ in store

in store 准备着，保存着；将要出现

☞ I'll run through the rest of today's programme, so that you can get a general idea of what else is ***in store*** today. 我会简单介绍一下今天其余的计划，这样你们就能大概了解今天还有哪些内容。

☞ If he had known what lay ***in store*** in him, he would never have agreed to go. 要是他事先知道会有什么遭遇的话，他是绝不会同意去的。

在听力过程中不要把 in store 和 in-store(店内的)混淆：如

in-store display 店内展示　　in-store positioning 店内布局

in terms of 根据，按照；在…方面

☞ A: Is there any difference between the two libraries?

B: Not ***in terms of*** their facilities.

A：这两个图书馆有什么不同之处吗？

B：设备方面没什么区别。

☞ I guess the next big step ***in terms of*** development of technology was to have people actually talking on the film, and the first step towards this was in 1926 when sound effects were first used on a film. 我猜技术发展接下来迈出的重大一步就是人们在电影中真正说话，而朝着这一目标迈出的第一步就是1926年第一次在电影中使用声效。

☞ according to

in that case 如果那样的话，在那种情况下

☞ ***In that case***, you will have to do without the help of your partner. 如果那样的话，你就不得不在没有搭档帮助的情况下自己完成(这项工作)。

🔍 雅思听力中常常出现 in no case，指“绝不”。

in the end 最后，终于

☞ The little boy has tried several times to pick up the ball, and ***in the end*** he succeeded. 那小男孩努力了好几次要拾起球，最后终于成功了。

☞ finally

in the first place 当初；究竟，到底(用于句尾)

☞ Why do you want to be a doctor ***in the first place***? 你究竟为什么想成为一名医生?

☞ firstly

in the heart of 在…中心

☞ A gem ***in the heart of*** Times Square, the hotel is located nearby the Broadway and the Rockefeller Center. 这家酒店犹如嵌在时代广场中心的一颗宝石，位于百老汇和洛克菲勒中心附近。

in the majority 占多数

☞ Our respondents were both men and women, but the women were just slightly ***in the majority***. 我们的调查对象中男性和女性都有，但是女性略占多数。

in the meantime 同时

☞ A: When do you want that dissertation done by?

B: Oh, it's not urgent. Um I should aim for the end of the term. But ***in the meantime***, I think you should also be thinking about Chapter Two.

A：你那篇论文想什么时候结稿?

B：不是很急。我的目标是这个学期末。但同时，我觉得你应该开始想想第二章了。

☞ at the same time, meanwhile

in the middle of 在…的中间

☞ Now I want you to look at the case study for Box Telecom as part of your exam assessment. It's interesting because they are ***in the middle of*** problems at the moment and I want you to track how they deal with them. 现在我想让你们思索一下博科斯电信的案例研究，这作为你们考试评分的一部分。他们正陷于麻烦之中，我想让你们追踪看看他们如何处理这些问题，这会很有意思。

in the middle of nowhere 在偏僻的地方，周围什么也没有

☞ As you can see, we're literally ***in the middle of nowhere*** here. There is no newspaper or TVs and there's only one phone and that's in the office. 正如你看到的，我们这里周围几乎什么都没有。没有报纸，没有电视，只有办公室里有一部电话。

☞ out of the way

🔍 go nowhere 和get nowhere 都可表示"没出息，一事无成"。

in that position 处在那种位置或境况

☞ Well, you're certainly not the only person ***in that position***, as I'm sure you've found. 你当然不是唯一处于那种境况的人，我相信你已经发现了这一点。

🔍 in one's shoes 表示"处于某人的位置，站在某人的立场上"。

in the region of （数量、重量、价格等）大约

☞ The cash price is going to be somewhere ***in the region of*** seven and a half thousand. 现金价格大概是 7500 元。

in the same vein 同样地

☞ A: Which type of programmes would you like to see more of?

B: Well, I certainly don't think we need any more factual programmes like news and documentaries. I think we need more about things like local information...And ***in the same vein***, perhaps more for younger viewers...good quality stuff.

A：你更想看到哪类节目？

B：当然我认为我们不再需要事实类节目，如新闻和纪录片。我觉得我们需要更多地方信息类的东西。同样，可能需要更多面向年轻观众的节目……高品质的节目。

☞ as well, in the same way

in this case 在这种情况下；假若这样；既然是这样

☞ You'll notice when you receive your room allocation in a few minutes that your room number either begins with the letter N, S, or W like this one here, the first letter refers to the three wings of the college which come away from this main building. Of course the letters represent the three directions—***in this case***—north, south and west. 几分钟后你们会知道房间分配情况，到时你们会发现房间号码都是以 N、S 或 W(就像这间房)开头的，首字母代表学院从主楼分离出来的三座翼楼。当然这三个字母在这里代表方向——北、南和西。

in total 总共，总计

☞ A: And you graduated in 1989. And I see you have been doing some teaching...

B: Yes. I worked as a volunteer teacher in West Africa. I was there for almost three years ***in total*** from 1990 to...umm...1992.

A：你毕业于 1989 年，而且一直做教学工作……

B：是的。我在西非做过教师志愿者。从 1990 年到 1992 年在那大概一共待了三年。

☞ The mountain was 900 miles ***in total*** and we managed to climb 32 peaks that were over 3,000 metres high, including Toubkal, which is of course the highest in North Africa. 这条山脉长达 900 英里，我们成功攀登了 32 座超过 3000 米的高峰，包括北非的最高峰图卜卡勒山。

☞ in all

in...faculty 在…系(或院)

☞ A: Are you an undergraduate or a postgraduate? Arts or Sciences?

B: Undergraduate, and I'm ***in*** the Business ***Faculty***.

A：你是本科生还是研究生？文科还是理科？

B：本科生。我在商学院。

incineration plant 焚化厂，焚烧厂

☞ Recycling can help to achieve UK's goal in two main ways: the production of recycled glass and paper uses much less energy than producing them from virgin materials, and also recycling reduces greenhouse gas emission from landfill sites and ***incineration plants***. 回收主要可以帮助英国实现两个目标：生产可回收的玻璃和纸所耗费的能量要比用原材料来生产它们少得多，并且回收可以减少垃圾填埋场和焚化厂排放的温室气体。

incorporate...into 将…融入

☞ An artist will ***incorporate*** that story ***into*** the painting. 艺术家会将故事融入画作。

indifference to 对…的冷漠

☞ We feel sorry for Jim's ***indifference to*** the poor. 吉姆对穷人漠不关心，我们对此深感惭愧。

individual circumstance 个人情况

☞ Now, as an international student you will need to provide evidence that you can fund yourself for however long your course lasts. Banks have different policies and the services that they'll offer you will depend on your ***individual circumstances*** and on the discretion of the bank manager involved. 现在，作为一名国际学生，你需要证明不管课程持续多久你都有足够的资金继续学业。每家银行的政策都不一样，所提供的服务取决于你的个人情况以及相关项目的银行经理的判断。

☞ personal circumstance

information desk 服务台，问询处

☞ Please show your invitation letter at the ***information desk***. 请在服务台出示您的邀请函。

information desk 经常出现在与图书馆(library)和学生会(Student Union)有关的听力场景中。

information explosion 信息爆炸

☞ In the ***Information Explosion*** Era, it's important to know what is going at home and abroad every day. 在这个信息爆炸的时代，知道国内外每天发生了什么很重要。

相关表达：

information age/era 信息时代　　informative 充满信息的

population explosion/boom 人口爆炸

insight into 深入了解，洞悉

☞ I like the way we're exploring the subject, and working towards getting ***insight into*** it. 我喜欢我们对研究题目进行探索的方式，不断努力以深入了解。

☞ The novel gives us fascinating ***insights into*** life in the remote village. 那部电影生动地描述了那个偏远小村庄的生活。

insist on 坚持

☞ For the recreation officer's course we offer a six-month certificate. Entry to this course normally includes applications of a wide range of ages and experiences, but we do not ***insist on*** any prerequisites for this course. 对于娱乐从业人员课程，我们提供为期六个月的课程的结业证书。一般情况下申请这门课的人的年龄段不同，有着各种各样的经历，但是我们对这门课程坚决不附加任何前提条件。

☞ stick on

inspire...to do 激励…去做

☞ The journalist said he hoped the story of Emily's life would ***inspire*** others ***to*** take up her causes in the future. 这位记者说他希望埃米莉的人生故事能激励其他人在未来继续她所走的路。

☞ encourage...to do

instant coffee 速溶咖啡

☞ A: Would you like something to drink?

B: Just a cup of ***instant coffee***.

A：你想喝点什么吗？

B：只要一杯速溶咖啡。

instant 的另一常考词组是instant noodle，指“方便面”，是一种快餐食品(fast food)。

instant hit 刚出现就立刻热卖的商品，一出现就大受欢迎的东西

☞ Since its launch last June the car has become an ***instant hit*** to rival the Mini Cooper enabling buyers to join in the craze of customizing their cars. 自去年六月上市以来，这种车就立即热卖，成为 Mini Cooper 的有力竞争对手，掀起消费者争相订购的狂潮。

dead stock 指"滞销品"。

instead of 代替，而不是

☞ The box office has been reoriented with its own access from the side of the building ***instead of*** through the foyer, which means it can be open longer hours, and has more space, too. 原先要穿过门厅才能到售票处，现在售票处的入口被重新单独安排到大楼的一侧，这样就能延长售票时间，空间也更宽敞了。

☞ in place of

insufficient for 不够做，不能胜任；不够，不足

☞ The early polar explorers' diet was commonly ***insufficient for*** their health. 早期极地探险家们的食物通常不能满足他们的健康需要。

☞ be incompetent to; be in short supply

insurance for 面向/针对…的保险

☞ A: Good morning. Diana Davies. Can I help you?

B: Yes, I'd like to get some ***insurance for*** the contents of my home.

A：早上好。我是黛安娜·戴维斯。有什么能为您效劳的吗？

B：我想给我的家庭财产上保险。

integrate into 融入，并入

☞ It's difficult to ***integrate*** foreign immigrants ***into*** our society. 要让外国移民融入我们的社会并不容易。

☞ merge with

intensive reading 精读

☞ ***Intensive reading*** is to read between the lines. 精读就是细致品读字里行间。

interest rate 利率

☞ The bank has been forced to slash the ***interest rate*** for the savings account. 银行被迫大幅降低储蓄存款的利率。

与“银行”相关的常用表达：

exchange rate 汇率	foreign exchange 外汇
gold reserve 黄金储备	national/public debt 国债
interest-free loan 免息贷款	discount rate 贴现率
bad debts 坏账	idle capital 游资
deposit 存款	endorse 背书

interest-free overdraft 免息透支

☞ Overdrafts usually incur charges though some banks offer ***interest-free overdrafts*** to some students. 尽管一些银行向一些学生提供免息透支，但透支经常会产生费用。

interfere with 干涉；打扰，妨碍

☞ These chemicals released from the explosion can kill people, badly damage the immune systems, cause cancer and ***interfere with*** normal infant and child development. 爆炸释放的化学物质可置人于死地，严重破坏免疫系统，致癌，损害婴儿和孩童的正常发育。

☞ get in the way of, hamper

interior decoration 内部装饰，室内装饰

☞ The ***interior decoration*** of this restaurant is like a small kindergarten with a lot of cartoon posters on the walls. 这家餐馆内部装饰得就像一个小幼儿园，墙上贴着许多卡通画报。

inter-library service 图书馆馆际服务

☞ Can you introduce me to the ***inter-library service*** in the UK? 你能给我介绍一下英国的图书馆馆际服务吗？

与“图书馆”相关的常用表达：

catalogue 目录	delivery/circulation desk 借书台
renew 续借	reserve 预借
classification 分类	bibliography 书目

international trade 国际贸易

☞ What is the difference between ***international trade*** and domestic trade? 国际贸易和国内贸易有什么不同之处？

introduce...to 把…介绍给

☞ Now I'd like to ***introduce*** you ***to*** the new committee for the Soccer Club for this season. 现在我要把你介绍给这个赛季足球俱乐部的新委员会。

☞ I would like to ***introduce*** my favourite hotel ***to*** you and the name of the hotel is Happy Home. 我要为你介绍我最喜欢的酒店——快乐之家。

iron out　熨平；消除；解决

☞ A: Could you ***iron out*** the wrinkles in the trousers for me?

B: Of course, just leave them on the table.

A：你能帮我把裤子上的褶子熨平吗？

B：当然可以，放在桌子上吧。

irreversible damage　无可挽回的破坏

☞ The resettlement and reconstruction after the tsunami are thought to have the potential to cause more ***irreversible damage*** to the local environment than did the tsunami itself. 人们认为，在海啸过后，重新安置和重建工作对当地环境造成的无可挽回的破坏可能要比海啸本身的破坏大得多。

严重的自然灾害都会导致 irreversible damage，下面介绍一些与"自然灾害"相关的词汇：

earthquake 地震	flood 洪水	tsunami 海啸
drought 干旱	heat wave 热浪	hurricane 飓风
tornado 龙卷风	famine 饥荒	landslide 泥石流

it makes no sense to　…是不明智的，…是不合情理的

☞ The economists said that ***it made no sense to*** continue paying the mortgage when the value of your home started going down. 经济学家说，在房子开始贬值时继续付房贷是不明智的。

☞ it's unreasonable to

it's a pleasure for...to do　对…来说做…很愉快（或荣幸）

☞ ***It's a great pleasure for*** me ***to*** welcome back Ms Diane Greenbaum who is a professional dietician and who has been kind enough to give up her time, in what I know is a very hectic schedule, to come along and talk to us today. 我很荣幸地欢迎黛安娜·戈林鲍姆女士归来，她是一位专业营养学家，今天，她在百忙之中抽出时间过来和我们聊聊，真是太好了。

it is/becomes absolutely essential for...to　必须要…

☞ With global rivals entering India and with cheap imports from other countries flooding the local market, ***it became absolutely essential for*** India ***to*** reform its tax rates. 随着国际竞争对手进入印度以及从其他国家进口的大量廉价货物涌入当地市场，印度必须对税率进行改革。

for 后面常加表"人、政体、国家"等的词汇，to 后面加的是 for 所接的主语的动作、行为等。

it's no exaggeration to say that 毫不夸张地说…

☞ ***It's no exaggeration to say that*** what distinguishes a great character from common person is the contribution they made to the society. 可以毫不夸张地说，伟人和普通人的区别就在于他们对社会所做的贡献不同。

NOTES

Unit 12

it's worthwhile to do 值得做

☞ I need some help in determining whether ***it's worthwhile to*** invest in industry. 我需要有人帮我决定投资该行业是否值得。

it's necessary to do 有必要做

☞ The questionnaire shows that most students think ***it's necessary to*** hold music courses at high school. 问卷调查显示，大多数学生认为在高中开设音乐课是必要的。

☞ it's essential to do

job description 工作说明，职位描述

☞ Our ***job description*** has been posted on our web. 我们的工作职位说明已经在我们网页上贴出来了。

job responsibility 工作职责

☞ To qualify for the post you have to fully understand the ***job responsibility***. 要胜任该项工作，你必须完全理解它的工作责任。

joint account 联名账户

☞ A: Will this be a ***joint account***?

B: No, just myself.

A：您要开联名账户吗？

B：不，只是我的个人账户。

joint effort 共同努力

☞ They are making a ***joint effort*** to catch those responsible for Monday's devastating bomb attack in Northern Ireland. 他们正共同努力去抓捕周一北爱尔兰破坏性爆炸事件的责任人。

just as well 幸好；无妨

☞ You know nothing about food catering, so you may ***just as well*** quit applying for that job. 你根本不懂餐饮业，不去申请那份工作也无妨。

keep fit　保持健康

☞ The research stations are really self-contained communities of about twenty people. There's living and working space, a kitchen with a huge food store, a small hospital and a well-equipped gym to ensure everyone ***keeps fit*** in their spare time. 研究站是相当自给自足的社区，约有 20 人。研究站内有生活区和工作区，一个存有大量食物的厨房，一家小医院和一个设备齐全的健身房，以保证每个人都能在业余时间锻炼身体来保持健康。

keep in touch with　与…保持联络

☞ What I do in this period is to ***keep in touch with*** you and reassure you that things are moving along. 在这个阶段我要做的就是和你保持联系并且确保事情进展顺利。

☞ Nowadays most of the parents use phones to ***keep in touch with*** their children. 如今大多数父母用电话与子女保持联络。

☞ stay in touch with, keep in contact with

keep on the file　存档，记录在案

☞ What you do in college will be ***kept on the file*** and go with you through your whole life. 你在大学期间的行为会被记录在案并伴随你一生。

☞ keep in the archives

keep...in mind　牢记

☞ A: We do offer to arrange special trips if, you know, there are more than twelve people.

B: Oh right, I'll ***keep*** that ***in mind***.

A：如果超过 12 人，我们会安排特别旅行。

B：好的，我会牢牢记住的。

☞ bear...in mind

keep to oneself　保守秘密；不与人交际

☞ A: To be honest, people seem to ***keep to themselves***; they're not really very friendly.

B: Oh I'm sorry to hear that. Well, what about the actual course? You're studying... uh?

A：坦白地说，人们似乎都不怎么与他人交往，不是十分友好。

B：真遗憾，那你现在的课怎么样，你是在学……？

keep watch on　密切注视，密切注意

☞ About two thousand years ago there were many soldiers standing there to ***keep watch on*** the Great Wall. 大约两千年前，那儿站立着很多士兵守卫着长城。

☞ keep an eye on, watch out

keep-fit studio 健身室

☞ A: I've played badminton in Fresham Sports Center.

B: Have you? They've got a lot of facilities our sport center doesn't have and vice versa. We do have a ***keep-fit studio***, which is very popular with members.

A：我在弗莱沙姆运动中心打过羽毛球。

B：真的吗？ 他们那有很多我们运动中心所没有的运动器材，反之亦然。我们这里有一个健身房，备受会员们欢迎。

☞ fitness room, fitness center

雅思听力中也会出现一些和"健身"有关的场景，常用的词组有：

physical fit 健身	keep fit/stay in shape 保持体型
lose some weight 减肥	gain some weight 增肥

kick...out of 开除，解雇；逐出

☞ Please rethink the idea of ***kicking*** Linda ***out of*** work. She has been working very hard. 请重新考虑一下解雇琳达的事。她工作一直很卖力。

☞ give...a sack

kill off 灭绝，杀光

☞ Despite living in a sanctuary, which makes the lions safe from hunters, they still face a number of problems that threaten their survival. One of these is the ever-present danger of disease. This is what killed more than a third of Africa's Serengeti lions in 1994, and people are fearful that something similar could happen in the sanctuary and ***kill off*** many of the Asiatic lions there. 尽管狮子生活在保护区内，可以免受猎人的追捕，但仍面临很多威胁它们生存的问题。其中之一就是疾病一直以来所带来的危险，这就是 1994 年杀死 1/3 以上非洲塞伦盖蒂草原狮的原因，人们担心保护区内会发生类似事情而导致大量亚洲狮死亡。

☞ get rid of

kind of 有点

☞ It is ***kind of*** weird to see the teacher in the dormitory again. 在宿舍里又看到这名老师，有点奇怪。

☞ sort of

knock down 拆除；（使）降低（价格），低价售出（尤指拍卖）

☞ Plans have been unveiled to ***knock down*** an entertainment center in the city. A famous architecture said he did not believe the building should be ***knocked down***. 已经宣布了市中心一座娱乐中心的拆除计划。但是一位著名建筑师认为这座建筑不应该被拆除。

know...backwards and forwards 精通；全面而深入地了解

☞ You can treat the instruction as material for a test you'll take and get to ***know*** it ***backwards and forwards*** in several days. 你可以把这个说明当做考试的复习材料，在几天内把它弄明白。

☞ know...inside out

known as 被认为是，被称为

☞ The Bachelor of Social Science is in one faculty within the university; that is the faculty where I work, ***known as*** Arts and Social Sciences. 社会科学学士学位由我们学校的一个系颁发，我就在该系工作，它被称做社会科学和艺术系。

landfill site 填埋场

与"垃圾"相关的词组：

rubbish bin 垃圾桶

solid waste 固体垃圾

disposal of rubbish 垃圾处理

hazardous waste 有害废物

living garbage 生活垃圾

waste-paper basket 废纸箱

last but not least 最后但同样重要的

☞ ***Last but not least***, you can go out and have a short rest at any time. 最后但同样重要的是，你随时可以出去休息片刻。

在英语口语或写作中，我们常用 first、second 等词来表示列举，最后就常用 last but not least 来表示最后但同样重要的一点。

late fee 滞纳金，过期附加费

☞ Read the credit card statement carefully to find out how much time you've got to pay your bill before triggering ***late fees***. 仔细阅读信用卡声明，明确什么时候支付账单才不致产生滞纳金。

☞ late fine, past due fee

常见的一些"费用"：

admission fee 入场费

cost 成本，原价

rent 土地、建筑物、房舍等定期的租费

toll 道路、桥梁、港口、市场的捐税及电话费等

launch new products 投放新产品

☞ Our company is planning to ***launch new products*** at the end of this quarter. 我们公司打算在本季末投放新产品。

laundry fee 洗衣费用

☞ In your fees you've paid a ***laundry fee*** which covers the cleaning of bed linen and towels. 你所付的费用涵盖了洗衣费，包括床单、枕套和毛巾的清洗费。

lead into 导致，引起；通向

☞ The gate ***leads into*** the courtyard. 这扇门通向院子。

lead to 导致；通向

☞ At that time there was a real possibility of having films of more than two or three minutes, and this ***led to*** the making of *The Great Train Robbery*—the very first movie. 那时，已经完全有可能制作出超过两三分钟长的电影了，这就促成了第一部电影《火车大劫案》的制作。

Exam failure can ***lead to*** worrying changes in the way you normally behave. 考试失利会导致你的正常行为方式发生令人担心的变化。

☞ give rise to, bring out

learn through 通过…学习

☞ A: That essay we have to write...the one on how children ***learn through*** the media... how are you planning to write it?

B: Well, I've given it some thought and I think that the best way to approach it is to divide the essay into two parts. First of all, we'd have to look at some examples of each type of media.

A：我们那篇关于孩子是如何通过媒体学习的论文，你计划怎么写呢？

B：我想过了，我觉得最好的办法是把论文分成两部分。首先我们应该针对各种媒体都找几个例子来看看。

lecture on 作演讲，讲课

☞ A: Hello, this is the School of Economics.

B: Oh good. I'm a new student and I was wondering if someone could give me some information.

A: Well, I might be able to help. I ***lecture on*** that program. What do you need to know?

A：你好，这里是经济学院。

B：太好了。我是一名新生，想得到一些信息。

A：或许我能帮助你，我教那个学科，你想知道些什么？

letter of acceptance 录取通知书

☞ Until I receive the ***letter of acceptance*** I will stay at my house. 在拿到录取通知书前，我会一直待在家里。

leisure time 闲暇时间

☞ Listening to music can both enrich my ***leisure time*** and satisfy my spiritual needs. 听音乐既能丰富我的闲暇时间又能满足我的精神需求。

☞ spare time

lend an ear 耐心而同情地听着，倾听

☞ I am willing to ***lend an ear*** to your story of your hard life. 我愿意倾听有关你艰辛生活的故事。

letter of recommendation 推荐信

☞ You can't expect a boss to hire you just because of a ***letter of recommendation***. 你别指望单凭一封推荐信老板就会录用你。

life expectancy 平均(期望)寿命，预期寿命

☞ I'm sure the ***life expectancy*** in China will increase in the future. 我相信未来中国人的平均寿命将会增加。

light rail 轻轨

☞ The ***light rail*** line runs from the Disney Land to the downtown. 轻轨线路是从迪斯尼乐园到市中心。

> 随着城市的发展，交通越来越便捷。常见的交通工具：
>
> bus 公共汽车　　coach 大客车　　tram 有轨电车
>
> elevated train 磁悬浮　　ferry 渡船　　subway 地铁

line up 排列成行；组织；邀请

☞ The Scotsman designed a camera, a projection device and the film. The system was first shown in New York in 1894 and was really very popular. People ***lined up*** around the block to see the wonderful new invention. 这名苏格兰人设计了一台照相机、一个投影装置和胶片。这个系统于1894年第一次在纽约展示并广受欢迎。人们在街区排队来看这个奇妙的新发明。

live music 现场音乐

☞ A: We should have known how the interviewees listen to their music.

B: The medium. Let's include radio, CD—and then I guess there's TV.

A: What about concerts? You know, in pubs and halls.

B: We should include ***live music*** of course.

A：我们应该知道这些受访者是如何听音乐的。

B：媒体。应该包括广播、CD——我猜还应该有电视。

A：音乐会呢？你知道的，在酒吧和音乐厅里。

B：我们当然应该包括现场音乐。

几种常见的音乐类型：

world music 世界音乐，常指发展中地区的传统音乐，如非洲及南亚洲地区的音乐

classic pop 带古典交响乐味道的流行曲

electrophonic music 电子音乐

chamber pop 室内乐，指一种典雅、高贵、精致的流行乐

bossa nova 带有爵士乐味道的巴西音乐

living condition 生活条件；生存境况

☞ These cottages were built for workers towards the end of the eighteenth century and they are still furnished from that period so you can get a good idea of ordinary people's ***living condition***. 这些棚屋建于18世纪末，是为当时的工薪阶层建的，内部陈设还保留当时的样子，因此你们可以对当时普通人的生活状况有个很好的了解。

另一常考的相关词组是 living standard，意为"生活标准"。

loads of 很多

☞ The cell phone produced by the South Korean company is only a couple of weeks old, but it has already dropped a big firmware update that fixes ***loads of*** bugs. 这种由韩国公司生产的手机才上市几周，但该公司已经发布了一个大的固件更新，能修复大量漏洞。

☞ a host of, a load of

local resident 当地居民

☞ I asked an old ***local resident*** about the history of the small town. 我向当地一位老人打听这座小镇的历史。

☞ local people

log on/in 注册；登录，进入(计算机系统)

☞ We'll give you a booklet with all the details when you join the library. You can always renew items if the books are not required by anyone else by telephoning or ***logging on*** to our website. 你成为图书馆会员后，我们会给你提供一本小册子，内附所有详情。只要没有人要求借你已借出的书，你就可以通过打电话或登录我们的网页一直续借。

☞ register

long jump 跳远

☞ In his ten years' athletic career he has won numerous medals in the ***long jump***. 在十年的运动生涯中，他赢得了许多跳远奖牌。

常见的"体育运动"：

swimming 游泳	diving 跳水
water polo 水球	discus 铁饼
javelin 标枪	beach volleyball 沙滩排球
baseball 棒球	softball 垒球
table tennis 乒乓球	high jump 跳高

look ahead 向前看；为将来设想，规划未来

☞ Women today need to ***look ahead***, think ahead—not wait until they're under pressure. 当今女性需要展望并思考未来——而不是迫于压力才如此行动。

look back 回头看；回顾，回忆

☞ As the final words are spoken by the team leader, it's difficult to ***look back*** over the past months without feeling a swirl of emotion. 队长话音落下，我们回顾过去几个月的时光，心情跌宕起伏。

look forward to 期盼，盼望

☞ My husband and I ***look forward to*** seeing you all next weekend. 我们夫妇都期待下周末见到你们。

☞ expect to

look through 快速阅读，浏览；快速查看

☞ What I decided to do was to ***look through*** catalogues specializing in IT. 我决定快速阅读一下 IT 行业的目录。

Before Friday, I think we should all ***look through*** the reading list. 我认为周五前我们所有人都应该浏览一下书单。

☞ skim through

另一个和 through 有关的词组：go through 可指"东西消耗得快"，也可指"乱翻东西"，如：go through one's shoes 穿鞋很费，go through one's stuff 乱翻某人的东西。

look up 好转，改善；查找；拜访

☞ A: I found it frustrating to have so few teaching resources in West Africa, but I did decide to stay and in the end I extended my tour to a third year.

B: Right. Things have ***looked up*** in the third year.

A：西非的教学资源如此之少，令人沮丧，但我决定留下，最终把这次行程延长到三年。

B：是的，第三年情况好转了。

☞ improve

lose sight of 忽略，看不见

☞ At the bottom of the diet pyramid are the things that you can eat lots of! Because they're the things that are really good for you, and here we have bread, vegetables and fruit. So don't ***lose sight of*** your healthy diet pyramid when you do your shopping. 处于饮食金字塔底层的是一些可以大量摄取的东西！这些东西对你大有益处，它们包括面包、蔬菜和水果。所以购物时千万不要忽略健康饮食金字塔。

☞ neglect, pay no attention to

lose temper 失态，发脾气

☞ It is really ashamed of you to ***lose temper*** in front of kids. 你在孩子们面前发脾气，真是太丢人了。

> temper 的常用搭配：
> control/keep one's temper 耐住性子　　fly into a temper 勃然大怒
> good temper 心情好　　a quick temper 急性子

lottery ticket 彩票

☞ I always dream of buying a ***lottery ticket*** and getting rich overnight. 我总梦想买张彩票一夜致富。

lower the rate of 降低…的概率

☞ To ***lower the rate of*** unqualified product, the factory has tried many methods. 为了降低不合格产品率，这家工厂已尝试了许多方法。

low-risk investment 低风险投资

☞ Many women are unwilling to invest in stocks and shares, but these can be extremely profitable. Financial advisors usually advise that at least 70% of a person's savings should be in ***low-risk investments***. 很多女性都不愿意投资股票，但股票会带来丰厚回报。金融顾问通常建议人们至少应该拿出70%的存款进行低风险投资。

loyalty to 对…的忠诚

☞ They swore their ***loyalty to*** the queen. 他们宣誓效忠女王。

lucky you 你真幸运

☞ A: Hi there, Martin. How are you going with your Australian studies tutorial paper?

B: Oh good. I've finished it actually.

A: ***Lucky you***.

A：你好，马丁，你关于澳大利亚人的研究小论文弄得怎么样了？

B：哦，好的，事实上我已经完成了。

A：你可真幸运。

lunar calendar 农历

☞ A: When is the Dragon Boat Festival in your country?

B: It is on the fifth day of the fifth month of the ***lunar calendar***.

A：你们国家的端午节是什么时候？

B：农历五月初五。

solar calendar 指“阳历”。

maid of honor 伴娘，女傧相

☞ Would you like to be our ***maid of honor*** in our wedding ceremony? 你愿意给我们当伴娘吗？

在西式婚礼(wedding ceremony)上，新郎(groom)和新娘(bride)在男傧相(best man)和女傧相的陪同下举行婚礼。仪式结束后，新郎和新娘会一起去度蜜月(honeymoon)。

main branch 银行总行；本店

☞ Banks used to be open from 9:30 am until 3:30 pm from Monday to Friday but many ***main branches*** are now open until 4:30 or 5 pm on weekdays and some of the bigger branches in London and other major cities are now open for a limited time on Saturdays. 过去，银行通常在周 到周五的上午 9:30 到下午 3:30 营业，但是现在很多银行的总行在周一到周五都要到下午 4:30 或 5 点才关门。在伦敦及其他一些大城市，一些大支行在周六也会开门，但营业时间是有限制的。

main course 主菜

☞ In that country fish cannot be used for the ***main course***. 在那个国家，鱼不能作主菜。

☞ main dish

NOTES

Unit 13

main topic 主题

☞ The ***main topic*** of conversation was Jim's new hairstyle. 交谈的主要话题是吉姆的新发型。

make a complaint 抱怨；投诉

☞ If you want to hear about special offers, please press one. If you want to hear our latest price lists, please press two. If you want to ***make a complaint***, please press three. If you want information about our new walking holidays, please press four now. 如果您想了解特惠活动，请按 1。如果您想了解我们最新的报价单，请按 2。如果您想投诉，请按 3。如果您想了解我们新的徒步旅行活动，现在请按 4。

☞ complain to

make a deep impression 留下深刻的印象

☞ During an interview, it is very important to ***make a deep impression*** on the employers. 面试中，给面试官留下深刻的印象很重要。

☞ be greatly impressed with

make a detour 绕行，迂回

☞ It seems we have to ***make a detour*** as the road is blocked by a fallen tree. 一棵树倒下挡住了路，看来我们不得不绕道而行了。

make a hit 给予极其良好的印象；成功；大受欢迎

☞ The new teacher does ***make a hit*** with students. 新老师着实给学生们留下了极好的印象。

make a nominal charge 收取少量费用

☞ A: What about the computers? Can I use them free of charge?

B: For college students it's free, but for external members like yourself, the first hour is free and then we ***make a nominal charge*** of £1 per hour thereafter.

A: 我可以免费使用这些电脑吗？

B：学生可以免费使用，但是对于像您这样的外部人员，第一个小时是免费的，之后每小时象征性地收取一英镑的费用。

nominal value 和 face value 都表"市值，面值"。

make (a) note of 记录，把…记下

☞ A: What would be your preferred time?
B: Any time up to 5pm would be fine.
A: OK, I've ***made a note of*** that.
A：你什么时间方便？
B：下午五点前任何时间都可以。
A：好的，我记下了。

☞ Please ***make note of*** my new address. 请把我的新地址记下来。

☞ keep an account of

make a provisional booking 进行临时预约

☞ A: What I'll do is to talk to my partner and get back to you.
B: Fine. So I'll ***make a provisional booking***, shall I? Two for the Whale Watch Experience. Let me issue you with a customer reference number for when you call back.
A：我去和我的搭档说一下，然后再打电话给你吧。
B：好的，我先为您做一个临时预订吧？两个人参加观鲸体验之旅。我给您注册一个顾客编号吧，以便您回电时进行查找。

🔍一般而言，做 booking（预订）时都要填表（booking form），其内容大致包括：Date（日期）、Number of People（人数）、Time（时间）和 Type of Ticket（票的类型）等。

make a quick getaway 快速离开，迅速逃脱

☞ Men were very aware that muggers or whatever might be concealed behind the car. They also made the point that you should leave plenty of room when you park your car so you can ***make a quick getaway*** if you need to. 男性对抢劫者或其他有可能藏在车后的任何人或物都非常警惕。他们还指出在停车时应该留出足够的空间，若有需要的话就可以快速逃脱。

☞ speed away, move quickly

make a reference to 涉及，提到

☞ A: I'd be quite interested to have a few more statistics about the schools in the different zones.
B: Oh, that wouldn't be a problem. I can get them from the Internet.
A: Great, and although you did ***make a reference to*** quite a few different writers, I think you should aim to cite more works written later than 2000.
A：我很想得到更多不同地区学校的数据。
B：这不成问题。我能从网上得到这些数据。
A：太好了，尽管你的参考书目确实涉及很多作者，但我认为你应该多引用2000年以后的作品。

☞ touch upon, involve

make a wish 许愿

☞ You can ***make a wish*** while directly throwing a coin into the well. 你可以直接向这口井投一枚硬币许愿。

make allowances for 体谅，谅解；考虑到，估计到

☞ I'm afraid the lectures will ***make*** little or no ***allowance for*** the presence of non-native speakers in the audience. 恐怕讲座不会考虑到听众中有非母语人士。

make an application 进行申请

☞ If you do decide to ***make an application*** to this position, what you should do is to send your résumé directly to me in my department. 如果你真的想申请这个职位，把简历直接寄到我工作的部门即可。

make an appointment 预约

☞ May I ask a favour of you to ***make an appointment*** with your manager? 你能帮我预约一下你们经理吗？

make an effort/efforts to 努力，致力于

☞ We were quite shocked to discover that only 9% of people in this country ***make an effort to*** recycle their household waste. 我们非常震惊地发现在该国，只有 9%的人在努力回收生活垃圾。

☞ These schools have ***made*** great ***efforts to*** improve the practical ability of their students in oral English. 这些学校在提高学生英语口语实际能力方面做出了巨大的努力。

☞ endeavour to, strive to

effort 与前面的 an 和后面的 to 都有连读，听录音时要注意。

make an exception (of) 允许例外，让…成为例外

☞ Most of the people think that the railway shouldn't have ***made an exception of*** foreigners and only a few people think that it is understandable. 大多数人认为铁路方不应该对外国人搞特殊，只有小部分人对这一做法表示理解。

make clear 讲清楚；表明，显示

☞ Thomas's silence ***makes clear*** that he isn't interested in this kind of consulting sessions. 托马斯的沉默表明了他对这种咨询课程不感兴趣。

make difference 有影响；有关系

☞ You're supposed to ask for a home visit before 10:30 in the morning, but obviously, if it's an emergency, you can phone at any time, night or day. It might not be your doctor that comes, though. It's quite often one of the other doctors in the practice. It doesn't really seem to ***make*** much ***difference***. 你应该在上午 10:30 前要求医生出诊，当然如果情况紧急的话，则可以随时来电，不论白天或夜晚。不过来的可能就不是你的家庭医生了。通常会是医疗点的另外一位医生。这似乎真的没多大影响。

make friends with 和…交朋友

☞ He is that sort of person I really don't want to ***make friends with***. 他属于那种我极不愿意与之交朋友的人。

make great progress 取得巨大进步

☞ It's unbelievable that Linda has ***made great progress*** in such a short time! 琳达在如此短的时间内就取得了巨大的进步，真令人难以置信！

make headway 取得进展

☞ We have ***made headway*** with the new project. 我们在新项目上取得了进展。

☞ make progress

make it difficult for...to do 使得做…有困难

☞ We used to start all our performances at 7:30 pm, but that ***made it difficult for*** people to go home by public transport, so instead we're beginning at 7, because at 9:45, when it finishes, there are still buses running. 以前，我们所有表演都在晚上 7:30 开始，但这样一来，观众就很难乘公共交通工具回家，所以现在我们的表演都在晚上 7:00 开始，这样在 9:45 结束时还有公交车。

make notes 做笔记，记笔记

☞ While listening you can ***make*** some ***notes*** to help you better understand the article. 听录音时，你可以做一些笔记来帮助你更好地理解文章。

☞ take notes

make one's blood boil 使…非常生气，使…怒发冲冠

☞ It can ***make your blood boil*** when the services and stores people depend on are forced to shut their doors. 当你目睹人们生活所依赖的服务设施和商店都被迫关门时，你会非常生气的。

make out of 用…制造；用…得出；理解

☞ The pieces we ***made out of*** old wood cost $5. 我们用旧木头做的零部件要价是五美元。

make seat reservation 预订座位

☞ The cheapest tickets are called Advance and you have to buy them at least six days ahead. Only a certain number are available and you have to ***make seat reservations*** for these. 最便宜的票是"预售票"，至少要提前六天购买。数量有限，而且得预订座位。

make sure 弄清楚，查明，确定

☞ We recommend that, if you are buying a cot, do ***make sure*** that any metal present is not rusted or bent in any way. 我们建议，在购买婴儿床时得确保任何金属都没有生锈或弯曲。

☞ make certain

make up one's mind 做决定，拿定主意

☞ A: How can I help you?

B: Well, I'm thinking of buying a new car and I'd like some advice.

A: Sure, yes. Have you got any particular make in mind?

B: I'm interested in a Lida—I've had one before and liked it. But I haven't really ***made up my mind***.

A：我能帮你什么吗？

B：我在考虑买一辆新车，想听听你的建议。

A：当然可以。有什么中意的车型了吗？

B：我对利达的一款车很感兴趣——我之前买过一辆并且很喜欢，但我还没有拿定主意呢。

☞ make a decision

make up 编造（故事、谎言等）；凑数；作出补偿；铺床；形成，构成；拼装，组成

☞ There's a final category as well...computers, that ***make up*** the so-called electronic media. In the United Kingdom and Australia, they say that one in three families has a computer now. 还有最后一个类别……计算机，其构成了所谓的电子媒体。在英国和澳大利亚，据说现在每三个家庭中就有一个拥有计算机。

☞ A significant proportion of the lions' diet is ***made up*** of the livestock and poultry of these farmers—goats, chicken and so on—as much as a third, in fact. 狮子的绝大部分食物是这些农民的牲畜家禽——山羊、鸡等——实际上，占的比例高达 1/3。

☞ constitute

make use of 使用，利用

☞ For the second part of the assignment, we have to choose one method of data collection, and carry out a small-scale study, ***making*** appropriate ***use of*** the method chosen to gather data from at least five subjects. 对于作业的第二部分，我们要用一种数据收集的方法完成一项小规模研究，要求恰当使用所选方法来收集至少五门学科的数据。

☞ avail oneself of

make waves 惹麻烦

☞ The best way to stay out of trouble in companies is not to ***make waves***. 在公司里避免麻烦的最好方法就是不要惹是生非。

☞ make trouble

make/draw the...conclusion 得出结论

☞ These two detectives have ***drawn*** different ***conclusions*** from the clues left in the crime scene. 这两位侦探从犯罪现场留下的线索中得出了不同的结论。

☞ It took the jury some time to ***draw the conclusion*** that he was innocent. 陪审团花了很长时间才得出结论，认为他是清白的。

☞ reach the conclusion

man of the year 年度新闻人物，年度风云人物

☞ It is very tantalizing to know who is elected as ***man of the year***. 真想知道谁将成为年度风云人物。

management layer 管理层

☞ A more ambitious approach, and one which I think would have more chances of success, would be to alter how they're running things—the ***management layer*** and the processes. 我认为一个更雄心勃勃且有着更大成功率的方法是改变他们的运营方式——管理层和管理过程。

man-made object 人造物

☞ He said the Great Gall was the only ***man-made object*** that could be seen from space. 他说，长城是唯一能从太空看到的人造建筑物。

manual gear 手动换挡，手动挡

☞ A: Is there anything else to do with the engine? What kind of gear change do you want? I presume you'd want a manual?

B: I'd want automatic—I've never driven a car with ***manual gears***.

A：对发动机还有什么要求吗？你想要什么样的变速器？我猜是手动的。

B：我想要自动挡的——我从没开过手动挡的车。

many thanks to...for doing 十分感谢…做

☞ Firstly, let me welcome Robert Young, the new president, who will manage the meetings for the next two years. Robert's son has been playing football with the club for over five years now, and ***many thanks to*** Robert ***for*** taking on the job of president. 首先，让我们欢迎新的大会主席罗伯特·扬，接下来的两年将由他主持会议。到现在为止，罗伯特的儿子已经在这个俱乐部里踢了五年的球，非常感谢罗伯特先生接受主席一职。

☞ have gratitude to/towards...for doing

market economy 市场经济

☞ Nowadays, the living standard is higher and higher with the development of ***market economy***. 如今，随着市场经济的发展，生活水平也不断提高。

market share 市场份额

☞ The company's long-term problems, which were affecting their ***market share***, were eventually credited to poor training—and having looked at the details in their last report I think that's right. 长期影响这家公司市场份额的问题最终归结于糟糕的培训——认真研究过他们上一次的报告后我认为情况的确如此。

marketing consultant 营销顾问

☞ Good morning. Welcome to this talk on Space Management. And today I'm going to look particularly at space management in the supermarket. Now since the time supermarkets began, ***marketing consultants***, like us, have been gathering information about customers' shopping habits. 早上好。欢迎来听这场"空间管理"的报告。今天我们要着重讨论一下超市的空间管理。自超市出现以来，营销顾问(比如我们)就开始收集一些有关顾客购物习惯的信息。

mass media 大众传媒

☞ The questionnaire shows that most young people think that the modern ***mass media*** such as the Internet is more popular than the traditional ***mass media***. 问卷调查显示，大多数年轻人认为如网络之类的现代大众传媒比传统大众传媒更受欢迎。

大众媒体通常包括以下几种：

newspaper 报纸　　magazine 杂志　　Internet 网络

television 电视　　radio 收音机

maximum profit 最大利润

☞ Space Management is now a highly sophisticated method of manipulating the way we shop to ensure ***maximum profit***. 如今，空间管理是一个高度复杂化的方法，其通过支配我们的购物方式来获取最大利润。

medium-sized city 中型城市

☞ In the past, only few graduates chose to work in the small or ***medium-sized city***. 过去，只有极少数毕业生选择去中小城市工作。

相关词汇：

metropolis 大城市　　town 城镇　　county 郡

meet the deadline 在截止日期前完成

☞ There's always a lot of homework every day and I can hardly ***meet the deadline***. 每天总有很多的作业，我几乎不可能在期限内完成。

meet one's needs 满足某人的需求

☞ If ***one's*** accessibility ***needs*** are not ***met***, he or she can contact the hotel manager on duty. 顾客如果想进入却未得以许可，可以联系酒店的值班经理。

☞ satisfy/suit one's needs

meet up (with)（按照安排）会面，见面

☞ A: I've got a tutorial now. Can we ***meet up*** again later this week? What about Friday morning?

B: Suits me. Eleven o'clock?

A：我现在要去上一门辅导课。我们这周晚些时间还能再见面吗？周五早上怎么样？

B：我没问题，11 点可以吗？

☞ A: It was in many ways a social trip, wasn't it?

B: Yes, yes...we've arranged to ***meet up with*** friends at various points on the journey.

A：这次旅行在很大程度上来说是一次社交旅行，不是吗？

B：是的，在旅程中我们安排了多处地方与朋友会面。

☞ come across

metropolitan area 市中心地区，大都市区

☞ There is a famous coffee shop in ***metropolitan area*** which serves good coffee. 市中心有一家著名咖啡店，供应优质咖啡。

☞ downtown area

military use 军用

☞ The third gizmo is called the Army Flashlight because it was developed initially for ***military use***. 第三件小发明被称作军用手电筒，因为它最初是为军用而开发的。

🔍“民用”则是 civilian use。

mind doing 介意做

☞ Would you ***mind explaining*** that again, please? 请你再解释一遍好吗？

☞ I don't ***mind helping*** if you cannot find anyone else. 如果你找不到别人，我乐意帮忙。

mind you 请注意，留心

☞ The first experiment is called "Make your own hovercraft," which sounds very ambitious! ***Mind you***, you only need twenty balloons and a table. 第一个试验叫做“自制气垫船”，听起来很是野心勃勃，但要注意，你只需 20 只气球和一张桌子。

☞ take care

misplace trust in 看错，误信

☞ I don't want to ***misplace*** my ***trust in*** someone who is irresponsible. 我不想错信了不负责任的人。

🔍与 trust 相关的词组：

be based on trust 建立在信任的基础上　　earn one's trust 赢得信任

put trust in 信赖　　a position of trust 重任

take...on trust 听信，轻信

more or less 或多或少，差不多，几乎，大约

☞ In 1895, the projection systems were all developed, ***more or less*** at the same time and independently of each other. 1895 年，这些放映系统几乎在同一时间独立发展了起来。

🔍相关表达：

no more no less 不多不少

More hasty, less speed. 欲速则不达。

motivate...to do 激励…做

☞ The seminar is aimed at students like you who are uncertain about what to expect at college, and looks at a fairly wide range of approaches to university learning, to ***motivate*** you ***to*** begin your study and build on your own learning strategies. 该研讨会旨在为像你这样不清楚在大学干什么的学生而开，探讨大学学习的多种方法，激励你开始学习并形成自己的学习策略。

☞ The plan is designed to ***motivate*** employees ***to*** work more efficiently. 这个计划旨在促使员工更加卓有成效地工作。

☞ spur...to do

mountain climbing 爬山

☞ I like ***mountain climbing*** because it is a good exercise to keep me fit. 我喜欢爬山，因为它能使我保持健康。

🔍常见的“户外运动”：

jogging 慢跑	hunting 打猎	mountaineering 登山
hiking 徒步旅行	skating 滑冰	skiing 滑雪
cycling 骑自行车	swimming 游泳	

move along 向前移动

☞ What I do in this period is to keep in touch with you and reassure you that things are ***moving along***. 我在这个阶段要做的就是和你保持联系并且向你确保事情进展顺利。

move away from...to 从…移到

☞ The steam engine was invented and then the railways came and the centers of the industry were able to ***move away from*** the rivers and the countryside ***to*** the towns. 蒸汽机被发明了，接着铁路问世了，工业中心便从河流沿岸和乡村转入城镇。

move forward 向前移动，往前走

☞ As you know, sharks are very quick swimmers. This is made possible by their fins, one set at the side and another set underneath the body, and the tail also helps the shark ***move forward*** quickly. 众所周知，鲨鱼游得非常快。其原因在于它们的鳍，一个在其身体侧面，另一个在其身体下方，而且鱼尾也能帮助鲨鱼快速前行。

move on (to) 开始做(别的事)；前进；出发，离开；换话题

☞ Well that's a good list to start with...we're really getting somewhere with this essay now...so let's ***move on to*** when each type of media could be used. I guess we could start by trying to identify the best situation for each type of media. 这个列表是个好的开始，我们对这篇论文已经有了点思路，所以让我们开始看一下各种媒体何时可使用。我觉得我们应该从找出每种媒体最适用的场合着手。

NOTES

Unit 14

multiple entry visa　多次入境签证

☞ Can you explain why you apply for ***multiple entry visa***? 你能解释一下为什么申请多次入境签证吗?

常见的签证:

student visa 学生签证　　tourist visa 旅游签证
business visa 商务签证　　employment visa 工作签证
visit visa 访问签证　　residency visa 居留签证
re-entry visa 再入境签证　　single entry visa 单次入境签证

musical instrument　乐器

☞ I am not good at playing ***musical instrument***. How about you? 我不擅长演奏乐器,你呢?

常见的乐器:

piano 钢琴　　guitar 吉他　　cello 大提琴
violin 小提琴　　saxophone 萨克斯　　harp 竖琴
viola 中提琴　　flute 长笛　　pipe organ 管风琴
trumpet 喇叭　　bagpipe 风笛

natural resources　自然资源

☞ It is wicked for some countries to deprive others of their ***natural resources***. 掠夺其他国家自然资源的做法是卑鄙的。

一些常见的自然资源:

coal 煤　　petroleum/oil 石油
natural gas 天然气　　solar energy 太阳能
mineral 矿物　　wind energy 风能
tidal energy 潮汐能

natural scenery　自然风光

☞ The country boasts of the world's most spectacular ***natural scenery***. 这个国家自夸拥有世界上最壮丽的自然风光。

never mind 没关系，不要紧

☞ A: Was the briefcase locked?

B: No, I'm afraid not.

A: ***Never mind***. Any distinct features?

A：公文包锁了吗？

B：恐怕没锁。

A：没关系，有什么显著特征吗？

nine-year compulsory education 九年制义务教育

☞ Some students in the poor areas cannot finish their ***nine-year compulsory education***. 贫困地区的一些学生无法完成九年义务教育。

相关表达：

kindergarten 幼儿园 | day-care center 幼儿园；托儿所，日托中心

nursery school 托儿所，育幼院 | primary/elementary school 小学

secondary school 中学 | junior high school 初中

senior high school 高中 | university 大学

no charge 免费

☞ There is ***no charge*** for the sample. 样品不收费。

☞ without charge, free of charge

雅思听力中常见的 charge 搭配：

commission charges 佣金，手续费 | charge the ticket 买票

charge out 把…借出来 | service charge 服务费

no exception 没有例外，无一例外

☞ No company has the right to discriminate employees based on race, and this one is ***no exception***. 任何公司都没有权利种族歧视员工，这家公司也不例外。

no substitute for 不可替代

☞ Vitamin pills should be labeled with warnings that they are ***no substitute for*** a healthy diet in Europe. 在欧洲，维生素药片必须注明其不可取代健康饮食。

non-native speaker 非母语人士

☞ I'm afraid the lectures will make little or no allowance for the presence of ***non-native speakers*** in the audience. 恐怕讲座不会考虑到听众中有非母语人士。

non-smoking section 无烟区，禁烟区

☞ The boss wanted to make reservation for a room in a ***non-smoking section***. 老板想在无烟区预订一个房间。

🔍 smoking section 表"吸烟区"。

nose dive 俯冲；暴跌，急剧下降

☞ After breaking up with Mary, Tom's study took a ***nose dive***. 跟玛丽分手后，汤姆的学习成绩一落千丈。

not always be the case 情况不会一直是这样的

☞ Most people think that lions only come from Africa. And you would be forgiven for thinking this, because in fact most lions do come from Africa. But this ***hasn't always been the case***. 大多数人都认为狮子只生活在非洲，这样想情有可原，因为实际上大多数狮子的确都来自非洲，但并非一直如此。

not for circulation 不外借

☞ Sorry, all of the books in this library are ***not for circulation***. 对不起，这个图书馆的所有书籍概不外借。

not have a clue about 不了解，不知情

☞ Do not ask the old man which key to press—he ***doesn't have a clue about*** computers. 不要问这个老人应该按哪一个键，他对计算机一窍不通。

not mean any offense on 不是有意冒犯

☞ You know, I ***don't mean any offense on*** these disabled people. 你知道，我并非有意冒犯这些残疾人。

not only...but also 不但…而且，不仅…还

☞ There are an increasing number of opportunities for young people to work for a period in Antarctica—***not only*** as research assistants in projects like mine, ***but also*** in a wide range of junior administrative and technical positions including vacancies for map-makers. 年轻人有越来越多的机会在南极洲工作一段时间——不仅在采矿类项目中担任研究助理，还可任职于各种中级管理和技术岗位，如地图绘制员。

not to mention 更不用说

☞ It's far too early for you to go out and play basketball, ***not to mention*** the fact that it's snowing. 你现在出去打篮球太早了，更何况还在下雪。

☞ needless to say

not...but rather 不是… 而是

☞ Actually, Thomas Edison ***didn't*** do the work himself ***but rather*** asked a young Scotsman in his employ to design a projection system. 实际上托马斯·爱迪生并没有亲自做这件事，而是雇用一个苏格兰人设计了一个放映系统。

note down 记录，记下

☞ A: Should I be drafting the chapter two of my dissertation?

B: No, but I think you should ***note down*** its main sections.

A：我应该开始为论文的第二章打草稿了吗？

B：不用，但是我认为你应该记下第二章的主要部分。

notice board 布告板，布告牌，布告栏

☞ A: After the procedure we have to go to the ***notice board*** to find out about lectures and then we have to put our names down for tutorial groups and go to the library.

B: Great. Well, first let's sit down and have our lunch.

A：完成这道程序后，我们得在布告板上找讲座的信息并登记申请参加辅导小组，然后得去图书馆。

B：好的。我们先坐下来吃午饭吧。

☞ A: How do we reserve a place?

B: You sign your name on the ***notice board***.

A：我们怎么预订位置？

B：在布告板上签上姓名即可。

now that 既然，由于

☞ Right, ***now that*** everyone knows what team they're in, we'll get on with the orientation and training program. 好了，既然每个人都已经清楚自己属于哪个组，我们就开始介绍会和培训项目吧。

🔍 in that 表"在于，因为"。

nuclear family （包括父母和孩子两代的）小家庭，核心家庭

☞ The concept of ***nuclear family*** with just one or two children has become universal in the developed countries and even in several developing countries. 在发达国家甚至一些发展中国家，只有一两个孩子的小家庭的观念变得普遍。

🔍 和 nuclear family 相对的是 extended family （大家庭），尤指三代以上同堂的家庭。

nursing care 护理

☞ The old people who are left without a partner may have to pay for ***nursing care***, because they don't have a spouse to look after them. 丧偶的老人也许不得不在护理上花钱，因为没有配偶照顾他们。

🔍 nursing diploma（护理证书）也曾出现在雅思听力的医学类文章中。

ocean current 洋流

☞ Within this general field, surveying changes in the volume and stability of the ice-cap is vital, since these may have profound effects on world sea levels and on ***ocean currents***. 在这个总的研究范围内，对冰帽容量和稳定性变化进行调查至关重要，因为它们对全球的海平面和洋流有着深远的影响。

ocean current 常出现在环境类场景中，常用的相关词组：

marine environment 海洋环境	marine ecosystem 海洋生态系统
marine pollution 海洋污染	marine sediments 海洋沉积物

off campus 在校外

☞ He leads a wonderful life ***off campus***. 他的校外生活很精彩。

"在校内"是 on campus。

off topic 离题

☞ He was supposed to talk about food shortage at the conference but he was ***off topic***. 他本该在会上谈论食物短缺问题，可他却离题了。

☞ off the track

offer/give opportunity for...to do 给…提供机会做

☞ The new policy ***offers opportunity for*** the disabled ***to*** earn their living by themselves. 新政策给残疾人提供了自行谋生的机会。

☞ give...a chance to do

office staff 办公室文员，办公室职员

☞ A: Now we ought to be thinking about invitations...who mustn't we forget to invite?

B: The ***office staff***.

A：现在我们应该考虑一下请柬的问题……我们必须邀请谁呢？

B：办公室职员。

on a roll 连连获胜；连续交好运；进展顺利；（与修饰词连用，表）处于…势头

☞ A: We're ***on a roll*** now! Next point could be about where the interviewees actually get their music.

B: You mean that, do they buy it in music shops, or department stores?

A: Yes, or download it from the Internet.

A：现在一切进展顺利！下一步是关于受访者在哪里获取音乐。

B：你是指他们是在音像店还是在百货商店购买吗？

A：是的，或是从网上下载。

on average 按平均数计算；一般说来

☞ Maybe you know that an adult in the UK will probably need about 1,700 kilocalories a day ***on average***; someone in Antarctica will need about 3,500—just over double! 你们也许知道，在英国一个成年人平均每天可能需要 1700 大卡能量，在南极洲则需要 3500 大卡，是在英国时的两倍还多！

☞ A: How many hours a day ***on average*** do you watch TV?
B: Not a lot really...I should say just over an hour.
A：你平均每天看多长时间的电视？
B：真的不是很多……应该是一小时多点儿。

above/below average 表"在平均水平上 / 下"。

on business 因公

☞ A: What about trains to London? I'll need to go there ***on business*** for one day.
B: Then you need to go to Central Station—that's for all the national services. There are regular trains to London.
A：能介绍一下去伦敦的火车吗？我需要去那出差一天。
B：你得去中央车站，那儿提供国内所有车次服务。有火车定点开往伦敦。

与 business 相关的常用表达：
in business 经营；准备就绪
out of business 停业，歇业
be the business 很好
business in business 公事公办
get about your business 忙自己的事，做通常做的事
none of one's business 与某人无关

on campus 在校内

☞ A: Are you familiar with the bus route of the downtown area?
B: No, I am not at all because I have been living ***on campus***.
A: 你熟悉市中心的公交线路吗？
B: 不，一点儿也不熟悉，因为我住校。

on display 展出，展览，陈列

☞ Samples of all the tools that were used widely at that time are ***on display*** in the showroom. 所有当时广泛使用的工具的样品都在陈列室展出。

on hand 现有(尤指帮助)；在场，出席

☞ Entertainment is laid on nearly every night with tour leaders ***on hand*** to organize lectures, games, quizzes and respond to any special requests from guests. 几乎每晚都有娱乐活动，领队会在场组织演讲、游戏和测试，并应对客人提出的所有特殊要求。

与 hand 相关的常用表达：

(at) first hand 第一手；亲自	have one's hands full 忙得不可开交
in hand 在手头，可供使用；在控制中	off one's hands 不再由某人负责
out of hand 难以(或无法)控制	to hand 在手边，随时可得到

on impulse 一时冲动

A: I really didn't know you were looking for some new clothes.

B: I just bought them ***on impulse*** last weekend.

A：我真的不知道你要买一些新衣服。

B：上周末只是一时冲动才买的。

on one's behalf 为了…的利益，代表

We have a full-time accommodation officer available to help all students. She'll get in touch with you when you're accepted—she's got plenty of contacts in the town and will deal with the agencies ***on your behalf***. 我们有一个全职的住宿管理员，她会给所有学生提供帮助。你被录取后她会和你联系，她在镇上有很多熟人，会代表你和中介打交道。

on one's way to 在去…的路上

A: I'm starving!

B: So am I.

A: Actually, I was ***on my way to*** the canteen to get something for lunch.

A：我饿了！

B：我也是。

A：事实上我正要去餐厅买午餐。

on request 应要求

The hotel can provide special services to guests ***on request***. 该旅馆可以根据顾客的要求提供服务。

on second thoughts 经重新考虑，进一步考虑后，继而一想

A: What would you like? Pizza, sandwich, hot dog, fried rice, the canteen does everything...

B: Oh, something easy. Take-away fried rice sounds good.

A: OK, fried...

B: No, ***on second thoughts***, I'll have a cheese and tomato sandwich.

A：你想要什么？比萨、三明治、热狗或是炒米饭，餐厅里什么都有……

B：要些简单的吧。可打包的炒饭听上去不错。

A：好的，要炒……

B：不，想了想，我还是要奶酪和番茄三明治吧。

相关词组：
have second thoughts 改变想法，改变主意
without a second thought 立即，马上，不假思索

on strike 罢工

☞ Transport workers are ***on strike*** in Melbourne over a pay claim and the strike looks set to spread to other states. 墨尔本的运输工人举行罢工要求加薪，这场罢工很可能会波及其他州。

雅思口语考试中，曾考过 strike 的另一个词组：strike up a conversation，意为“攀谈，搭讪”。

on the margin of 接近于，近乎

☞ When I learn that I have gone bankrupt, I'm ***on the margin of*** breaking down. 当得知自己已破产，我几近崩溃。

☞ in the brink of, on the edge of

on the minus side 不利的一面

☞ ***On the minus side***, our testers did not like the fact that the side of the cot did not drop down, making it difficult to pick up newborn babies. 我们的测试者觉得这个婴儿床不好的一点是，侧板不能降下，要抱起新生儿很困难。

minus 常出现在雅思听力的地理场景中，多用来表示温度，如：minus five degree（零下五度）。

on the other hand 另一方面

☞ On the one hand they'd love to have kids, but ***on the other hand,*** they don't want to give up their freedom. 一方面，他们想要孩子，但另一方面，他们又不想放弃自由。

☞ on the other side

on the phone 在打电话；在电话里

☞ Let me explain ***on the phone***. I'm a counsellor here at the Student Services Section of the university and I'm interviewing overseas students to help me draw up a guide for new students. 我在电话里解释吧。我是大学生服务中心的顾问，我正在采访留学生，这有助于我草拟一个为新生服务的指南。

on the same wavelength 具有相同的思路，合拍

☞ Although we don't work together all the time, we are really ***on the same wavelength***. 尽管我们并不总是一起工作，但我们真的很合拍。

☞ be sympathetic to

on the weaker side 不利的方面

☞ I felt the small size was a real advantage. ***On the weaker side***, I find the noise the key gives off unpleasant. 我觉得形状小巧确实是个优点。要说缺点，我发现钥匙发出的声音不悦耳。

on the whole 总之；总体上，基本上，大体上

☞ My opinion is ***on the whole*** the same with yours. 我的意见与你的大体相同。

☞ all in all, in general

on top of 除…之外；紧接着，紧靠着；在…上方；控制着，掌握着

☞ A: You'd be expected to write an essay each month, which counts towards your final assessment. You have a case study to do by the end of the course, which might involve doing a survey or something like that, and also you need to hand in a short report every four weeks.

B: So, that's quite a lot of work, then, ***on top of*** working every day. It sounds like a lot of studying—and really tiring.

A：每个月要写一篇论文，这将包括在你的期末评估里。在这门课程结束时还要做一个案例研究，这可能会是一个调查或类似的事，而且每四周还要交一份简短的报告。

B：除了每天的学习外，还真有不少作业，听起来学习任务很繁重，而且很令人厌烦。

☞ Please put this record ***on top of*** this pile of books. 请把唱片放在这堆书的上面。

☞ in addition to

one's/the best bet 最好的方法

☞ A: Where do you think I should put up the notice? Where everyone's guaranteed to see it.

B: On the café notice board I should think.

A: Hardly anyone looks at that.

B: Well, the newsletter is probably ***your best bet***.

A：你认为我应该把通知贴在哪儿？得是一个保证每个人都能看到的地方。

B：我认为可以贴在咖啡馆的布告牌上。

A：几乎没有人会看那里。

B：登在时事通讯栏可能是最好的办法。

open a bank account　开银行账户

open a bank account

☞ A: Good morning, I'd like to ***open a bank account***, please.

B: Certainly. If you'd like to take a seat, I'll just get some details from you.

A：早上好，我想开一个银行账户。

B：当然可以。您先请坐，我需要问您一些细节问题。

open admission　免试入学制，开放式入学

☞ When did ***open admissions*** begin within the university system in the United State? 美国的大学是从什么时候开始纳入免试入学制的？

open stacks　开架式书库

☞ In this library, students have free access to books and magazines located in ***open stacks***. 在这个图书馆，学生可以自由阅读开架式书库里的图书和杂志。

与"图书馆"相关的常用词组：

closed stacks 闭架式书库	closed shelves 闭架式书库
alphabetical index 著者索引	call slip 索书单
classified index 分类索引	catalogue room 目录室
periodical index 期刊索引	newspaper file 报纸夹
subject index 主题索引	title index 书名索引

open ticket　不定期客票

☞ There's a standard ***open ticket*** which doesn't have any restrictions. This can be bought in advance or on the day. 有一种普通的不定期客票，没有任何限制，可以提前购买，也可以当天购买。

open ticket（不定期客票）指票已经出了，但具体的出发日期、航班都没有确定，乘客在行程确定后需告知航空公司或铁路公司。

open shelves　开架式书库

☞ In the past these books were read by teachers only, but they are now on ***open shelves*** for all the students. 以前，这些书只供老师阅读，但它们现在被放置在开架式书库供所有学生借阅。

opening time　开放时间；营业时间

☞ Would you please tell me the ***opening times*** for the two tourist places? 你能告诉我这两个旅游景点的开放时间吗？

与 opening 相关的表达：

opening ceremony 开幕式
opening hours 营业时间
opening night 首夜演出，演出放映
opening up 开放，解禁；落成
opening remarks 开场白

other than 除了；不同于，而不

☞ I've checked the whole house. There's nothing here ***other than*** a bed. 我已经检查过整幢房子了，除了一张床，什么都没有。

☞ except

ought to do 应该做

☞ Teachers ***ought to*** earn more. 教师的薪资应该高一些。

☞ be supposed to do

out of bounds 禁止进入

☞ If a place is ***out of bounds***, no people are allowed to go there at any time. 如果某地被列为禁区，那么无论何人何时都不得入内。

out of character 与自身特性不相符，不符合个性

☞ On both the really high summits, the two people took diversions that were quite ***out of character*** and I can only assume that it must have been due to tiredness. 在两座高耸的山峰上，那两个人选了与他们的个性相当不符的方向，我只能猜测是疲劳所致。

out of date 过期的，过时的

☞ I'm afraid the information is ***out of date***, and you're probably better talking to the tutor on the research method course. 恐怕这个信息已经过期了，你最好和研究方法课程的导师谈谈。

☞ old-fashioned

out of print 已售完，已绝版

☞ This book was the first edition and the bookshop said it had been ***out of print*** soon after it was published. 这本书是第一版，而且书店说出版后不久就脱销了。

☞ sold out

Unit 15

out of shape 状态不好，处于不良的健康状况；变形，走样

☞ It is difficult for a player totally ***out of shape*** to get fit in a few weeks time, and the fitness gained quickly can be lost equally quickly. 对于身体状况极度不佳的运动员来说，要在几周内恢复健康是很困难的，而且快速形成的健康体态也同样会快速消失。

out of temper 生气

☞ A: Don't be ***out of temper***, John. There's bound to be a way out.

B: Thank you, Joe.

A：约翰，不要生气，一定会有办法的。

B：谢谢你，乔。

out of the way 不再挡路，不再碍事；结束，完成，已解决；不寻常的；偏僻的

☞ Philip got one of the toughest lawsuit cases ***out of the way***. 菲利普打赢了最费力的一场诉讼。

☞ A: Could you tell me your date of birth please?

B: 25 July 1977.

A: That's the most important part ***out of the way***, but could I just ask you a few questions for a survey we're conducting?

A：能告诉我你的出生日期吗？

B：1977年7月25日。

A：最重要的部分已经解决了，我们正在做一个调查，能问你几个问题吗？

与 way 相关的常用词组：

in a/one way 在某种程度上

in the/sb.'s way 妨碍，挡路

in the way of 关于，就…而言

under way 已经开始，在进行中

the other way round 相反，反过来；相反的情况

out on loan 借出的

☞ Sorry, the book you asked for is ***out on loan*** right now. 不好意思，你要的书现在已借出。

over and above 此外，另外

☛ There are other factors ***over and above*** those we have discussed. 除了我们所讨论的以外，还有其他因素。

☞ besides, in addition to

over the phone 在电话里

☛ I need to take down a few details of the actual damage ***over the phone*** before you put it in a full report. 在你提交完整的报告之前，我需要先通过电话记录一些有关实际损毁情况的详细信息。

☞ on the phone

overseas student 留学生

☛ If you are an ***overseas student***, you may feel that your grant is insufficient to see you through college life. 留学生也许会觉得奖学金不足以维持读完大学。

owe...to 起源于，归因于；归功于

☛ "We ***owe*** our lives ***to*** the skill of the pilot," said one of the boys, but the pilot replied modestly that it was "all part of a day's work." 一个男孩说："我们把自己的生命交给飞行员的技术。"但飞行员谦逊地回答说："那仅是日常工作的一部分。"

🔍 雅思口语常出现的另一个有关 owe 的词组是 owing to，意为"由于，因为"。

ozone layer 臭氧层

☛ An important thing is monitoring the size of the hole in the ***zone layer*** above Antarctica, since this is an indicator of global ultra-violet radiation levels. 监测南极上方臭氧层空洞的大小是一件重要的事，因为它是全球紫外线辐射水平的一个指示器。

🔍 相关词组：

atmospheric particulates 大气颗粒物	atmospheric circulation 大气环流
greenhouse gases 温室气体	atmospheric processes 大气过程
carbon dioxide 二氧化碳	carbon cycle 碳循环
solar radiation 太阳辐射	global warming 全球变暖

pace of life 生活节奏

☛ In the modern society ***pace of life*** is becoming faster and faster. 现代社会的生活节奏变得越来越快。

packing list 装箱单

☛ Make sure you paste the ***packing list*** on the package. 你要确保把装箱单贴在包裹上。

pain killer 止痛药，镇痛剂

☞ Bed rest, giving up exercise and ***pain killers*** are traditional responses to back pain. 卧床休息、停止锻炼和服止痛药是应对背部疼痛的传统方法。

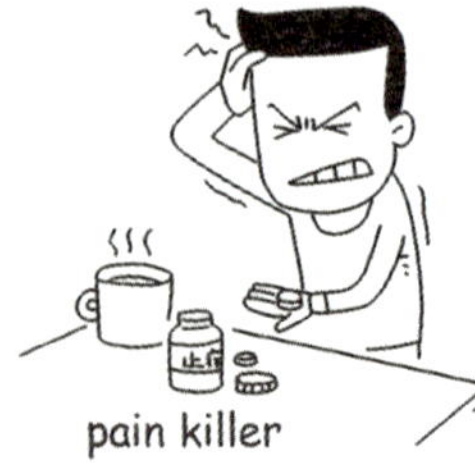

pain killer

🔍相关表达：

febrifuge 退烧药　　penicillin 盘尼西林
antibiotic 抗生素　　ointment 药膏
medication 药物　　aspirin 阿司匹林
cold cure 感冒药　　sweating medicine 发汗药

parallel to 与…平行(的)

☞ Beach-netting, or meshing, involves setting large nets ***parallel to*** the shore. 沙滩设网就是沿海岸平行铺设大网。

parent organization 母公司

☞ The ***parent organization*** is far different than the one that first caught worldwide attention 10 years ago. 十年前母公司刚受到世界瞩目，现在已经今非昔比。

🔍与“职场”相关的一些词汇：

officially 职务上　　assumption 就职　　career 职业
resign 辞职　　promote 升职　　dismiss 解雇

parking lot 停车场

☞ There is a ***parking lot*** sign over there, so let's drive straight ahead. 那儿有一个停车场标志，我们直接开过去吧。

☞ stopping place

parking permit/sticker 停车证

☞ A: Where do I get a ***parking sticker*** from?

B: I think you can get that from the administration office.

A：我该去哪儿办停车证呢？

B：我觉得可以去行政办公室办理。

part exchange 部分抵价交易，以旧换新交易

☞ Would you be interested in taking your present car as ***part exchange***? 你有兴趣将现在的车折价吗？

🔍在国外买卖汽车可采用交换的方式，即 part exchange。要是自行进行买卖的话可以看报纸上的广告，常见表达有：good 指“车况良好的”，bargain 或 good buy 指“特价”，parts 指“车子的零部件”。

part-time job 兼职工作

☞ He did several ***part-time jobs*** to support himself. 他做了好几份兼职维持生活。

participate in 参与

☞ You may wish to ***participate in*** outings or trips if you don't know many people at the moment. 在目前并不认识很多人的情况下，你可能会想参加远足或短途旅行。

☞ take part in

passport photo 护照用照片

☞ A: Could you tell me what I have to do to join the library?

B: Well, you'll need to come in to the library and fill out some forms. You'll also need to bring two ***passport photos*** with you.

A: 您能告诉我要成为图书馆会员需要做什么吗?

B: 你需要到图书馆来填写一些表格，还需要带两张护照用照片。

pay a...deposit 交付…押金

☞ If you cancel within seven days of departure you will have to pay 50% of your total booking. And you also need to ***pay a*** 20% ***deposit*** at the time of booking. 如果你在起程前七天内取消预订，就必须支付全部预订费的 50%，而且预订时还要交 20%的押金。

pay a/the mortgage 还贷款

☞ Many Americans face losing their homes as they struggle to ***pay the mortgage*** during tough economic times and increasing unemployment. 在经济困难和失业率逐步上升的时期，很多美国人在努力偿还按揭贷款的同时面临流离失所的危险。

和"贷款"相关的常用表达：

mortgage assets 抵押资产	by installment 分期付款
joint account 联名账户	extension 延期
down payment 首付	personal housing loan 个人住房贷款
time loan 定期贷款	student loan repayment 学生贷款还款

pay attention to 注意

☞ I've told you many times to ***pay attention to*** your spelling when you are writing. 我已经告诉过你很多次，写作时要注意拼写。

☞ take notice of

pay for 付款

If you just want to relax, you are free to sit by the hotel pool or go down the beach. Oh, and they also have tennis courts at the hotel, but you have to ***pay for*** those by the hour. 如果你只是想放松一下，可以随意去宾馆的泳池边坐坐或是去海滩走走。宾馆里还有网球场，但要按小时付费。

☞ foot the bill, shell out

pay off 还清(债务);付清工资后解雇,遣散;赢利;取得成功,奏效;用钱买通(某人)

☞ We are the first local habitat homeowners to ***pay off*** the mortgage within the mortgage terms. 我们是当地购房者中第一个在贷款期内还清贷款的。

pay tribute to 向…表示敬意

☞ The female singer sang a modified version of that famous song to ***pay tribute to*** the King of Pop. 这名女歌手演唱了那首著名歌曲的改编曲向这位"流行音乐之王"致敬。

☞ show respect to

peak time 高峰时期;(收听广播、收看电视的)高峰时间,黄金时间

☞ A: Does your company run these tours often?

B: Well, it depends on the time of year. Of course in ***peak times*** like the summer holidays we do them every weekend, but at the moment it's usually once a month at most.

A: 你们公司经常开设这些旅游路线吗?

B: 这要看一年中的不同时间。当然,在高峰期,比如暑假,我们每周末都有,但现在最多是一个月一次。

☞ rush hour, prime time

相关词组:

morning peak 早高峰	off-peak time 非高峰时间
non-service time 非运营时间	off-running time 收车时间
one-line monthly ticket 专线月票	special line 专线

per person 每个人

☞ The house owner paid 50 dollars ***per person*** for their works. 房主付给每人 50 美元作为他们的酬劳。

personal contents insurance 个人财产保险

☞ He is not going to pay ***personal contents insurance*** for his valuable stuff. 他不打算为贵重物品上个人财产保险。

常见的保险种类:

social insurance 社会保险	medical insurance 医疗保险
unemployment insurance 失业保险	endowment insurance 养老保险
property insurance 财产保险	luggage insurance 行李保险

personal possession 个人财产

☞ A: When did you move into the house?

B: A couple of weeks ago, and it's an apartment actually. I was told by the landlord that it would be a good idea to get some insurance for the furniture and other ***personal possessions***.

A：你什么时候搬入这幢房子的？

B：几周前，实际上是一间公寓。房东告诉我应该给家具及一些其他个人财产上保险。

☞ personal property

personal statement 个人陈述

☞ ***Personal statement*** is an opportunity to tell admission office why you are an excellent applicant for their university. 个人陈述让你有机会告诉招生办公室，你为什么是他们大学的优秀申请者。

PS(personal statement)是留学申请中最重要的部分，是申请者最主要的自我包装。写个人自述要求独具创意，最大忌讳就是写得毫无特色，枯燥乏味。

personality questionnaire 性格问卷

☞ More and more employers around the world are making use of what are called ***personality questionnaire*** to help them select new staff. 全世界越来越多的雇主都借助性格问卷来挑选新员工。

personally speaking 从个人角度来看，就个人而言

☞ ***Personally speaking*** I prefer to play football rather than play basketball. 就个人而言，我更爱踢足球而不是打篮球。

personnel management 人事管理

☞ A: Are you working at the moment?

B: Yes, I've been working in the administration section of the local hospital for the last three years. And before that I worked in the office of a computer engineering company for two years. So I've got about five years of relevant work experience. And what I'm hoping to focus on is ***personnel management***.

A：你现在工作了吗？

B：是的，过去三年我一直在当地一家医院的管理部门工作，在那之前我还在一家计算机工程公司工作过两年，所以我有大约五年的相关工作经验。我现在希望能主要从事人事管理方面的工作。

与"公司人事管理"相关的表达：

achievements 工作成就，业绩
responsibility 职责
professional history 职业经历
work experience 工作经验
position desired 期望职位
career objective 职业目标
work permit 工作证
salary raise 加薪
punch the clock 打卡
agreement of employment 聘书

phone bill 电话费账单

☞ You don't need to pay for gas, electricity or water, but you will need to pay your proportion of the ***phone bill***. 你不需要付煤气费、电费及水费，但是你需要支付自己的那部分电话费。

各种常见"账单"：

water bill 水费单
electricity bill 电费单
gas bill 煤气费单
heating bill 暖气费单

phone up 给…打电话

☞ What you can do is to ***phone up*** a student from your own country who is present studying in this college—we will, of course, liaise between you—and discuss your concern with them. That way you can get an objective opinion of what you can expect if you come to live and study at Rexford. 你可以给目前就读于该学院且与你来自同一国度的学生打个电话，当然我们可以帮你联系，你可以和他们聊聊你关心的问题。这样你就能得到在雷克斯福德生活和学习的客观意见。

☞ ring up, call up

pick one's brain 向某人请教，征求某人的看法

☞ You'd better go see the professor and ***pick his brain***; maybe he can make it clear to you. 你最好去请教一下教授，没准他能把问题给你解释清楚。

☞ consult with sb.

pick out 精心挑选；分辨出；(经仔细研究)找出，认识到；使显著；(不用乐谱)慢慢地弹奏

☞ He was ***picked out*** from hundreds of applicants for the job. 他从数百名求职者中被选中承担这项工作。

☞ I can ***pick out*** my mother's voice among so many people. 我能从这么多人中分辨出母亲的声音。

☞ seek out, tell from

pitch in 投入，参与；支援

☞ When I bought this second-hand car, all my relatives ***pitched in*** to help fix it up. 在我购入这辆二手车时，所有亲戚都出力帮我修理。

places of historical interest 历史名胜，名胜古迹

☞ A: What sort of places shall we pay a visit to this week?

B: Well, obviously it varies, but always ***places of historical interest*** and also which offer a variety of shopping.

A：本周我们要去参观哪些地方？

B：很明显，现在情况尚未定，但肯定会有些名胜古迹，也会包括购物场所。

与"旅游"相关的词组：

natural beauty 自然美景
tourist attraction 游览胜地
tourist resort 度假村
summer resort 避暑胜地
tour route 旅游路线
tourist association 旅游协会
off/off-peak season 淡季
on/peak season 旺季

plan on 计划，打算

☞ A: How long would you want to stay with the host family?

B: I'm ***planning on*** staying a year. I have to get an extension to my permit.

A：你准备在寄宿家庭住多久？

B：我计划待一年。我必须去延长许可证的时间。

plastic bag 塑料袋

☞ The growers put ***plastic bags*** around the bunches to protect the banana trees and keep them warm. If you go up to the banana growing districts, you'll see all these banana trees with ***plastic bags*** on them. 种植者给香蕉束套上塑料袋以保护香蕉树，同时也起到保暖作用。你去香蕉种植区的话就会看到所有香蕉树上都会有塑料袋。

play a significant role 扮演重要角色，起重要作用

☞ Which do you think ***play a*** more ***significant role*** in our life, music or dance? 你认为音乐和舞蹈哪个在我们生活中起着更重要的作用？

plenty of evidence has shown that 充分的证据已经表明

☞ ***Plenty of evidence has shown that*** people learn best when they are entertained. 充分的证据已经表明人们在兴趣的驱动下学得最快。

point of view　观点

☞ A: Christina, what did you find? What was the most useful aspect of the project from the ***point of view*** of the English practice?

B: When we were being shown how to edit the film, we had to follow the instructions. And that was very good practice for me. And I also learned some technical terms that I hadn't heard before.

A：克里斯蒂娜，你发现了什么？从英语练习的角度来看，这个项目最有用的一面是什么？

B：在我们观看如何剪辑电影时，我们必须遵照说明。这对我来说是个很好的练习。并且我也学到了一些以前未曾听过的专业术语。

☞ standpoint, viewpoint

point out　指出

☞ I'd just like to ***point out*** where everything is and then you can take a look at everything for yourself. 我只想指出每样东西所处的具体位置，然后你们可以自己参观。

population growth　人口增长

☞ The speed of ***population growth*** in that region is appalling. 该地区人口增长的速度令人震惊。

pose a threat to　对…构成威胁

☞ Substandard water supply and sanitation ***pose a threat to*** human health via exposure to pathogens such as intestinal parasites. 不达标的水源和卫生条件会使人易受肠道寄生虫等病原体的侵袭，从而对健康造成威胁。

🔍 pose a threat to 常出现在与环境保护相关的雅思口语话题中。

postgraduate student　研究生

☞ It is the university's policy to give priority in the allocation of residence places to three categories, and those are: visiting students, exchange students and new ***postgraduate students***. 大学的政策允许以下三类学生优先选择住处：访问学生、交换生和研究生新生。

potential customer　潜在顾客，潜在消费者

☞ As a salesperson, you should know who are your ***potential customers***. 作为销售人员，你应该知道谁才是你的潜在顾客。

☞ prospective customer

相关词组：

potential market 潜在市场	target market 目标市场
pricing policy 价格策略	price promotion 价格促销
market potential 市场潜力	market share 市场份额
sales analysis 销售分析	sales personnel 销售人员

potential problem 潜在问题

☞ With increasing industrial development around the world, the discharge of toxic pollutants is a ***potential problem*** for many countries. 随着世界范围内工业的逐步发展，对很多国家来说，有毒污染物的排放是一个潜在问题。

prefer...to 喜欢…胜过…

☞ I much ***prefer*** coffee ***to*** tea. 我喜欢咖啡远胜过茶。

present oneself 出席(会议等)，到场

☞ Make sure you wear neatly while ***presenting yourself*** in the seminar. 出席研讨会时一定要衣着整齐。

prevent...from 阻止

☞ In Australia, where people spend a lot of time at the beach, the government has realized that it must ***prevent*** sharks ***from*** swimming near its beaches. 在澳大利亚，人们在沙滩上度过大量时间，政府已经意识到必须阻止鲨鱼游到沙滩附近。

☞ stop...from

price range 价格范围

☞ A: Before I ring, we'd better just make sure the hotels are within the ***price range***.

B: Up to £15 a head?

A: I think you'll find some people won't be able to go that high.

A：打电话前，我们最好确保这些旅馆的房价在我们能承受的价格范围之内。

B：每人最多15英镑？

A：我觉得你会发现有些人不能承受那么高的价格。

price structure 价格结构，价格构成

☞ A: How much are the tickets?

B: We've introduced a simpler ***price structure***. Ticket prices used to range from £6 to £30 but now they're all £18.

A：票价是多少？

B：我们启用了一套更单一的价格结构。原先票价是从6英镑到30英镑不等，但现在一律18英镑。

pride oneself on 以…自豪，为…感到骄傲（或得意）

☞ We *pride ourselves on* our friendly service, which are particularly important for the increasing number of people who choose to holiday alone. 我们为能提供舒适的服务感到自豪，舒适的服务对日益增多的独自度假的人而言尤其重要。

☞ be proud of

pride oneself on

proficient in/at 熟练，精通

☞ The candidate for this position must be *proficient in* English and is willing to travel in remote areas. 该职位要求申请者必须精通英语并愿意去偏远地区出差。

profound influence 深刻的影响

☞ The UV-B radiation has *profound influence* on the immune system in human beings as well as in laboratory mice. UV-B 辐射对人体和实验用小鼠的免疫系统都会产生很大的影响。

projection system 放映系统

☞ The single problem with all the *projection systems* was they couldn't really project the film onto a screen. 所有放映系统共有的一个问题是它们都不能真正地在大屏幕上放映电影。

promote sustainable development 促进可持续发展

☞ The President and the authorities of the country are committed to positively tackling poverty and *promoting sustainable development*. 该国的总统和当局都承诺要积极解决贫困问题并促进可持续发展。

该词组常用于环保、发展等话题中，其他常用表达：

ecosystem 生态系统	environment-friendly 环保的
recyclable 可回收的	biodegradable 生物所能分解的
renewable 可再生的	sanitation 卫生设施

property insurance 财产保险

☞ I don't have extra money to take *property insurance*. 我没有闲钱买财产保险。

propose a toast 敬酒，祝酒

☞ I *proposed a toast* for all the guests here and our relationship through the training course. 我提议为在座的所有客人和我们在培训中建立起来的友谊干杯。

该词组常用在婚礼等喜庆场合。与“婚礼”相关的常用表达：

wedding ceremony 结婚典礼
wedding reception 婚宴
wedding anniversary 结婚纪念日
trousseau 嫁妆
wedding day 结婚日
bride 新娘
wedding march 婚礼进行曲
bridegroom 新郎
wedding dress 结婚礼服
groomsman 伴郎
bridesmaid 伴娘
honeymoon 蜜月

protect...from 保护，防护以免于

☞ Because the farmers can use incubators and hatched chicks are nourished well and ***protected from*** danger, the failure rate in farms is very low. 农民能使用孵化器，孵出的小鸡能得到很好的饲养，并且免受危险，所以农场孵鸡的失败率很低。

provide...with 提供

☞ We are here to ***provide*** the public ***with*** a service. 我们来这里是为公众服务的。

☞ A: Did you have a question?

B: Yes, does the Students Union also ***provide*** help ***with*** any problems, I mean advice on financial problems, for example? Or does the university provide that?

A: Yes, the union runs their own advice service, offering help with financial matters such as grants.

A：你有什么问题吗？

B：是的，学生会也为任何问题提供帮助吗？我的意思是比如经济问题方面的建议，或是由学校提供这项服务。

A：是的，学生会有它们自己的建议服务，就补助金等经济问题提供帮助。

NOTES

Unit 16

public transport system 公共交通系统

☞ People criticized the ***public transport system*** as frustrating and disappointing. 人们批评公共交通系统令人灰心丧气，极其失望。

常见的公共交通工具：

subway/underground/tube 地铁	minibus 小公共汽车
train 火车	taxi 出租汽车
coach 大客车	express train 特别快车
airliner 班机，客机	sailing boat 帆船

publicity leaflet 宣传册

☞ First of all, those who will be looking after the phones and handling all calls regarding the exhibition, you will be on the red team. Now, we've also put the entrance staff on the red team and you'll be stamping the entrance tickets and giving out ***publicity leaflets***. 首先，那些照管电话及负责接听与展览有关的电话的人员被分在红组。我们把入口处的工作人员也分在红组，负责在入口处验票和分发宣传册。

☞ brochure

pull out 拔出，取出；撤退，撤离；使摆脱困惑

☞ One of the subjects decided to ***pull out*** when it came to the second round. 到了第二阶段，有一位受访者决定退出。

☞ back off

pull up 拉起；（使车辆）停住

☞ She ***pulled up*** at the crossing. 她在十字路口停住了车。

☞ A: So how do we open a can of coke?

B: Mmm...first of all there's the tab which we ***pull up*** to open the can and that's held in place by a rivet.

A：那么我们怎么开可乐罐呢？

B：首先，有一个用铆钉固定住的拉环，拉起拉环就能打开可乐罐。

punch in 上班打卡

☞ A: Have all the workers ***punched in*** yet?

B: Linda is an exception.

A：所有员工都打卡了吗？

B：琳达除外。

punch line 画龙点睛的结束语，(笑话、故事中最后几句点题或抛出笑料等的)妙语，警句；好笑的部分

☞ A: What kind of video do you prefer to watch? Have a look at this list.

B: Well, I love anything that makes me laugh. I love to hear jokes and funny ***punch lines***.

A：你想看哪种录像节目？看看这个单子吧。

B：我喜欢任何能让我发笑的东西。我喜欢听笑话和故事最后几句点睛之语。

punch out 打卡下班

☞ It is weird that Laurence ***punched out*** at 3 pm this afternoon. 劳伦斯今天下午三点就打卡下班了，真是奇怪。

push up 增加，提高

☞ A: The house price is depending on a number of different factors.

B: What does it depend on?

A: Well, obviously the quality of the area. And then whether there's a garden.

B: Well, as I said, we'd want a garden.

A: A garage ***pushes up*** the price.

A：房价取决于很多因素。

B：取决于什么？

A：很显然，所处地域，以及有没有花园。

B：我说过，我们想要一个花园。

A：如果你想要一间车库，房价会更高。

push-up 指"俯卧撑"。

put aside 储存(尤指金钱)以备他日之需；把…放到一边，把…撇开不理

☞ The main priority for men when saving money is their retirement. When they're earning, they're far more likely to ***put*** money ***aside*** for their old age than women are. 男人存钱主要是为退休后作准备。他们在赚钱时，要比女人更可能为了养老而存钱。

☞ prepare for a rainy day

put down 记下；放下；批评，奚落，贬损

☞ I'll ***puts*** that ***down*** as a definite. 我肯定会记下的。

☞ write down

put emphasis on 强调；重读

☞ My mom ***puts*** great ***emphasis on*** who makes friends with me. 妈妈极其重视我的交友对象。

☞ place emphasis on

put one's feet up 休息，放松

☞ A: What sort of programs do you go for?

B: Some news bulletins but I also really like to ***put my feet up*** with some of the old comedy shows.

A：你喜欢看哪种电视节目？

B：新闻简报，但我也很喜欢看看老的喜剧节目来放松放松。

☞ have a rest

put...at risk 使…处于危险境地，使…冒险

☞ You have no excuse to ***put*** your family ***at risk***. 你没有理由让你的家人身陷险境。

☞ put...in danger

put...on to 替…接通与…的电话

☞ Glenda Roberts is our dietician in the Health Service and we can ***put*** you ***on to*** her. 格伦达·罗伯茨是我们健康服务中心的营养学家，我们可以帮你接通她的电话。

put...through 为…接通电话；顺利完成

☞ A: Oh, hello. I'm ringing to report an accident.

B: Just hold the line a moment please. I'm ***putting*** you ***through*** to our insurance department.

A：您好，我打电话来上报一场事故。

B：请稍等片刻。我给你接到我们的保险部。

put together 把…合在一起；装配；组成，凑成

☞ Charles has ***put together*** a video about the journey and continues to lead groups to the Attora mountains, so if you want further information... 查尔斯已经把这次旅行的视频整合到了一起，并继续带领小组向奥特拉山前进，所以如果你想进一步了解……

put up　张贴；建造，搭起；增加，提高；为…提供膳宿；推举，提名

☞ I'll ***put up*** a notice with details of the restaurant and the menu. 我将张贴一则通知，上面会详细列出饭店和菜单的信息。

queue up　排队(等候)

☞ A: Does the Business Center cover all the main areas of business?

B: Yes, topics like finance, and of course marketing—that's a popular one. Local managers usually ***queue up*** to borrow the videos!

A: So it isn't just for students, then?

B: It's for members only, but anyone can join.

A：该商务中心是否涵盖了商务的所有主要领域？

B：是的，比如金融，当然还有营销——这个非常受欢迎。当地的经理们经常都排着队来借录像带看呢！

A：这么说来该中心不只是针对学生？

B：它只对会员开放，但任何人都可以成为会员。

☞ line up

range from...(to)　在…范围内变动；延伸

☞ A: Could you give me some idea about the house prices?

B: Certainly. It really ***ranges from*** £250 per month.

A: Only £250?

B: Yes, to about £500 depending on a number of different factors.

A：你能说说房价吗？

B：当然，每月250英镑起。

A：只有250英镑？

B：250英镑到约500英镑不等，取决于很多因素。

rather than　宁愿…(而不)；不是…(而是)

☞ It was the availability, ***rather than*** the condition, of the housing that was the major concern for tenants and landlords. 住房的可用性而非房屋状况，是房客与房东主要关心的问题。

☞ Nowadays people spend more time watching TV and playing on the computers after dinner ***rather than*** going out for a walk. 如今，人们晚饭后花更多的时间看电视和玩电脑，而不是外出散步。

🔍注意和词组 other than(除了)区别开来。

raw materials 原材料

☞ The water and the availability of ***raw materials*** in the area, like minerals and iron ore, and also the abundance of local fuels, like coal and firewood, all made this site suitable for industry from a very early time. 该地区有水和可利用的原材料，如矿物质和铁矿石，并且当地煤、木柴之类的燃料丰富，这一切都使得该地很早就适合工业发展。

🔍在工业革命(industrial revolution)时，工业中心常建在水资源(water resources)和矿产资源(mineral resources)丰富、交通便利(convenient transportation)的地方。

recommend...to/for 向…推荐，介绍

☞ My name's Brian Ardley. I've decided to enroll in a management course. A friend of mine took one last year, and ***recommended*** it ***to*** me. 我名叫布赖恩·阿德利。我已经决定注册这门管理课程了。去年我的一个朋友上了这门课，并推荐给我。

☞ If you want to ***recommend*** some people ***for*** the job, please contact us. 如果你们想推荐谁来做这项工作，请联系我们。

☞ put forward, nominate

recover from 恢复

☞ Henry has ***recovered from*** his operation. 亨利已经从手术中恢复过来了。

refer to 有关，涉及；提及；参考，查询；提交…作决定(或处理)

☞ A: It's a workshop on dissertations.

B: What do you mean—how to write one?

A: Er, no, it's more to do with academic writing conventions, you know—writing a bibliography and how to ***refer to*** sources in your text. That sort of thing. Here's a leaflet with information.

A：这是一个关于论文的研讨会。

B：什么意思——是告诉我们如何写作吗？

A：不是，更多是关于学术写作的规则——如何写参考书目和在文章中标注引文来源之类的东西。这儿有一张单页，上面有相关信息。

reference letter 推荐信

☞ A: What sort of things do I need to get done to rent this house?

B: A letter from your bank and a ***reference letter*** from your employer.

A：租这间房子前我需要做些什么呢？

B：需要你账户所在的银行开具证明，以及你的雇主给你写封推荐信。

🔍letter of recommendation 表"推荐信；表扬信"。

reference materials 参考资料

A: Is there any difference between the two libraries?

B: Not in terms of their facilities. Access to online databases and the Internet is available at both sites and each site has a range of ***reference materials*** on education.

A：这两个图书馆有什么不同之处吗?

B：设备方面没什么区别。两个地方都可以链接到在线数据库和网络，并且都有一系列的教育类参考资料。

reference 一词经常出现在图书馆场景中，图书馆场景常用的相关表达：

reference stacks 书库	delivery/circulation desk 借书台
call slip 借书单	check out 登记并借出
admission/library card 借书卡	renew 续借
date of expiry 期限	reserve 预借
not for circulation 不外借	out circulation 借出
in circulation 在书库里	

reference number 咨询号码

This page provides guidance to students on making universities' ***reference number*** available. 这一页为学生提供向导，方便他们查询大学的咨询号码。

reference source 参考源

You'll also find that the library has loaded several CD-ROMS onto the computers from specialist ***reference sources*** such as the MLA. 你也会发现图书馆从现代语言学会等专家参考源处下载了一些 CD-ROMS(只读光盘)装在电脑上。

reference number（参考编号）、reference stacks（书库）、reference books（参考书）等都是 reference 一词在雅思听力中的高频搭配。

reference stacks 书库

You can consult the ***reference stacks*** for information you want. 你可以查询书库以获得所需信息。

refrain from 克制，抑制

The brave boy in the movie ***refrained from*** tears. 影片中那个勇敢的小男孩忍住了没哭。

desist from

refresh one's memory　唤起记忆，回忆

☞ A: Where should we meet? I could come and pick you up at your house, if you like.

B: Yes, that would be wonderful. My car is still off the road.

A: Just ***refresh my memory***. What's the address again?

B: It's 15 Chesterfield Road, Paddington.

A: 我们应该在哪里会合呢？如果你愿意的话我可以去你家接你。

B: 那太好了。我的车还没修好呢。

A: 再告诉我一次你的地址吧。

B: 帕丁顿区切斯特菲尔德路 15 号。

☞ remind sb. of

refresher course　进修课程

☞ I want to know more about the ***refresher course*** that you run. 我想进一步了解一下您开设的进修课程。

regard as　认为…是，视做

☞ Confucius is ***regarded as*** the greatest philosopher in the history of China. 孔子被认为是中国历史上最伟大的圣哲。

☞ think as

regardless of　不理会，不顾，不管

☞ ***Regardless of*** the fact that he was born in a humble family, he was a gentlemen through and through. 尽管出身卑微，但他完全是一位绅士。

☞ in spite of

register with　向…登记；注册

☞ What we should do is to ***register with*** a family doctor. 我们应该注册一个家庭医生。

> 在英国，从理论上说，除了急诊外不可以直接上医院，必须先去看家庭医生进行治疗。所有在英国停留时间超过六个月的学生可就近注册家庭医生。

registered mail　挂号信

☞ I wonder why he sends me a ***registered mail***. 不知他为什么寄给我一封挂号信。

registration fee　报名费；挂号费；登记费

☞ It is said that the ***registration fee*** for the contest is very high, but I won't let go. 据说那项竞赛的报名费很贵，可我不会错过的。

regular meeting 例会

☞ A: Could anything be done to improve the course in your opinion?

B: Well, I think it would be helpful to have meetings with lecturers on the course. Say once a fortnight—something like that.

A: ***Regular meetings***. Yes, that could certainly help.

A：你认为怎样能提高课程质量？

B：我认为就课程与老师进行讨论会有帮助，比如两周一次。

A：例会，是的，那肯定会有帮助。

relate to 有关，涉及；有良好关系；欣赏，认同

☞ At this library we hold materials ***relating to*** primary education, as well as special needs, but of course you'll need to familiarize yourself with both the two libraries to make the most of our resources. 在这个图书馆里我们有关于初级教育的资料，也有别的资料能满足你的特殊需求，但是当然，为了最大限度利用我们的资源，你需要了解这两个图书馆。

☞ touch upon

relay race 接力赛跑

☞ The city organized a ***relay race*** to celebrate Independent Day. 这个城市组织了一次接力赛跑来庆祝独立日。

release pressure 释放压力

☞ Some scientists say a slow earthquake could be helping to ***release pressure*** of the earth, and able to prevent powerful quakes. 一些科学家称小地震可以帮助地球释放压力，并阻止强烈地震的发生。

religious practice 宗教习俗

☞ When you are in a different country you have to abide by their ***religious practice***. 身处异国就应遵循该国的宗教习俗。

rely on/upon 依赖，依靠

☞ Babies ***rely*** entirely ***on*** their parents for living. 婴儿完全依靠他们的父母生活。

☞ Of course, you have to cope with all the pressure without your usual social network—the social contacts, family and friends you could normally ***rely on*** for help. 当然，你必须在没有平时的社交网的情况下，应对所有压力，社交网即你通常所能求助于的社会关系，包括家人和朋友。

☞ In fact, extensive underground water resources are available over more than half of Australia's land area, but most of the water is too salty to be used for human consumption or for the irrigation of crops. However, most inland farmers do ***rely on*** this water for watering their animals. 事实上，澳大利亚有一半多的土地都有着丰富的地下水资源，但是大多数的水含盐量太高，无法供人类使用或灌溉庄稼。尽管如此，大多数内陆农民还是用这种水来喂养家畜。

☞ depend on/upon

remind...of 使…回想起或意识到，提醒

☞ The museum ***reminds*** him ***of*** the one he visited last year. 这个博物馆让他想起去年参观的那一个。

☞ As you can see, the Maritime Museum is a very modern building built in the post modern style and it was in fact opened by the Prime Minister of Australia in November 1991. It has been designed with a nautical flavor in mind to ***remind*** us ***of*** our links with the sea. 你们可以看到，这个海事博物馆是一栋非常现代的建筑，采用后现代主义风格建造而成，事实上是由澳大利亚总理于 1991 年 11 月宣布开放的。博物馆的设计带有海洋风情，意在提醒我们和大海之间的联系。

☞ put...in mind of

removals van 搬家卡车

☞ With the ***removals van*** it becomes easier to move from one place to another. 有了搬家卡车，搬家就方便多了。

常见的交通工具：

truck 卡车	train 火车	bus 公共汽车
car 小汽车	lorry 卡车	minibus 小型公共汽车
carriage 马车	wagon 四轮马车	tractor 拖拉机

research assessment 研究评估

☞ At Rexford we have a strong research capability. We came 7th out of 101 universities in last year's ***research assessment***. 雷克斯福德研究实力雄厚，在去年的研究评估中，我们在 101 所大学里排名第七。

在雅思考试中，assessment 常出现在与学习相关的场景中，同时也出现在看病场景中，the assessment of patients 指"对病人状况的评估"。

research method 研究方法

☞ Well, you should see your course tutor to agree on your final title and you should also be aware that there's a special program running on ***research methods*** for anyone who wants some extra help on this problem. 你应该去见见课程导师并就最终的标题达成一致，此外你也应该知道还有一个关于研究方法的课程，专门针对在这方面需要额外帮助的人。

与"研究"相关的常考词组：

design research 设计研究 | research approach 研究方法
research technique 研究技巧 | scientific research 科学研究

research methodology 研究方法（法）

☞ You should read the article by Jackson, but just look at the part on the ***research methodology***—how they did it. 你应该读读杰克逊写的那篇文章，但只需读有关研究方法的那部分——看看他们是如何进行调查的。

resistant to 对…抵制的，对…有抵抗力的

☞ Through interview, employers may find out whether someone is ***resistant to*** change. 通过面试，雇主可以发现面试者是否能随机应变。

respond to 回答；对…作出反应；对医疗有良好反应

☞ The disease failed to ***respond to*** the drugs. 这些药对这种病未能奏效。

☞ react to

response rate （问卷的）回复率，有效率

☞ There are some problems you will get if the ***response rate*** is too low. 如果问卷回复率太低，你就会遇到一些问题。

response to 回答；对…的反应

☞ The body's ***response to*** back injury can be very counter-productive. 身体对背部损伤的反应可能会起到严重的反作用。

☞ reaction to

result from 归因于

☞ It turns out that nothing has ***resulted from*** our effort. 结果，我们的努力付诸东流。

☞ Very serious consequences can ***result from*** people or organizations not considering the possible results of their actions seriously enough. 人或组织若没有慎重考虑自己的行为，可能会造成极其严重的后果。

☞ arise from, attribute...to

result in 导致，带来

☞ The game ***resulted in*** another victory of the Phoenix. 比赛以凤凰队的又一次胜利而告终。

☞ lead to

ringback tone 振铃音，回铃音

☞ Young men choose distinctive ***ringback tones*** to reflect their personalities. 年轻人选择与众不同的振铃来彰显个性。

roam about 漫游，漫步

☞ To start your visit I'm just going to give you a brief account of the history of the museum before letting you ***roam about*** on your own. 开始参观前我要向大家简要介绍一下博物馆的历史，然后大家可以随意参观。

☞ amble, wander

root for 支持

☞ This man is not likely to succeed in the impending election because very few voters ***rooted for*** him over the recent months. 此人似乎不大可能在即将举行的竞选中胜出，因为最近几个月支持他的选民微乎其微。

☞ be in favor of

round-trip ticket 往返票

☞ A: One-way or a ***round-trip ticket***?

B: A ***round-trip ticket***, please.

A：单程票还是往返票？

B：一张往返票。

☞ return ticket

"单程票"也可表达为 single ticket。

roundabout route 迂回路线，绕道；曲折的历程

☞ According to my research, the banana, which is the first type to be cultivated here, actually originated in China but they had a fairly ***roundabout route*** before they got to Australia. 我经过研究发现，这种香蕉是此处培育的第一个香蕉品种，它实际上源于中国，在被引进到澳大利亚前经历了一个相当曲折的过程。

☞ We drove home by a ***roundabout route***. 我们绕道驾车回家。

Unit 17

routine work　日常工作；例行工作

☞ I'm tired of the ***routine works*** in the library. 我厌倦了图书馆的日常工作。

☞ daily work

run across　偶然碰见，与…不期而遇

☞ I just ***ran across*** several old friends when I went to the interview. 我在去面试的路上遇见了几个老朋友。

run into　（使汽车）撞在…上，猛撞；偶然碰见；遭遇

☞ The car went out of control and ***ran into*** a tree. 汽车失控，撞上了一棵树。

☞ A: Hi Tim! How are you? I'd been wondering when I'd ***run into*** you. Have you been here long?

B: I arrived yesterday, on Sunday.

A：嗨，蒂姆！你好吗？我一直在想什么时候能遇到你。你来这里已经很久了吗？

B：昨天，也就是星期天到的。

run out of　用完，耗尽

☞ I has ***run out of*** sugar. Could you help me to buy some in that shop? 糖用完了。你能帮我去那家商店买一些吗？

☞ In August 2000, we ***ran out of*** money. We had containers of bikes ready to send, but no money to pay the bills. 2000 年 8 月，我们的钱花完了。我们有数个集装箱的自行车要发货，却没有钱付（发货）账单。

☞ exhaust, use up

🔍 run out of steam 和 run out of gas 常用于日常生活中，表"精力或热情的耗尽"。

run risks　冒风险

☞ You are ***running risks*** in marrying some guy whom you have known less than a month. 跟一个认识不到一个月的人结婚是在冒险。

☞ Investment is all about ***running risks***. 投资就是要冒风险。

run the risk of 冒…的险

☞ If you don't acknowledge the source of your information then you ***run the risk of*** failing the subject or in very serious cases you might be denied entry to the university. 如果你不明确信息来源，那么你就要冒该科不及格的风险，情节严重的话会被学校拒之门外。

🔍在雅思听力考试中，run 常用的词义是"经营"，如：He wants to open a new shop, which is running sport articles. 他想开一家商店，经营体育用品。

run through 反复练习，排练；刺穿；贯穿；浏览，匆匆阅读；挥霍，很快用完

☞ A sad feeling ***runs through*** the poetry written by the famous female writer. 那位著名女作家的诗中贯穿着一股忧伤之情。

☞ A: Where is the main hall?

B: I'll show you in a minute. Just let me quickly ***run through*** this morning's events first and then I'll explain how to get there.

A：主会场在哪里？

B：我一会儿指给你看。先让我快速浏览下今天上午要做的事，然后我会告诉你怎么去那里。

run wild 变得荒芜；到处撒野；(价格)暴涨；失去控制(或约束)；自由驰骋

☞ In this case, I'd say pictures are best with individual children, because they give them an opportunity to let their imaginations ***run wild***. 在这种情况下，我想图片最适用孩子个体，因为它们给予孩子们一个自由想象的机会。

☞ be out of control

🔍的与 run 有关的常考词组：

run across 偶然碰见　　run down 撞倒；诋毁

run into 偶然碰见；猛撞　　run up against 遇到(困难)

rush hour 高峰时间

☞ I think it's wise of you not to go out in ***rush hour***. 我认为你高峰时间选择不出门真是明智。

rush off 赶紧做，匆匆生产；匆忙走开

☞ If you lack vitamins in any way the solution isn't to ***rush off*** and take vitamin pills, though they can sometimes help. It's far better to look at your diet and how you prepare your food. 如果你缺乏某种维生素，解决方法不是赶紧吃些维生素片，虽然它们有时能有点帮助。更好的做法是注意饮食和烹饪方法。

sanitary condition 卫生条件，卫生状况

☞ Those who could afford to live in more pleasant surroundings moved out from the East End, and the area became one where the vast majority of people lived in extreme poverty, and suffered from appalling ***sanitary conditions***. 那些负担得起更好住房条件的人都搬出了伦敦东区，该地区便沦为绝大多数处于极度贫困、忍受极其恶劣卫生条件的人居住的地方。

sanitary 在雅思听力中的其他常见搭配：

sanitary landfill 卫生填埋　　sanitary wares 洁具

satisfy the need of 满足…的要求

☞ The foreign steel manufacturer is one of our main customers and we must try our best to ***satisfy the need of*** the factory at any cost. 这家国外钢铁制造商是我们的一位主要客户，我们必须竭尽全力并不惜一切代价满足他们的需求。

save a back-up copy 保存副本

☞ The tutor suggested that I should ***save a back-up copy*** of any work I did. 导师建议我应该保存一个任何已完成作业的副本。

save up 储蓄，存钱；贮存，节省

☞ They are ***saving up*** for a house. 他们正在存钱买房。

saver ticket 优惠票，打折票

☞ The man was sentenced to 200 hours of community service for his part in making fake airline ***saver tickets***. 该男子因参与伪造打折机票被判做200小时的社区服务。

雅思考试中各种常见的“票”：

open ticket 开放机票　　one-way ticket 单程票　　round-trip ticket 往返票

savings account 储蓄存款账户

☞ You should learn to save money, so you'd better open a ***savings account*** in the bank. 你应该学会存钱，所以最好去银行开一个储蓄存款账户。

与“存款”相关的常用词组：

bank/pass book 存折　　open an account 开户
current account 活期存款账户　　deposit account 定期存款账户
signature card 签名卡　　credit card 信用卡
full refund 全额偿还　　service charge 服务费，手续费

scare off　吓走，吓跑

☞ This is a fake video camera which you fix to your wall to ***scare off*** burglars. 这是一款仿真摄像机，可以安在墙上吓走窃贼。

scenic spot　景点，景区

☞ Tourism authorities in this city have closed all ***scenic spots*** along the coast and evacuated more than 300,000 tourists who had flocked to seaside. 这个城市的旅游机构已关闭了所有沿海景点并疏散了 30 多万去海边游玩的游客。

science fiction　科幻小说

☞ The innocent kids believe that superman exists not only in the ***science fiction*** stories but also in the real life. 天真的孩子们相信，超人不但存在于科幻小说中，而且也存在于现实生活中。

文学作品的常见分类：

prose 散文	poem 诗
autobiography 自传	detective story 侦探小说
fairy tale 童话故事	thriller 惊悚读物
satire 讽刺文学	novel 小说
reportage 报告文学	romance 传奇故事

security entrance　安全入口

☞ I do need to tell you that there's a ***security entrance*** to the house, so you need to press the green button for someone to let you in. Don't press the red button please, but don't worry, it's all clearly labeled. 我需要告诉你们这房子有一个安全入口，所以需要按绿色按钮叫人带你进去。请不要按红色按钮，不用担心，这些都标得一清二楚。

sell out　卖完；卖掉（商店等），出售（股份）；（尤指为了钱）出卖原则（或朋友）

☞ Tickets are already selling fast. The Friday and Saturday performances ***sold out*** almost immediately and, in fact, now there are only tickets for Monday and Thursday. 票卖得很快，星期五和星期六的演出票几乎马上就售罄了，实际上，现在只剩星期一和星期四的票了。

☞ be out of stock, be unavailable

semi-detached house　半独立式住宅

☞ A ***semi-detached*** house with five bedrooms is for sale. 出售一幢带五个卧室的半独立式住宅。

雅思考试中常见的“家庭住宅”：

apartment/flat 公寓　　bungalow 平房　　cottage 村舍

villa 别墅　　house 独立住宅

send out　发出，发送；派遣

☞ The demand for bikes there is enormous, which makes them very expensive locally. So we sell them for 75% of the normal price. But in order to continue operating we need to have a constant supply of bikes which we ***send out*** every six months. 那里对自行车的需求量很大，因此自行车在当地极其昂贵。所以我们的价格是平常价格的75%。但为了持续运作，我们需要长期的自行车供应，每六个月就要发货一次。

senior citizen　老年人

☞ ***Senior citizens*** should be deemed as a treasure to our country. They have worked hard all their lives for the development of the nation as well as the society. 老年人应该被视为我们国家的一笔财富。他们为国家和社会的发展辛苦工作了一辈子。

在西方，senior citizen 作“老人”讲时是委婉语，因为很多人对自己的年龄比较敏感，为了表示尊重，一般称老人为 senior citizen。

serve...with　向…提供，把…交给

☞ This hotel offers an impeccable service, ***serving*** guests ***with*** welcoming sweetmeats. 这家旅馆为顾客提供至善至美的服务，还有迎宾甜品。

☞ supply...with

service charge　服务费，手续费

☞ A: Ann, do you know the ***service charge*** of this bank?

B: Sorry, I have no idea.

A：安，你知道这家银行的服务费吗？

B：对不起，我不知道。

set aside （为某种目的）留出，拨出；节省；对…不予考虑，置于一旁；取消，驳回，宣布…无效

☞ Fears of the new round outbreak of bird flu have not been fully ***set aside***. 人们对爆发新一轮禽流感的恐惧尚未完全消除。

set back　耽搁（或阻碍）…的进展，使受挫，延缓；使花费，使破费

☞ It would be easy to say the company had invested too heavily, or at the wrong time, but in fact the signs were good and what they were ***set back*** by was high interest rates. 我们可以很轻松地说是这个公司投资过度，或是投资的时机不对，但实际上，征兆是好的，导致他们失败的是高利率。

☞ hinder from

set down 停下让(乘客)下车；制订，规定，记下

☞ A: And how many times have been ***set down*** for the tutorials, do you have that information?

B: That's a very well-attended course so there's a number of tutorial times.

A：已经确定下来的辅导课有多少次啊，你知道吗？

B：那门课很受欢迎，所以会有很多次辅导课。

set out 陈列，摆放，安排；出发，动身，开始；陈述，阐明

☞ He ***set out*** his objections to the plan. 他陈述了对这个计划的反对意见。

☞ The several students are ***setting out*** on an American tour this summer. 这几名学生今年夏天要去美国旅行。

set off 触发，引起；出发，动身；衬托，使更明显

☞ Though it won't ***set*** back pain ***off*** in the first place, the body weight will increase the strain and make things worse. 虽然体重不是引起背痛的第一位因素，但它会增加压力，使事情变得更糟。

set the table 放餐具，布置餐桌

☞ Do our modern lifestyles mean that we no longer have the time to ***set the table*** with various delicate china? 现代生活方式意味着我们再也没有时间在餐桌上摆放精致的瓷器吗？

set up 创造，建立，开创；设置，竖起；造成，产生，引起；安装(机器等)

☞ A number of initiatives have been ***set up*** to help women deal with the economic problems. 已采取了很多措施来帮助女性处理经济问题。

☞ A: If you had to give the new directors some specific advice when they ***set up*** the channel, what advice would you give them?

B: I think I'd advise them to pay a lot of attention to the quality of the broadcast, you know, the sound system.

A：如果你必须在新导演们开设新电视频道时提出一些具体的建议，你会提什么建议呢？

B：我会建议他们多关注广播的质量，也就是音响系统。

☞ establish

settle down 安顿下来，过安定的生活；习惯于某种生活方式(或职业等)；开始专心于，认真地着手去做

☞ A: You really should find a right person and ***settle down***.

B: You're right, but that's not easy.

A：你真的应该找到一个合适的人并安顿下来。

B：你说的对，但那并不容易。

share the view on 对…持相同观点

☞ I'm glad we ***share the view on*** whom to take credit for. 我很高兴在谁是功臣的问题上我们达成了一致。

shift work 轮班工作，换班

☞ I would appreciate it if you can ***shift work*** with me. 如果你能跟我换班，我将不胜感激。

work overtime 指"加班"。

shock value 轰动效应

☞ Four years into her career, Tina realizes she no longer can rely on the ***shock value*** of her being the first Muslim female actress. 工作了四年后，蒂娜认识到她不能再依赖"第一位穆斯林女演员的身份"所造成的轰动效应继续下去了。

shoot a film 拍摄电影

☞ A: Have you heard the news that our favourite director is going to ***shoot a film*** in black and white?

B: Yes, I've got the news two days before.

A：你听说了吗？我们最喜欢的那个导演将拍摄一部黑白电影。

B：是啊，我两天前就知道了。

与"电影"相关的表达：

director 导演	producer 制片人
leading actor 主角	supporting role 配角
special effect 特效	premiere 首映
stunt man 特技替身演员	extra 临时演员
distributor 发行人	filmdom 电影业，电影界
trailer 预告片	

show off 炫耀

☞ Nowadays, many women like wearing tight dress to ***show off*** their nice figures. 如今，许多女性喜欢穿紧身裙来炫耀自己的好身材。

show up 显现；揭露，暴露；露面

☞ Most of my female friends like the same music as me. Different age groups would be much more likely to ***show up*** differences, I think. 我的大多数女性朋友都和我喜欢相同的音乐。我认为不同的年龄段更可能会表现出不同的兴趣。

☞ You spin the wheel around and if you can get the wheel spinning fast enough, hopefully the colors all merge and ***show up*** as white. 转动轮子，如果转得足够快，所有的颜色就会融为一体变成白色。

☞ come up, reveal, expose

shut down （使工厂等）停工，歇业，关闭

☞ If the company truly are cautious, then I suspect they will seek to ***shut down*** some of their shops. 这家公司如果真的很谨慎，那么我猜他们会关闭一些商店。

side effect 副作用

☞ Medical institution must be frank about the ***side effects*** of this newly invented treatment. 医疗中心必须坦白这种新研发出来的疗法的副作用。

sightseeing spot 观光景点

☞ I want to visit all the ***sightseeing spots*** of this country. 我想参观这个国家所有的观光景点。

🔍 go sightseeing 指"去观光"。

sign a contract with 与…签订合同

☞ A: Have you heard that the famous swimmer is going to ***sign a contract with*** the sportswear giant, Adidas?

B: Really? That's great.

A：你听说了吗？这个著名的游泳运动员将与运动品牌巨头——阿迪达斯签约。

B：真的吗？太棒了。

🔍 labor contract 指"劳动合同"。

sign up 报名参加（俱乐部、课程等）；雇用

☞ We do ask that you ***sign up*** three days in advance. 我们要求提前三天报名。

☞ enter for

single-speed cycle 单速自行车

☞ ***Single-speed cycles*** are really only suited to short, casual rides. 单速自行车只适合短途的休闲之旅。

sit in 旁听，列席；代替（某人）主持；参加（集体）静坐示威

☞ A: We like people to write a case study, describing an organization they know.

B: I've already done that, as my friends told me you wanted one. But would it be possible to ***sit in*** on a teaching session to see what it's like? I haven't been a student for quite a while.

A：我们希望学生能写个案例研究，描述一个他们熟悉的组织。

B：我已经完成了，因为我的朋友说你会需要的。但是我能旁听一节看看这课是怎样的吗？我的学生生涯结束好久了。

sit with 临时替人照看

☞ Can you do me a favour to ***sit with*** my daughter for half an hour? 你能帮我照顾我的女儿半个小时吗?

slip from...to 从…滑落到

☞ Because of the ache on her back the world ranking of the tennis player has ***slipped from*** first ***to*** third. 由于背部伤痛，这位网球选手的世界排名从第一位滑到了第三位。

slip on 穿上

☞ Please ***slip on*** the jeans and sweater you wore last week, along with a pair of shoes. 请穿上你上周穿的牛仔裤和毛衣，再穿双鞋子。

slip-on 指“(鞋子)无带扣的，易穿脱的”。

slow down (使)减速，(使)慢下来

☞ Business ***slows down*** at this time of year. 每年此时生意就会渐趋清淡。

反义词组是 speed up，指“(使)加速”。

snap up 抢购，抢先弄到手

☞ Products in the center of an aisle are ***snapped up*** and manufacturers pay a lot for these areas which are known in the trade as hotspots. Naturally everyone wants their products to be in a hotspot. 摆放在通道中心的商品经常被顾客一抢而空，因此制造商们不惜为这些区域花重金，这些区域在贸易上叫做“热点区域”。很自然，每个人都希望自己的产品被摆放在热点区域。

so forth 等等

☞ A: Good morning. I'm interested in the children's workshops and I'd like a little more information, please.

B: Do you mean the Art and Craft workshops?

A: Yes. A friend of a friend mentioned them—the children do painting and make models and ***so forth***.

A：早上好，我对儿童工作坊很感兴趣，想多了解一点。

B：你是说艺术手工作坊吗?

A：是的，一个朋友的朋友提起过它们，就是孩子们画画、做模型，等等。

soak up 吸收

☞ Many scientists believe global warming might get worse in ten years if the oceans ***soak up*** less of the greenhouse gas. 很多科学家相信如果海洋不能吸收那么多温室气体，那么十年内全球变暖问题就会恶化。

☞ draw in

social interaction 社会交往

☞ ***Social interaction*** is a great way to broaden your circle of friends. 社交是扩大朋友圈的好方法。

social welfare 社会福利

☞ The local government provides ***social welfare*** to the poor and the jobless. 当地政府向贫困人群和失业人员提供社会福利。

常见的“社会福利”：

pension 退休金，抚恤金 insurance 保险

public housing fund 住房公积金 medicare 医疗保险

soft drink （不含酒精的）软饮料

☞ “Dream” is the name of a ***soft drink*** made by the drink company. “Dream”是这家饮料公司生产的一种软饮料的名字。

soil conditioner 土壤调节剂，土壤改良剂

☞ Over a third of the waste paper can't be used in the recycled paper, leaving the question of what to do with it. One firm, Paper Save, currently sells this to farmers as a ***soil conditioner***, though this practice will soon be banned because of transport costs and smell, and the company is looking into the possibility of alternative uses. 超过 1/3 的废纸不能被回收利用，给人们留下一个难题。现在有一家名为“节约纸张”的公司把这些废纸作为土壤调节剂售给农民，尽管这种做法由于废纸的运输成本和气味很快将被禁止，但该公司正在寻找废纸其他可能的用途。

conditioner 的其他搭配：hair conditioner 护发素

solar energy 太阳能

☞ New cars powered by ***solar energy*** have become popular in this city. 以太阳能为能源的新型汽车已经在这座城市里流行了起来。

随着化石燃料(fossil fuel)的枯竭和环境污染(environmental pollution)的加剧，人类正在不断寻求新能源，如太阳能、水能(water energy)、核能(nuclear energy)和风能(wind energy)等。

sort...out 挑选；处理，解决；澄清；使情绪稳定

☞ If you're planning to live off campus, you've got to ***sort*** the problems ***out*** earlier.
如果你想住在校外，就应该早点解决这些问题。

NOTES

Unit 18

sound good 听起来不错

☞ It ***sounds good*** that we can visit the museum without charge. 我们可以免费参观博物馆，这听上去很不错。

☞ sound great

spare time 空闲时间

☞ In most interviews you usually ask candidates questions about their hobbies and what they like doing in their ***spare time***. 在大多数面试中，你通常会问求职者的爱好以及他们在闲暇时喜欢做什么。

☞ free time

spark off 引发，诱发

☞ Too much fat and sugar will ***spark off*** obesity and diabetes. 摄入过多的脂肪和糖会引发肥胖和糖尿病。

speak at natural speed 用自然语速说

☞ I think the people ***speak at natural speed***, so it forces me to get used to it. And they use a lot of slang. 我觉得这些人说话时是正常语速，这迫使我去适应它，而且他们用了很多俚语。

speak of 谈及，说到；表明，说明

☞ The woman refused to ***speak of*** her husband. 这个女人拒绝谈及她的丈夫。

☞ mention

speak up (for) 大声点说；明确表态，(为…)说好话，辩护

☞ please ***speak up***—we can't hear you at the back. 请大声点——我们在后面听不见。

☞ The woman ***spoke up*** in defense of her political beliefs. 那个女人为她的政治信仰力辩。

special clinic 专科门诊，特诊室

☞ Dr Williams holds a ***special clinic*** for people with back trouble. 威廉斯医生开了一家诊所，专治背部疾病。

🔍 与"看病"相关的表达：

out-patient department/OPD 门诊部
in-patient department 住院部
consulting room 诊察室
waiting room 候诊室
emergency 急诊室
dispensary 药房
isolation ward 隔离病房
maternity ward 产科病房
observation ward 观察室
blood bank 血库

specialized course 专业课

☞ We are going to discuss the project of ***specialized courses*** setting in foreign language education. 我们将探讨外语教学专业课程设置的方案。

🔍 雅思选课场景常见表达：

basic course 基础课
course arrangement 课程安排
required/compulsory course 必修课
optional/selective course 选修课
application form 申请表
project 需学生进行独立钻研的课外课题
syllabus 教学大纲
credit 学分
dissertation 论文
enrollment 注册

speed up 加速

☞ Products placed here, at the beginning of aisles, don't sell well. In tests, secret fixed cameras have filmed shopper's movements around a store over a seven-day period. When the film is ***speeded up***, it clearly shows that we walk straight past these areas on our way to the centre of an aisle. 放置在走廊入口的商品卖得不好。在测试中秘密安装的摄像头拍下了七天内顾客在商店内的活动。当加速放映录像时，很明显就可以看到顾客径直穿过走廊入口直奔中部。

☞ gather way, accelerate

split off （使）分离，（使）分裂

☞ My particular interest is Asiatic lions, which are a sub-species of African lions. It's almost a hundred thousand years since the Asiatic lions ***split off*** and developed as a sub-species. 我对亚洲狮尤其感兴趣，它们是非洲狮的一个分支。其分离出来成为一个单独的分支已长达近十万年。

spoken English 英语口语

☞ One or two of you asked me earlier about your level of ***spoken English***. Obviously most of you have already achieved a lot. 之前你们当中有个别人问我你们的英语口语水平（如何）。显然，你们大多数人都取得了很大进步。

spot on　一点不错，对极了，完全正确，很准确

☞ I think the survey checklist you made is good. Very much on the right lines. I'd say the first two sections of your dissertation are ***spot on***. 我认为你做的调查清单很好，相当切题。论文的前两部分极中要害。

spring up　萌芽；迅速出现，突然兴起；腾起

☞ A: How do the banana trees reproduce then?

B: Well, bananas are normally grown from suckers which ***spring up*** around the parent plant, usually just above the plant.

A：香蕉树是如何繁殖的？

B：香蕉一般是从母体植株周围的根出条中长起来的，通常直接在原植株上生长。

☞ Outdoor products stores are ***springing up*** all over the city in recent few months. 近几个月来，户外用品店如雨后春笋般出现在这座城市里。

☞ grow quickly, pop up

spring up 指"突然出现"时和 pop up 近义，但两者有细微差别：spring up 有"出现后继续发展"的意思，而 pop up 强调"突然出现"这个动作。

sprout up　发芽；大量出现

☞ As cyber cafes continue to ***sprout up*** all over the world, travel blogs have become a good place for keeping in touch with those stayed at home. 随着网吧在全球大量涌现，旅行博客成为与待在家里的人保持联系的一个好方式。

staff room　教研室；职员室

☞ The ***staff room*** is near the main entrance, just opposite the reception desk. 教研室在主入口附近，正对着接待处。

staff room 可用在很多场合，如"教师休息室、会议准备室、员工休息室等"，只要是"员工"休息或办公的地方就可以。在英国，staff room 侧重于"工作的地方"，而在其他国家亦有 rest room 的含义，不过都是对"员工"开放的。

stand for　代表；为…的缩略；支持，主张；容忍

☞ Do you know what do the letters UFO ***stand for***? 你知道 UFO 是什么的缩写吗？

☞ The organization ***stands for*** self-reliance. 该组织主张自力更生。

stand out　出色，杰出，更为重要；显眼；坚持

☞ The first chapter of your draft is fine but the middle section really ***stood out*** for me... most interesting. 你草稿的第一章不错，但是中间部分特别突出，是最有趣的部分。

☞ The warning sign ***stands out*** in the street and attracts the eyes of the passers-by. 大街上的警告标识很显眼，吸引了行人的目光。

standard of living 生活标准

☞ Because of our work, people in a number of countries now have a better ***standard of living***—so far we've provided 46,000 people with bikes. 我们的工作提高了很多国家人民的生活水平——迄今为止我们已经给4.6万人提供了自行车。

start off 开始活动；动身；开展起来；首先进行；以…起步(或起家)

☞ Don't you think it's a bit ambitious for this age group? I mean, I don't want to ***start off*** something and then have to abandon it if they just can't cope with it. 你不觉得对于这个年龄群来说有点冒险吗？我不想在开始了某件事后而仅仅因为他们处理不了却不得不放弃。

start up (使)启动，发起，开始

☞ I have many women patients who say they have completely given up exercise because the pain makes them so miserable. But of course that ***starts up*** a vicious circle. 我的很多女病人都说疼痛让她们痛苦得完全放弃了锻炼。但是很自然的这开始了一个恶性循环。

start with a clean slate 重新开始；改过自新；重归于好

☞ If you ***start with a clean slate*** and quit drinking, your wife will take you in again. 你如果改过自新戒酒的话，你的妻子会重新接纳你的。

☞ turn over a new leaf

state-run enterprise 国有企业

☞ It is understandable that many parents want their sons and daughters to find a job in the government or in the ***state-run enterprises***. 许多父母都希望子女能在政府部门或国有企业供职，这是可以理解的。

☞ public sector

stay in touch with 与…保持联系

☞ Last but not least, ***stay in touch with*** us. 最后但同样重要的一点是，要与我们保持联系。

stay within the budget 使预算在…范围内

☞ Today I'm going to talk about ways of making sure that you eat well while at the same time ***staying within the budget***. 今天我要讲讲如何保证吃得好同时又不超出预算。

stereo system　立体音响系统

☞ A: What things did you want to insure?

B: Well, what do you recommend?

A: Well, the most important things are those which you would normally find in a home. Things like the television, fridge and so on.

B: I see. Well, I've got a fridge and a ***stereo system*** which I've just bought from a friend.

A：你想为什么东西投保?

B：你们有什么建议?

A：家里常见的那些东西最应该投保，如电视、冰箱等。

B：明白了。我刚从一个朋友那买了一个冰箱和一套立体声音响。

常见家用电器：

electric fans 电风扇	toaster 烤箱，烤面包机
microwave oven 微波炉	radiator 电暖炉
air conditioner 空调	washing machine 洗衣机
hair dryer 吹风机	electric iron 电熨斗
blender 搅拌机	juicer 榨汁机

stick shift　手动挡；手动变速车

☞ My brother bought a car for me and tried to teach me how to drive ***stick shift***. But he didn't have the patience so I almost abandon that car. 哥哥给我买了一辆车并教我如何开手动挡。但是他没什么耐心教我，所以我几乎都要闲置那辆车了。

"自动挡"为 automatic shift。

stick in one's mind　（往事、形象等）经久不忘，铭记在心

☞ One of the paintings in particular ***sticks in my mind***. 有一幅画我尤其难忘。

stick to　继续（做某事），坚持（做某事）；维持，固守

☞ Even though he is unsatisfied with his job, John can ***stick to*** the job for a long period. 尽管对工作不满意，但约翰仍能坚持工作很长一段时间。

☞ adhere to

stock market　股票市场

☞ Personally I think the ***stock market*** is to blame. I think they were expecting too much of the company and then inevitably it looked bad when it didn't perform. 我个人认为，股票市场应该负责任，我认为他们过于依赖公司，而当公司经营不善时股票市场就必然会一蹶不振。

☞ share market

与“股票”相关的常用表达：

dividend 股息，红利	stockholder 股票持有人，股东
capital stock 股本	stock index 股指
stock exchange 股票交易所	stock transfer 股票转让

store...away/up 储存，保存；(在计算机里)存储

☞ Maybe we could ***store*** the idea ***away*** for later. 或许我们可以把这个想法留到以后(再用)。

straight away 立即，马上

☞ A: The first thing is the washing machine. It's been leaking a little and it's beginning to get worse. Because we have a small child, we really need to get that done ***straight away***.

B: OK...that's a washing machine for immediate repair.

A：第一件事就是洗衣机(的问题)。洗衣机一直都有点漏水，而且越来越严重了。我们家里有个小孩，所以需要马上修好。

B：好的，洗衣机需要马上修理。

☞ A: Can you also send me an application form?

B: Of course. I'll get that in the post to you ***straight away***.

A：你能给我寄一张申请表吗？

B：当然，马上就邮寄给你。

☞ right away

strip down 拆开，拆散；使精炼；脱光衣服

☞ If you do have a bike to donate, it doesn't matter what condition it's in—if we can't repair it, we'll ***strip*** it ***down*** for several parts. 如果你有自行车要捐，车况如何都没有关系——如果无法修理的话，就会把它拆开，用零部件。

☞ break up, tear apart

strive for 努力，奋斗

☞ The lyrics of the song aim to encourage fellow citizens to move away from the path of violence and ***strive for*** a bright future filled with peace. 这首歌旨在鼓励人们停止使用暴力，去努力创造一个充满和平的美好未来。

student account 学生账户

☞ Now, by far the most useful type of account to open is a current account. When you do this, you will actually get what is called a ***student account*** which is a current account with special concessions for students. 迄今为止最有用的账户类型是活期账户。申请这种账户时，实际得到的是学生账户，一个对学生有着特殊优惠的活期账户。

student handbook　学生手册

☞ You can find the school advice on the ***student handbook***. 你可以在学生手册上找到学校建议。

student/students' union　学生会

☞ We are going to elect the chairman of ***Student Union*** next Friday. 下周五我们将选举学生会主席。

☞ We're very grateful that the committee has agreed that a representative for the ***Students' Union*** can present students' suggestions. 我们非常感谢委员会同意学生会派出一名代表提出学生们的建议。

🔍这个短语在雅思考试中有时会缩写成 SU。

subscription fee　订阅费，预订费

☞ A: Is this kind of membership very expensive?

B: Well, it's now £500 for the annual ***subscription fee***.

A：要成为这种会员，费用贵吗？

B：现在的年费是 500 英镑。

suffer from　遭受；受苦，受折磨

☞ The old man ***suffers from*** heart disease. 那个老人患有心脏病。

☞ Many companies are ***suffering from*** a shortage of skilled staff. 许多公司苦于缺乏有经验的员工。

☞ inflict upon

suggestion box　意见箱，建议箱

☞ We invited all students to submit written suggestions for the design, placing cards in a ***suggestion box***. 我们邀请全体学生提交有关设计的书面建议，并把建议卡放入意见箱。

suitable for　适合

☞ I'd like to buy some books ***suitable for*** children under 5. 我想买一些适合五岁以下儿童阅读的书。

☞ fit for

summit conference/meeting　峰会，首脑会议

☞ At the ***summit conference***, the President presents his ideas on global warming. 在峰会上，该总统阐述了他对全球变暖的看法。

superior to　（在级别、重要性或职位上）高于；（在品质上）优于

☞ Instead of moving from place to place, the settlers needed permanent dwellings. The stone axes used to chop down trees to make these dwellings were far ***superior to*** any that the Stone Age hunter-gatherers used. 这些居民不再四处搬家，他们需要固定住处。他们用于砍树造房子的石斧比石器时代采猎者所用的要先进得多。

surf the Internet 网上冲浪，上网

☞ Betty is ***surfing the Internet*** to find useful information. 贝蒂正在上网寻找有用的信息。

🔍如今，网络已走进千家万户，人们通常上网聊天（chat on line）、玩游戏(play computer games)、发电子邮件（send e-mail）、搜索（search）和播放音乐(play music)等。

sweep across 席卷

☞ High winds and storm activity continued to ***sweep across*** the state yesterday, with the State Emergency Service fielding more than 100 calls. 昨天强风暴雨继续席卷整个州，州紧急情况服务中心接到了 100 多个电话。

swimming costume 游泳衣

☞ There are various ***swimming costumes***, mini skirts and cartoon T-shirts in this shop. 这家店里有各种各样的游泳衣、迷你裙和卡通 T 恤。

table tennis 乒乓球

☞ If you want to relax, you can play ***table tennis*** with us. 如果你想放松一下，可以和我们一起打乒乓球。

take a sip of 喝一小口

☞ The lecturer paused to ***take a sip of*** the hot coffee and then went on his story. 这名演讲者停下来喝了一口热咖啡又继续他的故事了。

take a stroll around 漫步，闲逛

☞ On the first day, tourists can enjoy the beauty of the rainforest and ***take a stroll around*** the famous lake. 第一天，游客可以观赏热带雨林，并在这个著名的湖边散步。

take a/an...view of/towards 对…抱…的见解

☞ I always ***take a*** negative ***view towards*** marrying for money. 我一直对为金钱而结婚的行为抱有成见。

☞ hold a/an...view of

take advantage of 运用，利用

☞ If one is visiting Manhattan, he or she can ***take advantage of*** the 24-hour shuttle to and from Kennedy Airport. 游客在曼哈顿旅行时，可搭乘往返于肯尼迪机场的 24 小时大巴。

☞ make use of

take ages 花费很长时间

☞ A: We have to do two groups, remember, and it looks like we have to interview fifteen for each group.

B: That's thirty altogether then. It's going to ***take ages***.

A: Yes, but remember we're working on this together, so we'll only have to do fifteen each.

A：记住，我们需要做两组调查，好像每组要采访 15 个人。

B：那就是 30 个人了。会花很长时间的。

A：是的，但是记住我们是共同完成的，所以每人采访 15 个就可以了。

take an interest in 对…感兴趣

☞ Do your parents ***take an interest in*** your friends? 你的父母有兴趣了解你的朋友吗？

take...as an example 举…为例

☞ We've looked in general at the telecommunications market in the UK over the last few sessions and I want you to ***take*** Box Telecom ***as an example*** and suggest some ways in which they might overcome their problems. 在前几节课中我们已经对英国的电信市场有了大概的了解，现在我想让你们以博科斯电信为例，为他们提出几点建议来克服困难。

☞ for example

take care of 照顾，照看

☞ Thank you very much for ***taking care of*** my baby for me this afternoon. 非常感谢你今天下午帮我照顾孩子。

☞ look after

take control of 控制，掌控；掌管

☞ I mean the biggest difference between college and school is that new college students have to do a lot of work on their own, and it's sometimes useful to get advice on how to ***take control of*** your time and work effectively. 我的意思是大学和中学的最大区别是大学新生要自己做很多事情，所以有时获得一些如何控制时间并有效工作的建议是很有用处的。

take down 写下，记下

☞ A: Can I book a place on the "Study for Success" seminar course now?

B: Yes, let me just get out a registration form and ***take down*** your details.

A：我现在能预订"为成功而学习"的研讨会课程吗？

B：好的，让我拿一份登记表记下你的详细信息吧。

☞ write down

take...into account / take account of 考虑到，虑及

☞ The designers ***take into account*** the possible changes in technology and lifestyle over the next 10 years when they design the new operating system. 设计师在设计新的操作系统时，考虑到了未来十年里科技和生活方式可能会发生的变化。

☞ take...into consideration

take...into consideration 考虑

☞ The noise factor will have to be ***taken into consideration*** with the layout of the house. 噪音因素和房屋布局都要考虑在内。

☞ take account of

take a heavy toll（on）/ take its toll（on） 造成重大损失（或破坏等）

☞ The tornado has ***taken a heavy toll*** in a large part of the country. 龙卷风给该国大部分地区造成了惊人的损失。

☞ The economy crisis is ***taking its tool on*** the housing markets. 经济危机使房地产市场遭受着重大损失。

take notes 做笔记

☞ A: Do you want me to ***take notes***?

B: That will be great, thanks.

A：你想让我做笔记吗？

B：那太好了，谢谢。

NOTES

Unit 19

take off 起飞；匆匆离开；（观念、产品等）突然大受欢迎，迅速流行

☞ A group of school children who were traveling in a privately chartered airplane from Sydney to Queensland to take part in a musical concert found themselves swimming for the shore when their airplane had to land in the sea just three minutes after ***taking off*** from Sydney airport. 一架从悉尼飞往昆士兰州的私人包机载着一群学生去参加音乐会，在从悉尼机场起飞三分钟后，不得不迫降在海面上，这些学生被迫游回岸边。

take one's breath away 使某人激动得喘不上气，使惊讶不止

☞ Not many things can ***take one's breath away*** these months, but this movie is something absolutely wonderful. 这几个月来，没有太多的事可以给人带来惊喜，但是这部电影实在是太棒了。

take one's temperature 量体温

☞ The nurse ***takes my temperature*** three times a day. 护士一天给我量三次体温。

take out insurance 买保险

☞ Nowadays everyone can ***take out insurance*** fast and uncomplicated via Internet. 现在，人们能够通过网络方便简易地购买保险。

与"保险"相关的一些表达：

insurance agent/broker 保险代理人，保险经纪人

insurance company 保险公司　　insurance claim 保险索赔

insurance policy 保单　　insurance premium 保险费

take over one's business 接管某人的生意

☞ My father wants me to ***take over his business*** when I graduate from college. 我父亲希望我毕业后能接手他的生意。

take pictures 照相

☞ A: Who likes to ***take pictures*** better, your husband or you?

B: Me, of course.

A: 你和你丈夫，谁更喜欢照相？

B: 当然是我。

☞ take photographs

take pity on 对…表示同情(或怜悯)

☞ But in the end they ***took pity on*** me, so now I've just about got enough money. 但最终他们对我表示了同情，所以现在我的钱差不多够了。

take responsibility for 对…负责

☞ Corporate crime can have very severe consequences. It's not just a matter of companies making bigger profits than they should do, but of event which may affect the lives of innocent people, and yet very often companies, because they say they didn't intend to harm everyone, can avoid ***taking responsibility for*** the results of their actions. And that has been a very dangerous loophole in the law. 公司犯罪会带来极其严重的后果，这不仅是公司获取本不属于他们的利润的问题，而可能会影响无辜人群的生活，通常公司会说他们无意伤害任何人，这样就可以避免为他们的行为所产生的后果负责任。这在法律上是个非常危险的漏洞。

☞ be responsible for

take the role of 扮演…的角色

☞ In the east, most men seem to be unwilling to ***take the role of*** house-husband whilst their wives go to work. 在东方，大多数男性似乎都不愿意在妻子上班时自己在家当家庭主"夫"。

☞ play the role of

take unpaid leave 请无薪假

☞ My boss has agreed to pay the cost of the course itself, but I would have to ***take unpaid leave*** if I want to study full-time and, I don't think I could afford to support myself with no salary for a whole year. 老板同意为我支付课程本身的费用，但如果我想全天学习的话就得请无薪假，而且一整年没有薪水恐怕我也无法维持生活。

与"假期"相关的表达：

paid leave 带薪假	annual leave 年假
maternity leave 婚假	sick leave 病假

take up 继续，接下去；填满，占据，占用；开始从事

☞ Although trees can significantly improve the local climate, they do ***take up*** a lot of space. 虽然树林可以大幅改善当地气候，但它们确实要占据很大的空间。

☞ You see you only get one bunch of bananas per tree and it can ***take up*** to three years for a tree to bear fruit if you don't do anything special to it. 你看，如果不对香蕉树采取点特殊措施的话，香蕉树要三年才结果实，而且每棵树只结一串香蕉。

☞ I'm very excited about the whole thing of ***taking up*** studying again. 可以继续学习，这整件事令我激动不已。

☞ We train you so that you can ***take up*** a particular kind of job. So it is important that you know the main roles of the jobs—what the work is like and what kind of qualities you need to succeed at them. 我们给你们培训以便你们可以从事具体的工作。因此，了解工作的主要职责——这项工作本身是什么以及需要什么素质才能成功做这项工作，是很重要的。

talcum powder　爽身粉；滑石粉

☞ A: We should get something for the baby. What do you think?

B: Yes, you're right. What do you think of something like baby shampoo or ***talcum powder***?

A: Or we could get a little hat, or something like that.

A：我们应该给孩子买些东西。你觉得呢？

B：是啊。婴儿香波和爽身粉之类的东西怎么样呢？

A：或者我们可以买顶小帽子之类的。

talk through　（经过精心准备后）讨论；把某事谈透

☞ As we explained in the letter, in this part of the interview, we'd like to ***talk through*** your application form...your experience to date, etc... 正如在信中所说，在这部分的面试中，我们想深入讨论你的求职表、你到现在为止的工作经历等。

tax revenue　税收

☞ ***Tax revenue*** for July exceeded targets for the first time this fiscal year in this country, thanks in part to increases in tax on fuel and alcohol. 该国七月的税收额在这个财年里第一次超过了目标额，部分归因于燃料税和酒精税的提高。

一些常见的"税"：

operation tax 营业税
stamp tax 印花税
consumption tax 消费税
income tax 所得税
corporate income tax 企业所得税
construction tax 建设税
resource tax 资源税
inheritance tax 遗产税

teaching facilities　教学设施

☞ A: How about the ***teaching facilities*** in your school?

B: They need improving.

A: 你们学校的教学设施怎么样？

B: 需要改善。

team spirit　团队精神

☞ Young people participate in tennis training camps that aim to engender ***team spirit*** and help bridge religious gaps. 年轻人参加网球训练营，这些训练营旨在培养团队精神，帮助消除宗教上的隔阂。

tear down 拆除，拆毁

☞ Many of the old classrooms in this district will be ***torn down*** to make way for an expanded library. 为给扩建一个图书馆腾出空间，会拆掉这个区的很多旧教室。

telephone interview 电话访谈，电话面试

☞ We have to do ***telephone interviews*** to collect data. 我们必须通过做电话采访来收集数据。

🔍 雅思考试中 interview 的一个常见搭配是 job interview(求职面试)。

telephone rental 电话月租费

☞ A: How much is the house?

B: It's £380.

A: 380. Is that including water?

B: No, I'm afraid not, but it does include the ***telephone rental***.

A：这间房子(月租金)多少?

B：380 英镑。

A：380 英镑。包括水费吗?

B：恐怕没有，但包括电话月租费。

🔍 雅思听力另一常考短语是 car rental，意思为“汽车租赁费”。

tell...from 辨认，辨别，区分

☞ How can you ***tell*** an Asiatic lion ***from*** an Africa lion, with which you're probably more familiar? 你如何区分亚洲狮和非洲狮，更熟悉哪一个呢?

tend to 趋于，倾向于；照料，护理

☞ The study have found that men ***tend to*** save for a car. 研究表明男人往往会为买一辆车攒钱。

☞ One drawback of the questionnaire was that its data ***tends*** not ***to*** reveal anything unexpected, because it is limited to the questions fixed in advance by the researcher. 问卷调查的一个弊端是收集到的数据往往不能反映任何意料之外的情况，因为它受限于研究者事先所设定的问题。

☞ incline to, have a tendency to; care for

thank goodness for 谢天谢地

☞ A: What did you have inside the briefcase?

B: Well, all my papers from college. It's so frustrating, but, ***thank goodness for*** computers, I haven't lost them completely!

A：你的公文包里都有什么?

B：我从学校里带出的所有论文。太糟糕了，不过，多亏有电脑，总算没有完全丢失论文。

thanks to 由于，因为；幸亏

☞ ***Thanks to*** their efforts, these scientists have won great honors for our country. 这些科学家的努力为我们国家赢得了巨大的荣誉。

the last thing...want to do 最不愿做的事

☞ To move back to my hometown with my brothers would be ***the last thing*** I ***want to do*** now. 现在我最不愿做的事就是跟我的兄弟们一起搬回家乡。

类似的表达：

the last person I want to see 最不愿意见到的人

the thing I like least 最不喜欢的事

the/your best bet 最好的办法

☞ A: Is parking available nearby the museum on Saturday?

B: ***Your best bet*** is to leave your car at the back of the library—on a Saturday morning there are plenty of spaces there. It's right next door to the museum.

A：周六博物馆附近能找到停车处吗？

B：你最好把车停在图书馆后面，周六早上那儿会有很多停车位。图书馆就紧挨着博物馆。

You bet. 是英语常用表达，指"肯定的"。

theme park 主题公园

☞ A: Are there lots of places to go to around Trebirch?

B: Oh yes. You can enjoy many days out. Um there's the Merthyr Mining Museum, which is only half an hour from Trebirch by train. Your children will find it just as fascinating as many ***theme parks*** and they can ride in the original miner's lifts and on the coal trains.

A：垂博克周边好玩的地方多吗？

B：是的。可以玩上很多天。有梅瑟蒂采矿博物馆，从垂博克坐火车过去只要半小时。你的孩子会发现那和很多主题公园一样好玩，他们可以乘坐矿工早先用过的升降梯，还可以坐运煤的火车。

through and through 完全，彻底，地地道道

☞ The man's British ***through and through***. 那个男人是地地道道的英国人。

tick away/by 过去，流逝

☞ As the minutes ***ticked away***, the kid became more and more impatient. 随着时间一分一秒地流逝，那个孩子变得越来越不耐烦了。

ticket office 售票处

☞ Now we're standing at the entrance, and immediately to our right is the ***ticket office***. 我们现在站在入口处，售票处就位于我们的右边。

☞ booking office

tie...in (to/with) 把…联系到，（使）连接在一起

☞ Banana's history is not as boring as you'd think. And I wanted to ***tie*** it ***in to*** the work I've been doing on primary industries and the economy. 香蕉的历史不像你们想得那么无聊，并且我想把它与我对主要行业和经济一直所做的研究联系起来。

time difference 时差

☞ You should learn about the ***time difference*** between here and Tokyo before you go there. 你在去东京前应该了解这儿与那儿的时差。

to be frank 坦白地说

☞ I think questionnaires are very good at telling you how people fill in questionnaires, but ***to be frank*** they tell you very little else. Avoid them! 我认为调查问卷可以很好地告诉你人们是如何填写调查问卷的，但是坦白地讲，它们所告诉你的其他事就少之又少了。所以不要用这种方法。

☞ frankly speaking

to be precise 确切地说

☞ In the eleventh century, in 1066 ***to be precise***, the Norman conquered England, and during the next few centuries London became one of the most powerful and prosperous cities in Europe. 在11世纪，确切地说是1066年，诺曼人占领了英国，在接下来的几个世纪中，伦敦成为欧洲最强大、最繁荣的城市之一。

☞ be more exact, properly speaking

to one's surprise 让某人惊讶的是

☞ ***To no one's surprise***, Mr. Robert was re-elected as company's chief executive officer. 毫无悬念，罗伯特先生又一次当选为公司的首席执行官。

to some extent/degree 某种程度上

☞ The exam stress affects nearly everyone ***to some extent***, but especially overseas students. 在某种程度上，考试压力几乎会影响每一个人，但对留学生尤甚。

to sum up 总而言之

☞ ***To sum up***, this is a fantastic journey and I enjoy it very much. 总而言之，这是一次奇妙的旅行，我非常喜欢。

☞ in a word

to the best of one's knowledge 就…所知

☞ Although the questions are beyond the topic for today, I will try to respond as much as I can and ***to the best of my knowledge***. 尽管问题超出了今天的话题范围，但我还是会尽我所能就我所知道的给予回答。

to the point 中肯，扼要，说到点子上，扣题

☞ A: Could I just ask—what do you think I should call the chapter one of my dissertation?

B: Well, I'd go for something like Context Review. What do you think?

A: Well, short and ***to the point***.

A：我能问一下，您觉得我论文的第一章应该叫什么呢？

B：我喜欢"背景回顾"之类的题目。你觉得呢？

A：简洁且切题。

tourist attraction 旅游景点

☞ Disney theme park is one of the most welcome ***tourist attractions*** in the world. 迪斯尼主题公园是世界上最受欢迎的旅游景点之一。

与"旅游"相关的表达：

guide 导游 | guidebook 旅行指南
travel agency 旅行社 | places of interest 名胜
resort 胜地 | package tour 包办旅行

tourist destination 旅游目的地

☞ The President declared that it is time to make the country the leading ***tourist destination***, because they have everything they need to do so. 总统宣布是时候把国家打造成一流旅游目的地了，因为他们已经万事俱备。

tow...away 拖走，拉走

☞ A: What happens to you if you don't buy a sticker? Do they clamp your wheels or give you a fine?

B: No, I think they ***tow*** your car ***away***.

A：如果不办停车证的话会怎样？他们会把你的车轮夹住或罚款吗？

B：不，我觉得他们会把你的车拖走。

雅思考试停车场景常用表达：

parking permit/sticker 停车许可证 | parking lot 停车场
parking ticket 违规停车罚单 | parking fee 停车费
fine 罚款 | speed limit 限速

track and field 田径运动

☞ Who is the first gold medalist in the ***Track and Field*** events of the Beijing Olympic Games? 谁是北京奥运会田径项目的第一位金牌获得者?

常见的田径项目:

marathon 马拉松

sprint 短跑

foot race 竞走

triathlon 铁人三项

long-distance running 长跑

triple jump 三级跳

trade fair/show 交易会，展销会

☞ Who are you going to send to the toy ***trade fair*** opening today? 今天召开的玩具交易会你打算派谁去啊?

trade...in 折价购买

☞ He wanted to ***traded*** his old desktop computer ***in*** for a new laptop. 他想把旧台式电脑折价然后添钱买台新笔记本电脑。

trade on 利用

☞ The officer is good at ***trading on*** his social status for personal gain. 那个官员善于以权谋私。

☞ make use of

trade up 以旧物折价添钱买较贵的东西，折价贴换：卖掉原有的以便买更贵的东西

☞ My mother likes to ***trade up*** our used electrical apparatuses for new ones. 我母亲想用旧家电换新的。

traffic congestion/jam 交通堵塞

☞ The critic does not believe the bridge will help ease ***traffic congestion*** in the city. 这位批评家认为这座桥不会缓解该城市的交通堵塞。

☞ Thomas was late again because of the heavy ***traffic jam***. 由于严重的交通堵塞，托马斯又迟到了。

与"交通"相关的表达:

rush hour 交通高峰期

traffic flow 车流

traffic police 交警

zebra crossing 斑马线

pavement 人行道

traffic lights 交通信号灯

temporary traffic regulation 临时交通管制

traffic warden 交通管理员

intersection 十字路口

traffic rules 交通规则

traffic noise 交通噪音

☞ A problem in built-up areas is that ***traffic noise*** is intensified by tall buildings. 高楼林立的区域存在的一个问题是高楼放大了交通噪音。

噪音是环境污染(environmental pollution)的一种，划分噪音等级(noise level)的单位是分贝（decibel)，长期处于高噪音环境下会导致精神失常(mental disorder)和听力丧失(hearing loss)等。

trail away/off 声音逐渐减弱，逐渐消失

☞ Her voice ***trailed away*** to nothing. 她的声音越来越小，最后消失了。

train of thought 思路

☞ And as a consequence, although your paragraphing and inclusion of subheadings help, it's quite hard to follow your ***train of thought*** at times. 结果是尽管分段和添加一些小标题有所帮助，但有时还是很难跟上你的思路。

transfer to 转到；搬迁；转让，让与；转乘

☞ A: Good afternoon. Can I help you?

B: Good afternoon. Yes, I've just ***transferred to*** the School of Education, and I'd like information about joining the library.

A: 下午好，有什么能帮你的吗？

B：下午好。我刚刚转入教育学院，想了解一些办理图书馆证件的事宜。

☞ switch to

NOTES

Unit 20

translate...into　把…转变成，变化；翻译成

☞ The pupil has to ***translate*** the two-dimensional design of ther hat ***into*** a form to fit the head. 学生要把帽子的平面设计图转变成适合头型的帽子。

☞ change...into

transportation system　运输系统

☞ I think ***transportation system*** should be improved in two years. 我觉得运输系统在两年内应该得到改善。

travel agency　旅行社

☞ There were a large number of respondents in favour of a ***travel agency*** and insurance centre. 很多受访者都支持成立旅行社和保险中心。

travel light　轻装上阵

☞ For those who hope to enjoy the journey, my suggestion is to ***travel light***. 对那些想享受旅行的人，我的建议是轻装上阵。

traveller's cheque/check　旅行支票

☞ You can replace your ***traveller's check*** if it is lost or stolen. 旅行支票如果丢失或被窃，可以进行更换。

☞ A: Why were you so late? Did something happen?

B: Yes, you know, I went to the bank to cash some ***traveller's checks***.

A：你为什么这么晚呢？发生什么事了吗？

B：是的，我去银行兑换旅行支票了。

常见的"支票"：

order check 记名支票　　rubber check 空头支票　　blank check 空白支票

try on　试穿(衣物)

☞ Please ***try*** the shoes ***on*** before you buy them. 买鞋子前请先试穿。

try one's best to do　尽力做

☞ Have you ***tried your best to*** solve the problem? 你尽力去解决这个问题了吗?

☞ do one's best to do

try out　试验，试用

☞ People with back pain can ***try out*** an orthopedic mattress or a spring slatted bed. 背痛患者可以尝试整形外科床垫或弹簧床。

turn a blind eye (to)　假装看不见，(对…)视而不见

☞ The tour is very interesting and impressive, so it makes many tourists ***turn a blind eye to*** the expense. 这次旅行很有趣且令人印象深刻，所以很多游客并不在意费用。

turn down　关闭；调小，调低；拒绝

☞ It was practically a year ago that I applied to my local council for a grant, and it took them six months to ***turn*** me ***down***. 差不多一年前，我向地方委员会申请助学金，他们花了六个月的时间拒绝了我的申请。

☞ freeze off

turn off　关闭；拐弯，转入另一条路；不再听(或想)；使厌烦，使失去兴趣

☞ We won't get a very good mark if the children don't enjoy the experiments, and I suppose we could ***turn*** them ***off*** science for good! 如果孩子们不喜欢这些实验，我们就不会得到很好的分数，而且我猜可能会使他们永远地远离科学！

☞ Please ***turn*** the lights ***off*** before you leave the office. 离开办公室前请关灯。

☞ switch off

turn to　转向，变成；求助于

☞ That brief outline takes us to the beginning of the twentieth century, and now we'll ***turn to*** housing. 这个概述把我们带入 20 世纪初期，现在我们要讲有关住房的内容了。

☞ The small country has ***turned to*** America for help. 这个小国家已经向美国求助了。

☞ go to...for help

turn up　出现，来到；露面；开大，调高

☞ Thanks for ***turning up*** today to this short talk. I'm going to give on student banking. 感谢来参加今天这个简短的介绍，我要讲的是学生金融服务。

tutorial paper　指导论文

☞ A: Well, you have to complete a ***tutorial paper***.

B: What does that involve?

A: Well, it's a piece of work on a given topic based on some set reading texts.

A：你需要完成一篇指导论文。

B：都包含些什么内容？

A：要在一个给定的主题下，基于一些指定的阅读材料完成一篇论文。

twice as many 两倍之多

☞ We already had a few seats which were suitable for wheelchair users, and now there are ***twice as many***, which we hope will meet demand. 我们已经有一些为使用轮椅的残疾人特设的座位，现在这种座位已多达以前的两倍，希望能满足需要。

ultra-violet radiation 紫外线辐射

☞ This technology uses high intensity ***ultra-violet radiation*** to kill bacteria and other micro-organisms. 这种技术借助高强度的紫外线辐射来杀死细菌和其他微生物。

uncertain about 对…不确定

☞ The boys are ***uncertain about*** what to do next. 那些男孩们都不确定下一步该做什么。

☞ unsure about

under pressure/stress 在压力之下

☞ Employers may ask the sort of questions that you might expect, like do you like working ***under pressure*** or are you good at keeping deadlines? 雇主可能问及你能想到的问题，如：你喜欢在压力下工作吗？你善于在期限内完成任务吗？

☞ The interesting side of sports physiology, at least in my view, is the side that looks at the micro level, looking at cellular changes. The researchers are doing cellular research, looking at changes in body cells when the body is ***under stress***. 至少在我看来，运动生理学有趣的一面是从微观上观察细胞变化。研究人员正在进行细胞研究，观察人处于压力下体细胞会发生什么变化。

undergraduate student 大学本科生

☞ A: Do you know anything about parking rights on the campus? I was wondering whether students are allowed to park their cars on the campus or not?

B: I think it's possible for postgraduate students but not for ***undergraduate students***.

A：你知道有关校内停车权的事吗？我在想学生是否可以将车停在校园内？

B：我想研究生可能可以，但本科生不可以。

union fee 会费

☞ Well, you'll have to go across to the Law Faculty and get this card stamped and then you come back here with it and pay your ***union fee***. 你需要去法学院给这张卡盖章，然后回到这里来交会费。

universal education 普及教育

☞ The official put forward ***universal education*** plans in the meeting. 该官员在会上提出普及教育计划。

与"教育"相关的词组：

elementary education 初等教育　　secondary education 中等教育
higher education 高等教育　　adult education 成人教育

up to 多达；直到，不多于，不迟于；(在体力或智力上)能胜任；由(某人)决定

☛ A: I can borrow books for ***up to*** three months—is that what you are saying?
B: Yes.
A：书最久可以借三个月——是这个意思吗？
B：是的。

☛ A: How often do you like to receive statements?
B: I haven't really thought. Um, what's the usual thing?
A: It's ***up to*** you. Some people like them weekly.
A：你想要多久收一次银行结单？
B：我还没考虑这个问题，通常是多久呢？
A：这取决于你。有些人喜欢一周收一次。

☞ no less than; as many as

upper class 上层社会，上层阶级

☛ The small supermarket can hardly attract the people from ***upper class*** because there are no expensive things. 这个小超市没有价格昂贵的商品，很难吸引上层社会的人来购物。

相关词组：

middle class 中层社会　　lower class 下层社会

upper limit 上限

☛ What's your ***upper limit*** for the rent? 你所能承受的租金上限是多少？

☞ maximum

vacant position 职位空缺

☛ If there is a ***vacant position***, please keep me posted. 如果有职位空缺，请告知我。

vacuum flask 保温瓶

☛ The ***vacuum flask*** is made of stainless steel which is guaranteed for 20 years. 这种保温瓶是用不锈钢制造的，保修期是20年。

various aspects of 各方面

☞ In the last few weeks, we've been looking at ***various aspects of*** the social history of London and this morning we're continuing with a look at life in the area called the East End. 前几周，我们了解了伦敦社会历史的各个方面，今天上午我们继续来了解伦敦东区的生活。

vary with 根据…而变化

☞ Her mood ***varies with*** the weather. 她的心情随天气而变化。

vice versa 反之亦然

☞ You should take into consideration the advice of your parents and ***vice versa***. 你应该考虑你父母的建议，反之亦然。

virgin forest 原始森林

☞ Scientists take great pains in preventing the last ***virgin forest*** from being spoiled by human being. 科学家竭力保护最后一片原始森林不受人类破坏。

☞ primitive forest

virtual reality 虚拟现实

☞ The ***virtual reality*** system which allows children to manipulate aircrafts or watch flowers spring to life has become a big hit in the National Science and Technology Center. 这个虚拟现实系统使得孩子们能够操控飞行器或观看花朵绽放的过程，在国家科技馆里广受欢迎。

vocational school 职业学校

☞ Most of the students graduating from that ***vocational school*** have found a satisfying job. 那所职业学校的大部分毕业生都已经找到了满意的工作。

voluntary organization 志愿者组织

☞ After three years of studying, I wanted adventure. I loved traveling, so I decided to join a ***voluntary organization*** and was sent to Ecuador to carry out land surveys. 在三年的学习之后，我想要惊险的刺激。我喜欢旅游，所以加入了一个志愿者组织并被派往厄瓜多尔进行土地调查。

volunteer to do 志愿做，义务做

☞ The little girl ***volunteered to*** organize the visit to the museum for us. 那个小女孩自告奋勇为我们组织去参观博物馆。

wake up 醒来；唤醒，使清醒；使活跃；打起精神

☞ Don't ***wake*** him ***up*** so early! Yesterday he worked till the midnight. 别这么早叫醒他！他昨天工作到午夜。

☞ If your bed doesn't give enough support, back muscles and ligaments work all night trying to correct spinal alignment, so you ***wake up*** with a tired aching back. 如果床不能给你足够的支撑，背部肌肉和韧带就要整夜工作来试图纠正脊柱，于是醒来时背部就会感到疼痛且疲劳。

☞ waken up

walk away with　轻易取胜，轻松获得

☞ She ***walked away with*** the gold medal. 她轻松摘走了金牌。

washing machine　洗衣机

☞ The ***washing machine*** doesn't work and I have to ask someone to repair it immediately. 我的洗衣机坏了，必须马上请人来修理。

waste disposal　垃圾处理，废物处理

☞ ***Waste disposal*** is one of the major problems for the government to tackle with. 垃圾处理是政府需要处理的一个重大问题。

watch for　观察等待（某人出现或某事发生）；守候；注意

☞ I was ***watching for*** my tram because sometimes it comes early. 我一直在注意电车，因为它有时候会早到。

watch out　留意，密切注视；当心，留神

☞ We are planning to open our first centre outside this area in the coming year, so ***watch out*** for developments. 我们计划来年在这一区域外建立我们的首个中心，敬请关注动态。

water-soluble vitamin　水溶性维生素

☞ There are fat-soluble vitamins which can be stored for quite some time by the body and there are ***water-soluble vitamins*** which are removed more rapidly from the body and so a regular daily intake of these ones is needed. 脂溶性维生素可以在体内储存很长时间，而水溶性维生素则很快就能排出体外，因此有必要每天都摄取一些水溶性维生素。

way off base　完全错误

☞ The engineer's budget was ***way off base***, much higher than the current prices for labor and materials. 这个工程师的预算是完全错误的，远远高于当前劳动力和材料的价格。

☞ totally wrong

website address 网页地址

☞ A: Now what was good about some sessions was the handouts.

B: Yes, I thought all the handouts were good actually, and some were great, with ***website addresses*** and everything.

A：一些课程的优点在于发放的课程资料。

B：是的，我认为所有的资料都很好，有一些真是棒极了，上面提供了网址等，内容很全。

wedding vow 结婚誓言

☞ Nowadays it is much more common for the couple-to-be to participate in writing their own ***wedding vows***. 如今，对于那些即将结婚的情侣来说，亲自参与撰写结婚誓言变得越来越普遍了。

西方婚礼有许多有趣的习俗，如婚礼上新娘要有 something old, something new, something borrowed, something blue （一些旧的、一些新的、一些借来的、一些蓝色的东西）。旧的东西由生活幸福的女人提供，表示幸福生活的传递；新的东西一般是礼服和鞋子；借来的东西一般是金的，象征财运滚滚；蓝色的东西则象征谦虚、忠诚和爱。

weigh the pros and cons 权衡利弊

☞ When these foreign businesses look to investment overseas, they need to ***weigh the pros and cons*** of various cities' public infrastructure. 这些外国企业在考虑海外投资时，需要对不同城市的公共设施的好坏进行权衡。

weight lifting 举重

☞ Besides strength and technique, what else are the requirements of ***weight lifting***? 除了力量和技巧，举重还有什么其他要求？

well done 做得不错；（食物，尤指肉）熟透的，煮透了的

☞ A: Where are we supposed to get the ideas for these experiment from?

B: Well, I managed to get hold of two books from the library.

A: Oh, ***well done***.

A：对于这些试验，我们应该从哪里汲取灵感呢？

B：我设法从图书馆借到了两本书。

A：做得不错。

wipe out 彻底消灭，全部摧毁；使疲惫不堪；擦去

☞ A campaign to ***wipe out*** discrimination was spread throughout the country. 一项反歧视运动在全国开展了起来。

☞ The city was ***wiped out*** by the earthquake. 地震把这座城市夷为平地。

☞ sweep away, cancel out

with a population of 有着…人口

☞ Clare's hometown once was a beautiful scenic spot ***with a population of*** two million. 克莱尔的家乡曾是一个拥有 200 万人口的美丽的旅游景点。

with the help of 在…的帮助下

☞ In the modern society people do many things ***with the help of*** the computer. 在现代社会，人们在计算机的帮助下做很多事情。

☞ with the aid of

without question 无疑，毫无疑问，毫无异议

☞ The famous philosopher said it was easy to follow the crowd, to blend with the trend, to accept whatever we encounter ***without question***. 那位著名哲学家说要随波逐流并无异议地接受所遇见的一切是很容易的。

☞ beyond all doubt, beyond question

word/data processing 文字/数据处理

☞ Can you explain the term ***data processing*** to me? 你能给我解释一下数据处理这个术语吗?

与"计算机"相关的词汇:

software 软件	hardware 硬件	copy 复制
paste 黏贴	cut 剪切	database 数据库

work out 锻炼身体，做运动；计划，思考；处理，解决；计算，算出；弄懂

☞ A: Do I have to pay for classes?

B: Yes, it's £3 for each class you join.

A: I see. And what are the hours then?

B: Between 10:30 and 15:30 weekends only and you pay a £50 joining fee. The annual fee is £180—it ***works out*** at £15 a month, so that would be quite a lot cheaper.

A：课程是收费的吗?

B：是的，每节课三英镑。

A：我知道了，上课时间是怎么安排的呢?

B：只安排在周末上午 10:30 到下午 3:30，入会费是 50 英镑。年费是 180 英镑——折算后是每月 15 英镑，这样要便宜得多。

☞ A: Have you ***worked out*** that complicated problem yet?

B: Sure, I've done it two days earlier.

A：那道难题你已经解决了吗?

B：当然，两天前就解决了。

☞ A: I know the conference is for three days but actually I want to attend on Friday and Saturday only. Will that ***work out*** to be any cheaper?

B: Let me have a look. Well, you could register for the two days separately, but that couldn't actually save you very much as it still costs £35 for each day.

A：我知道这个会议要持续三天，但实际上我只想参加星期五和星期六的会议。这样会便宜点吗？

B：让我看一下。你可以单独注册这两天，但事实上并不会省多少钱，每天仍需 35 英镑。

☞ solve; figure out; puzzle out; turn out

work through 完成，做完工作

☞ A: Excuse me, I'm sorry to bother you, but would you have time to answer a few questions?

B: What are they about?

A: We're doing some market research for a new television channel starting in two years' time.

B: OK, why not?

A: Lovely, we'll just ***work through*** this form. And if we could start with some personal background information...

A：劳驾，很抱歉打扰你，但是你有时间回答几个问题吗？

B：关于哪方面的？

A：我们正针对一个将在两年内成立的新电视频道做一些市场调查。

B：好的，为什么不呢？

A：太好了，只要完成这个表格。先告诉我你的个人背景信息吧……

☞ carry out; get through

working experience

working experience 工作经验

☞ The position requires at least five years' relevant ***working experience***. 该职位要求至少五年的相关工作经验。

与"工作"相关的表达：

job applicant 求职者	job description 职位描述
team spirit 团队精神	interviewer 面试官
personnel system 人事制度	office hour 办公时间
salary 薪水	wage 工资
salary raise 加薪	year-end bonus 年终奖
internship 实习	on probation 试用

worth doing 值得做

☞ Although the performers are very young, the show is still ***worth seeing***. 虽然表演者年龄不大，但演出仍值得一看。

☞ worthwhile to do

write back 写回信，复信

☞ I have invited Mary to come to my wedding ceremony but she ***wrote back*** saying that she couldn't come. 我写信邀请玛丽参加我的婚礼，但她回信说来不了。

write up 详细写出；把…写成文

☞ A: I have to talk for 25 minutes?

B: Yes, that's right. And then you have to ***write up*** your piece of work and give it to the lecturer to be marked.

A：我必须讲 25 分钟吗？

B：是的，然后你要详细写出论文，并把它交给讲师进行评分。

☞ We have to do the experiments and ***write up*** our results within a week. 我们要在一周内完成试验并写出结果。

☞ write down

you name it 应有尽有

☞ This is the largest supermarket in the city—***you name it***, and they have got it. 这是该市最大的超市——无论你想买什么都能在那买到。

youth hostel 青年旅舍

☞ I've made a reservation for two rooms in advance in this ***youth hostel***. 我已经提前在这家青年旅舍预订了两个房间。

NOTES

新东方大愚雅思系列精品图书推荐

新东方独家引进

《剑桥雅思考试全真试题集 8》
(含光盘 2 张)
剑桥大学考试委员会　编著

定价：110 元　开本：16 开　页码：176 页

《剑桥雅思考试全真试题集 7》
(含光盘 2 张)
剑桥大学考试委员会　编著

定价：110 元　开本：16 开　页码：176 页

《剑桥雅思考试全真试题集 6》
(含光盘 2 张)
剑桥大学考试委员会　编著

定价：110 元　开本：16 开　页码：176 页

《剑桥雅思考试全真试题集 5》
(含光盘 2 张)
剑桥大学考试委员会　编著

定价：110 元　开本：16 开　页码：176 页

◎ 4 套完整的学术类雅思全真试题
◎ 2 套培训类雅思阅读与写作全真试题

《剑桥雅思真题精讲 8》
周成刚　主编

定价：28 元　开本：16 开　页码：208 页

《剑桥雅思考试全真试题集 7 精讲》
周成刚　主编

定价：28 元　开本：16 开　页码：234 页

《剑桥雅思真题精讲 4、5、6》
周成刚　主编

定价：25 元　开本：16 开　页码：168 页

◎ 洞悉雅思出题规律，精确剖析雅思真题
◎ 针对中国雅思考生的特点和需求，分题型全面破解

《剑桥雅思常见错误透析》
Pauline Cullen，Julie Moore　编著

定价：18 元　开本：32 开　页码：136 页

《剑桥雅思语法》(附 MP3)
Diana Hopkins，Pauline Cullen　编著

定价：45 元　开本：16 开　页码：272 页

◎ 雅思备考资料官方出版机构推出的权威雅思语法教程
◎ 剑桥资深语法专家为全球雅思考生量身定做

《剑桥雅思词汇》(附 MP3)
Pauline Cullen　编著

◎ 错误警示：帮助考生避免常见错误
◎ 单元测试：协助考生检验自己的进步
◎ 试题练习：涵盖学术类、培训类阅读以及写作、听力测试内容

定价：40 元　开本：16 开　页码：180 页

《剑桥雅思写作高分范文》(附 MP3)
刘巍巍　方林　编著

◎ 收集十年雅思写作题目，全部写作话题一网打尽
◎ 从雅思写作题目出发，全面提高考生写作能力

定价：38 元　开本：16 开　页码：248 页

《剑桥雅思 12 周完全攻略——听力》
(附 MP3)　王超伟　编著

◎ 针对中国雅思考生的学习特点，制定 12 周科学备考方案
◎ 覆盖雅思听力考试核心话题，提供权威答案，帮助考生有的放矢地备考

定价：28 元　开本：16 开　页码：184 页

《剑桥雅思 12 周完全攻略——口语》
(附 MP3)　孙涛　王冬　编著

◎ 针对中国雅思考生的学习特点，制定 12 周科学备考方案
◎ 覆盖雅思口语考试核心话题，提供权威答案，帮助考生有的放矢地备考

定价：29 元　开本：16 开　页码：204 页

《雅思词汇词根+联想记忆法(加强版)》

(附 MP3)　　俞敏洪　编著

◎ 完整收录雅思常考词汇，大量真题例句

◎ “词根＋联想”实用有趣，配有插图，加深记忆

◎ 按字母顺序编排，增加返记菜单，便于考生进行自测

定价：58 元　开本：16 开　页码：528 页

《雅思词汇词根+联想记忆法(乱序版)》

(附 MP3)　　俞敏洪　编著

◎ 完整收录雅思常考词汇，大量真题例句

◎ “词根＋联想”实用有趣，配有插图，加深记忆

◎ 增加返记菜单和索引，便于查找定位

定价：58 元　开本：16 开　页码：528 页

《雅思词汇词根+联想记忆法》

(附 MP3)　　俞敏洪　编著

◎ 原汁原味的真题例句，收词全面，涵盖雅思四大题型词汇

◎ 标出听力、口语单词，有针对性进行记忆

定价：28 元　开本：32 开　页码：456 页

《雅思词汇词根+联想记忆法——写作》

(附 MP3)　　俞敏洪　编著

定价：12 元　开本：64 开　页码：200 页

《雅思词汇词根+联想记忆法——听力》

(附 MP3)　　俞敏洪　编著

定价：12 元　开本：64 开　页码：160 页

《雅思词汇词根+联想记忆法——口语》

(附 MP3)　　俞敏洪　编著

定价：12 元　开本：64 开　页码：192 页

《雅思词汇词根+联想记忆法——阅读》

(附 MP3)　　俞敏洪　编著

定价：12 元　开本：64 开　页码：232 页

◎ “词根＋联想”实用有趣，配有插图，加深记忆

◎ 涵盖雅思阅读词汇，收词全面，分类科学

《雅思考官口语实战指导》

(附 MP3)　　Mat Clark　编著

◎ 分析中国考生的成绩现状，阐释评分系统的逐项要求

◎ 详尽介绍考试三部分程式，收录最新问题与话题卡片

定价：35 元　开本：16 开　页码：212 页

《雅思听力胜经》(附 MP3)

新东方教育科技集团雅思研发团队　编著

◎ 以雅思听力真题为蓝本，细分常见题型和场景

◎ 提供大量听写和分项练习，帮助考生提高听力单项技能

定价：30 元　开本：16 开　页码：170 页

《雅思口语胜经》(附 MP3)

新东方教育科技集团雅思研发团队　编著

◎ 收录口语考试最新问题和卡片话题

◎ 精选口语考试常用词汇和句型

定价：35 元　开本：16开　页码：216 页

《雅思阅读胜经》

新东方教育科技集团雅思研发团队　编著

◎ 词汇、语法、语篇三大层次剖析雅思阅读

◎ 精选 16 篇时文，全真模拟雅思阅读考试情境

定价：30 元　开本：16 开　页码：224 页

《雅思写作胜经》

新东方教育科技集团雅思研发团队　编著

◎ 系统说明写作准备过程及步骤

◎ 提供同题各档次作文比较，方便考生自测自学

定价：25 元　开本：16 开　页码：188 页

邮购咨询电话：010－62605127

《词以类记：IELTS 词汇》

（附 MP3）　张红岩　编著

◎ IELTS 最新词汇：覆盖听说读写
◎ 按学科和意群分类：细分至最小同义词区间，符合大脑分类记忆规律

定价：35 元　开本：32 开　页码：400 页

《雅思分级词汇 21 天进阶》

耿耿　编著

◎ 电脑统计雅思高频词汇，释义准确并配真题例句
◎ 收录雅思最核心 1228 词，方便考生高效把握词汇考点

定价：25 元　开本：32 开　页码：484 页

《雅思词汇精选》（附 MP3）

孙涛　编著

◎ 词条精选自雅思权威语料库
◎ 中英文双解释义，确保词义注释的准确性

定价：39 元　开本：16 开　页码：482 页

《IELTS 9 分必考词汇·学术类》

（附 MP3）　李伯庆　著

定价：28元　开本：32 开　页码：364 页

《IELTS 9 分必考词汇·培训类》

（附 MP3）　马升骅　著

定价：28 元　开本：32 开　页码：368页

◎ 用已知单词揣摩未知单词
◎ 从上下文中理解词义
◎ 借由"背诵诀窍"巧学助记

《IELTS 9 分必考短语·学术类》

（附 MP3）　李伯庆　著

定价：25元　开本：32 开　页码：272页

《IELTS 9 分必考短语·培训类》

（附 MP3）　林昱伶　著

定价：25元　开本：32 开　页码：272页

从记忆、理解到应用，一次搞定 IELTS 应考短语！① 记忆公式：不用死记，让你迅速掌握短语意义；② 英语理解：英语释义，让你直接领略短语的精确含义；③ 例句应用：通过例句让你学会如何应用短语。

《雅思核心词汇》（附 MP3）

陆文玲　编著

◎ 根据雅思考试出现频率分为"高频单词"、"精选单词"及"挑战单词"三大类，由浅入深，循序渐进
◎ 4 项主题式单词分类，涵盖政治、经济、科技、教育与休闲等领域。核心单词配合实用例句，活学单词，即学即用

定价：32 元　开本：16 开　页码：260 页

《雅思 9 分口语》（附 MP3）

Patrick Hafenstein　编著

◎ 给出 4 大口试评分标准及 QPS 口试应考策略
◎ 提供实用笔记速记法及口语测试现场模拟
◎ 全面囊括 12 大常考主题，依照口语测试标准题型编排

定价：35 元　开本：16 开　页码：232 页

《雅思 9 分写作》

Julian Charles　编著

◎ 60 篇高分写作范文
◎ 阶段式写作学习法
◎ 高分词汇精准运用
◎ 综合练习精进写作

定价：40 元　开本：16 开　页码：324页

读者反馈表

尊敬的读者：

您好！非常感谢您对**新东方大愚图书**的信赖与支持，希望您抽出宝贵的时间填写这份反馈表，以便帮助我们改进工作，今后能为您提供更优秀的图书。谢谢！

为了答谢您对我们的支持，我们将对反馈的信息进行随机抽奖活动，当月将有20位幸运读者可获赠《**新东方英语**》期刊一份。我们将定期在新东方大愚图书网站www.dogwood.com.cn公布获奖者名单并及时寄出奖品，敬请关注。

来信请寄：

北京市海淀区海淀东三街2号欧美汇大厦19层

北京新东方大愚文化传播有限公司

图书部收

邮编：100080　　　　E-mail：bj62605588@163.com

姓名：________ 年龄：________ 职业：________ 教育背景：________

邮编：________ 通讯地址：________________

联系电话：____________ E-mail：________________

您所购买的书籍的名称是：________________________

1. 您是通过何种渠道得知本书的（可多选）：

□书店 □新东方网站 □大愚网站 □朋友推荐 □老师推荐

□@新东方大愚图书(http://weibo.com/dogwood) □其他____________

2. 您是从何处购买到此书的？

□书店 □新东方大愚淘宝网 □其他网上书店 □其他____________

3. 您购买此书的原因（可多选）：

□封面设计 □书评广告 □正文内容 □图书价格 □新东方品牌

□新东方名师 □其他____________

4. 您对本书的封面设计满意程度：

□很满意 □比较满意 □一般 □不满意

改进建议____________

5. 您认为本书的内文在哪些方面还需改进?

□结构编排 □难易程度 □内容丰富性 □内文版式 □其他____________

6. 本书最令您满意的地方：□内文 □封面 □价格 □纸张

7. 您对本书的推荐率：□没有 □1人 □1—3人 □3—5人 □5人以上

8. 您更希望我们为您提供哪些方面的英语类图书?

□四六级类 □考研类 □IELTS类 □TOEFL类 □GRE、GMAT类

□SAT、SSAT类 □留学申请类 □BEC、TOEIC类 □英语读物类

□初高中英语类 □少儿英语类 □其他____________

您目前最希望我们为您出版的图书是：____________

9. 您在学习英语过程中最需要哪些方面的帮助?（可多选）

□词汇 □听力 □口语 □阅读 □写作 □翻译 □语法 □其他____________

10. 您最喜欢的英语图书品牌：____________

理由是(可多选)：□版式漂亮 □内容实用 □难度适宜 □价格适中

□对考试有帮助 □其他____________

11. 您对新东方图书品牌的评价：____________

12. 您对本书(或其他新东方图书)的意见和建议：____________

____

____

____

____

13. 填表时间：________年______月____日